First World War
and Army of Occupation
War Diary
France, Belgium and Germany

16 DIVISION
49 Infantry Brigade
Royal Irish Regiment
2nd Battalion
23 April 1915 - 25 April 1915

WO95/1979/1

The Naval & Military Press Ltd
www.nmarchive.com
Published in association with The National Archives

Published by

The Naval & Military Press Ltd

Unit 10 Ridgewood Industrial Park,

Uckfield, East Sussex,

TN22 5QE England

Tel: +44 (0) 1825 749494

www.naval-military-press.com

www.nmarchive.com

This diary has been reprinted in facsimile from the original. Any imperfections are inevitably reproduced and the quality may fall short of modern type and cartographic standards.

© **Crown Copyright**
Images reproduced by permission of The National Archives, London, England, 2015.

Contents

Document type	Place/Title	Date From	Date To
Heading	1979/1 2 Battalion Royal Irish Regiment Oct 1916-Apr 1918		
Heading	16th Division 49th Infy Bde 2nd Bn Roy. Irish Regt Oct 1916-Apl 1918		
Heading	War Diary Month Of October, 1916 Volume 2nd Royal Irish Regiment		
War Diary	Papot	01/10/1916	02/10/1916
War Diary	Ploegsteert	03/10/1916	14/10/1916
War Diary	Kemmel Shelters	15/10/1916	15/10/1916
War Diary	Kemmel	16/10/1916	31/10/1916
Operation(al) Order(s)	2nd. Battalion, The Royal Irish Regiment. Operation Order No. 35	02/10/1916	02/10/1916
Operation(al) Order(s)	2nd. Battalion, The Royal Irish Regiment. Operation Order No. 35 Appendix 2	06/10/1916	06/10/1916
Operation(al) Order(s)	2nd. Battalion, The Royal Irish Regiment. Operation Order No. 37. Appendix 3	09/10/1916	09/10/1916
Miscellaneous	Officer Commanding 2nd. R. Irish Rgt.	08/10/1916	08/10/1916
Operation(al) Order(s)	2nd. Battalion, The Royal Irish Regiment. Operation Order No. 38 Appendix 5	13/10/1916	13/10/1916
Miscellaneous	Officer Commanding. 2nd. R Irish Rgt. Appendix 6	13/10/1916	13/10/1916
Operation(al) Order(s)	49th. Infantry Brigade Order No 64 Appendix 7	12/10/1918	12/10/1918
Operation(al) Order(s)	2nd. Battalion, The Royal Irish Regiment. Operation Order No. 29 Appendix 8	16/10/1916	16/10/1916
Operation(al) Order(s)	49th Infantry Brigade Operation Order No, 66 Appendix 9	17/10/1916	17/10/1916
Operation(al) Order(s)	2nd. Battalion, The Royal Irish Regiment. Operation Order No. 40. Appendix 10	19/10/1916	19/10/1916
Operation(al) Order(s)	Operation Order No 2 By. Captain. I.F.O Donnell MC. Commanding 7/8th Bn Royal Irish Fusiliers Appendix 11	19/10/1916	19/10/1916
Operation(al) Order(s)	49th Infantry Brigade Order No. 67 Appendix 12	19/10/1916	19/10/1916
Operation(al) Order(s)	2nd. Battalion, The Royal Irish Regiment. Operation Order No. 41	25/10/1916	25/10/1916
Miscellaneous	Orders For Raid on the 49th Infty. Brigade Front Appendix 14		
Miscellaneous	Appendix A		
Miscellaneous	Appendix B		
Miscellaneous	16th Division. Appendix 15	30/10/1916	30/10/1916
Miscellaneous	Headquarters, 16th. Division. 49th. Inf. Bde. S.O. 828/5d/	30/10/1916	30/10/1916
Miscellaneous	Headquarters, 49th Infantry Brigade.	30/10/1916	30/10/1916
Miscellaneous	Head-Quarters, 49th Infantry Brigade	29/10/1916	29/10/1916
Operation(al) Order(s)	49th Infantry Brigade Order No 69 Appendix 18	30/10/1916	30/10/1916
Operation(al) Order(s)	2nd. Battalion, The Royal Irish Regiment. Operation Order No. 43 Appendix 19	31/10/1916	31/10/1916
Miscellaneous	Report On Raid carried out by 49th Inf. Bde. on 29th October, 1916 Appendix 20	29/10/1916	29/10/1916
Miscellaneous	Notes	01/11/1916	01/11/1916
Map	Area of Raid Map "A"		

Heading	War Diary. For Month Of November 1916. Volume 2nd R. Irish Regiment		
War Diary	Kemmel	01/11/1916	30/11/1916
Operation(al) Order(s)	2nd. Battalion, The Royal Irish Regiment. Operation Order No. 43	31/10/1916	31/10/1916
Operation(al) Order(s)	2nd. Battalion, The Royal Irish Regiment. Operation Order No. 44 Appendix 2	06/11/1916	06/11/1916
Operation(al) Order(s)	Operation Order No 45 By Major L.L Farmer Commanding 2nd. Battalion, The Royal Irish Regiment.	12/11/1916	12/11/1916
Operation(al) Order(s)	Operation Order No 46 By Lieut-Colonel H.G. Gregorie, Commanding, 2nd Battalion, 1 Royal Irish Regiment Appendix 4	18/11/1916	18/11/1916
Miscellaneous	Tactical Progress Report 49th Infantry Brigade No. B.M.C. IX/2773	24/11/1916	24/11/1916
Operation(al) Order(s)	Operation Order No. 47 By Lieut Colonel H.G. Gregorie Commanding. 2nd. Battalion, The Royal Irish Regiment. Appendix 6	23/11/1916	23/11/1916
Miscellaneous	2nd R. Irish Regt	22/11/1916	22/11/1916
Miscellaneous	49th Inf. Bde. No. B.O. 74/6,	22/11/1916	22/11/1916
Miscellaneous	H.Q. 16th. Division. (G)	18/11/1916	18/11/1916
Operation(al) Order(s)	49th. Infantry Brigade. Operation Order No. 74	18/11/1918	18/11/1918
Miscellaneous	Appendix 17		
Miscellaneous			
Operation(al) Order(s)	49th. Inf. Bde. Order No. 74/1	19/11/1916	19/11/1916
Miscellaneous	49th Inf. Bde. No. B.O. 74/2	20/11/1916	20/11/1916
Miscellaneous	49th. Inf. Bde. No. B.O. 74/3	20/11/1916	20/11/1916
Operation(al) Order(s)	Operation Order No. 48 By Captain W.L Moors-Braoazon, Commanding 2nd. Battalion, The Royal Irish Regiment.	29/11/1916	29/11/1916
Heading	War Diary For Month Of December 1916 Volume 2nd Royal Irish Regiment.		
War Diary		01/12/1916	10/12/1916
War Diary	Kemmel	11/12/1916	30/12/1916
Operation(al) Order(s)	Operation Order No 49. Appendix I	03/12/1916	03/12/1916
Operation(al) Order(s)	49th Infantry Brigade Order No 77 Appendix 2	03/12/1916	03/12/1916
Miscellaneous	Table Showing Boundaries Of Brigade Area. To Accompany 49th Infantry Brigade Order No 77	03/12/1916	03/12/1916
Operation(al) Order(s)	48th Infantry Brigade Operation Order 83 Appendix 3	03/12/1916	03/12/1916
Miscellaneous	Table Showing Boundaries Of Brigade Areas. To Accompany 48th Infantry Brigade Order No. 83 Dated 3rd December 1916	03/12/1916	03/12/1916
Operation(al) Order(s)	7th. (S) Battalion Royal Inniskilling Fusiliers Operation Order No. 67 Appendix 4	00/12/1916	00/12/1916
Operation(al) Order(s)	Operation Order No. 50 by Lieut Colonel H.G. Gregorie Commanding 2nd. Battalion, The Royal Irish Regiment.	05/12/1916	05/12/1916
Operation(al) Order(s)	Operation Order No. 51. By Lieut Colonel H.G. Gregorie, Commanding, 2nd Battalion, The Royal Irish Regiment. Appendix 6	11/12/1916	11/12/1916
Miscellaneous	OC. B Coy Appendix 7	14/12/1916	14/12/1916
Miscellaneous	49th Infy Bde No. S.O. 904 Appendix 8	14/12/1916	14/12/1916
Operation(al) Order(s)	Operation Order No. 52 Lieut Colonel H.G. Commanding 2nd Battalion The Royal Irish Regiment Appendix 9	17/12/1916	17/12/1916
Miscellaneous	49th I. Bde. S.C.C. VIII/365 Appendix 10	19/12/1916	19/12/1916
Miscellaneous	16th. Division No. A/174	19/12/1916	19/12/1916

Operation(al) Order(s)	Operation Order No. 54 By Lieut-Colonel H.G. Gregorie Commanding, 2nd. Battalion. The Royal Irish Regiment.	23/12/1916	23/12/1916
Operation(al) Order(s)	Operation Order No. 53 By Lieut-Colonel H.G. Gregorie Commanding, 2nd. Battalion. The Royal Irish Regiment. Appendix 12	22/12/1916	22/12/1916
Miscellaneous	49th Infy Bde No. B.O. 81/1	21/12/1916	21/12/1916
Miscellaneous	49th Infy Bde No. S.C. 81/2 Appendix 13	22/12/1916	22/12/1916
Miscellaneous	C Form (Duplicate).Messages And Signals.		
Operation(al) Order(s)	49th Infantry Brigade Order No. 81	20/12/1916	20/12/1916
Miscellaneous	49th Infy Bde No. B.O. 84/1	28/12/1916	28/12/1916
Operation(al) Order(s)	49th Infantry Brigade Order No. 84	28/12/1916	28/12/1916
Operation(al) Order(s)	Operation Order No. 55 By Major L.L. Farmer, Commanding, 2nd. Battalion, The Royal Irish Regiment. Appendix 15	29/12/1916	29/12/1916
Heading	War Diary for month of January, 1917 Volume 2nd Royal Irish Regiment.		
War Diary	Locre	01/01/1917	29/01/1917
Miscellaneous			
War Diary		08/01/1917	29/01/1917
Operation(al) Order(s)	Operation Order No. 1. by Major L.L. Farmer Commanding. 2nd Battalion The Royal Irish Regiment.	04/01/1917	04/01/1917
Operation(al) Order(s)	49th Infantry Brigade Order No. 87 Appendix 2	05/01/1917	05/01/1917
Operation(al) Order(s)	Operation Order No. 2 By Major L.L. Farmer, Commanding 2nd. Battalion. The Royal Irish Regiment. Appendix. 3	05/01/1917	05/01/1917
Operation(al) Order(s)	Operation Order No. 2 By Major L.L. Farmer, Commanding, 2nd. Battalion, The Royal Irish Regiment.	04/01/1917	04/01/1917
Operation(al) Order(s)	Operation Order No. 3 By Major L.L. Farmer Commanding. 2nd. Battalion The Royal Irish Regiment. Appendix 5	16/01/1917	16/01/1917
Operation(al) Order(s)	Operation Order No. 4 By Major L.L. Farmer Commanding. 2nd. Battalion The Royal Irish Regiment. Appendix	22/01/1917	22/01/1917
Miscellaneous	Programme of work for week binding 5th Feby 19		
Heading	War Diary For Month Of February 1917 Volume 2nd Btn Royal Irish Regiment.		
War Diary		01/02/1917	27/03/1917
Operation(al) Order(s)	Operation Order No. 5 By Major L.L. Farmer Commanding 2nd. Battalion. The Royal Irish Regiment	05/02/1917	05/02/1917
Operation(al) Order(s)	49th Infantry Brigade Order No. 95 Appendix II	05/02/1917	05/02/1917
Operation(al) Order(s)	Operation Order No. 6 Major L.L. Farmer, Commanding 2nd Pro The Royal Irish Regt. Appendix 3	09/02/1917	09/02/1917
Miscellaneous	Office Report		
Miscellaneous			
Miscellaneous	Offence Report		
Operation(al) Order(s)	49th Infantry Brigade Order No. 96 Appendix IV	08/02/1917	08/02/1917
Operation(al) Order(s)	Operation Order No. 7 by Major L.L. Farmer. Commanding 2nd The Royal Irish Regt. Appendix V	13/02/1917	13/02/1917
Miscellaneous	2nd Bn. The Royal Irish Regt.		
Operation(al) Order(s)	49th Infantry Brigade Order No. 98 Appendix VI	11/02/1917	11/02/1917
Miscellaneous	O.R. No. 783 Appendix VII	13/02/1917	13/02/1917
Miscellaneous	2nd Bn. The Royal Irish Regt.		
Miscellaneous	Organisation Of An Infantry Battalion		

Type	Description	Date From	Date To
Miscellaneous	2nd Bn. The Royal Irish Regt.		
Miscellaneous			
Miscellaneous	2nd Bn. The Royal Irish Regt.		
Miscellaneous		07/02/1917	07/02/1917
Miscellaneous	2nd Bn. The Royal Irish Regt.		
Miscellaneous	21 The Royal Irish Programme Of Framing For Period 15-22/2/17	22/02/1917	22/02/1917
Miscellaneous	21 The Royal Irish Programme Of Framing For Bombers	14/02/1917	14/02/1917
Operation(al) Order(s)	Operation Order No. 8 by Lieut-Colonel H.G. Gregorie D.S.O. Commanding 2/The Royal Irish.	21/02/1917	21/02/1917
Miscellaneous	Offence Report		
Operation(al) Order(s)	Operation Order No. 9 Appendix X	25/02/1917	25/02/1917
Heading	War Diary For Month Of March, 1917 Volume 2nd Btn Royal Irish Regt.		
War Diary		01/03/1917	31/03/1917
Operation(al) Order(s)	49th Infantry Brigade Operation Order No. 16	22/02/1917	22/02/1917
Miscellaneous	Issued With 49th Inf. Bde. O.O. No. 16		
Operation(al) Order(s)	Spanbroek Operation Order No. 12 By Lieut-Colonel L.E.S. Ward, D.S.O., R.F.A.	01/03/1917	01/03/1917
Miscellaneous	Table Of Tasks		
Miscellaneous	Ref Spanbroek O.O. No. 12 1.3.17	01/03/1917	01/03/1917
Operation(al) Order(s)	Operation Order No. 10 by Lieut Colonel H.G. Gregorie, D.S.O. Commanding and Battalion The Royal Irish Regiment. Appendix II	01/03/1917	01/03/1917
Operation(al) Order(s)	Operation Order No. 11 by Lieut Colonel H.G. Gregorie, D.S.O. Commanding and Battalion, The Royal Irish Regiment. Appendix III	18/03/1917	18/03/1917
Operation(al) Order(s)	49th. Infantry Brigade Order No. 103 Appendix IV	16/03/1917	16/03/1917
Miscellaneous	Issued through Signals.		
Miscellaneous	Relief Table To Accompany 49th Inf. Brigade Order No. 103		
Operation(al) Order(s)	49th Infantry Brigade Order No. 104 Appendix V	21/03/1917	21/03/1917
Operation(al) Order(s)	49th Infantry Brigade Order No. 105 Appendix VI	26/03/1917	26/03/1917
Operation(al) Order(s)	Operation Order No. 13 by Lieut. Colonel H.G. Gregorie D.S.O. Commanding 2nd. Battalion. The Royal Irish Regiment. Appendix VII	28/03/1917	28/03/1917
Miscellaneous			
Operation(al) Order(s)	Operation Order No. 14 by Lieut. Colonel H.G. Gregorie D.S.O. Commanding. 2nd Battalion, The Royal Irish Regiment. Appendix VII	31/03/1917	31/03/1917
Operation(al) Order(s)	49th Infantry Brigade Order No. 103 Appendix VIII	27/03/1917	27/03/1917
Miscellaneous	Relief Table To Accompany 49th Infantry Brigade Order No. 106		
Heading	War Diary For Month Of April 1917 Volume 2nd R. Irish Regiment		
War Diary		01/04/1916	30/04/1916
Heading	War Diary Volume For Month Of May, 1917 2nd Royal Irish Regiment.		
War Diary		01/05/1917	30/05/1917
Operation(al) Order(s)	Operation Order No. 24 By Lieut. Colonel H.G. Gregorie D.S.O. Commanding, 2nd Battalion, The Royal Irish Regiment. Appendix I	01/05/1917	01/05/1917
Operation(al) Order(s)	Operation Order No. 25. By Lieut. Colonel H.G. Gregorie D.S.O. Commanding 2nd. Battalion. The Royal Irish Regiment. Appendix 2	04/05/1917	04/05/1917

Operation(al) Order(s)	49th Infantry Brigade Order No. 118 Appendix 3	08/05/1917	08/05/1917
Miscellaneous	Relief Table To Accompany Brigade Order No. 118		
Operation(al) Order(s)	49th Infantry Brigade Order No. 117	08/05/1917	08/05/1917
Operation(al) Order(s)	49th Infantry Brigade Order No. 119 Appendix 5	09/05/1917	09/05/1917
Operation(al) Order(s)	Operation Order No. 26 By Lieut. Colonel H.G. Gregorie, D.S.O. Commanding., 2nd. Battalion, The Royal Irish Regiment.	09/05/1917	09/05/1917
Operation(al) Order(s)	Operation Order No. 27 by Lieut Colonel H.G. Gregorie DSO. Commanding 2/The Royal Irish Regt.	13/00/1917	13/00/1917
Operation(al) Order(s)	49th Infantry Brigade Order No. 120 Appendix 7	12/05/1917	12/05/1917
Operation(al) Order(s)	Operation Order No. 28 By Lieut Colonel H.G. Gregorie D.S.O. Commanding. 2nd. Battalion, The Royal Irish Regiment. Appendix 8	17/05/1917	17/05/1917
Operation(al) Order(s)	49th Infantry Brigade Order No. 121 Appendix 9	14/05/1917	14/05/1917
Miscellaneous	Relief Table To Accompany 49th Infantry Brigade Order No. 121		
Operation(al) Order(s)	Operation Order No. 29 By Lieut. Colonel H.G. Gregorie D.S.O. Commanding 2nd. Battalion, The Royal Irish Regiment. Appendix 10	29/05/1917	29/05/1917
Heading	War Diary For Month Of June, 1917. Volume 2nd Battn Royal Irish Regiment.		
War Diary		01/06/1917	30/06/1917
Miscellaneous	G.O.C. 49th Infty Bde.		
Miscellaneous		26/05/1917	26/05/1917
Operation(al) Order(s)	Operation Order No. 3 By Captain J.D. Scott, Commanding "A" Battalion, The Royal Irish Regiment Appendix 15	16/06/1917	16/06/1917
Operation(al) Order(s)	Operation Order No. 3 By Captain J.D. Scott, Commanding. 2nd. Battalion, The Royal Irish Regiment. Appendix 16	00/00/1917	00/00/1917
Operation(al) Order(s)	Operation Order No. 36 By Captain J.D. Scott, Commanding. 2nd. Battalion, The Royal Irish Regiment.	21/00/1917	21/00/1917
Heading	War Diary. For Month Of July, 1917. 2nd Btn Royal Irish Regt. Vol 28		
War Diary	Tatinghem Area	01/07/1917	07/07/1917
War Diary	Roubouck Area.	08/07/1917	08/07/1917
War Diary	Winnizeele Area	09/07/1917	20/07/1917
War Diary	Watou Aka No. 2	26/07/1917	27/07/1917
War Diary	Brandhoek Area	30/07/1917	31/07/1917
Operation(al) Order(s)	Operation Order No. 41	30/07/1917	30/07/1917
Miscellaneous	Offence Report		
Heading	War Diary Of 2nd R. Irish Regt. for August 1917		
Heading	War Diary. For Month Of August, 1917. 2nd Royal Irish Regiment Vol 29		
War Diary	Derby Camp (near Vlamertinghe)	01/08/1917	02/08/1917
War Diary	Cambridge Rd	03/08/1917	05/08/1917
War Diary	Blue Line	06/08/1917	07/08/1917
War Diary	Blue Line & Vlamartinghe	08/08/1917	08/08/1917
War Diary	H.16.a.5.5	09/08/1917	11/08/1917
War Diary	Blue Line	12/08/1917	14/08/1917
War Diary	German And British F.L.	15/08/1917	15/08/1917
War Diary	Black Line	16/08/1917	16/08/1917
War Diary	Goldfish Chau	17/08/1917	18/08/1917
War Diary	Watou	19/08/1917	20/08/1917
War Diary	Eecke	21/08/1917	21/08/1917

War Diary	Achiet-Le-Petit	22/08/1917	28/08/1917
War Diary	Hamelincourt	28/08/1917	31/08/1917
Map	15th Division		
Operation(al) Order(s)	Operation Order No. 42 By Major J.D. Scott, Commanding, 2nd. Battalion, The Royal Irish Regiment. Appendix II	15/08/1917	15/08/1917
Miscellaneous			
Miscellaneous	Provisional Orders For The Attack 5th R. Innis. Fusiliers.	14/08/1917	14/08/1917
Miscellaneous	Officer Commanding 2nd. R. Irish Regt.	14/08/1917	14/08/1917
Operation(al) Order(s)	Operation Order No. 4 By. Lieut. Colonel. K.C. Weldon D.S.O. Comdg Royal Irish Fusiliers	14/08/1917	14/08/1917
Heading	War Diary. For Month Of September, 1917. Volume Unit 2nd Battn Royal Irish Regt. Vol 30		
War Diary	Hamelincourt	01/09/1917	04/09/1917
War Diary	Hindenburg Line	06/09/1917	10/09/1917
War Diary	Croisilles	10/09/1917	16/09/1917
War Diary	Hamelincourt	16/09/1917	28/09/1917
War Diary	Line	29/09/1917	30/09/1917
Miscellaneous	49th Inf. Bde. No. B.M.C. XII	01/09/1917	01/09/1917
Operation(al) Order(s)	Operation Order No. 26 By Lieut. Colonel J.D Scott Commanding 2nd Battn. The Royal Irish Regiment. App I	03/09/1917	03/09/1917
Operation(al) Order(s)	Operation Order No. 47 By Lieut. Colonel J.D Scott Commanding 2nd Battn. The Royal Irish Regiment. App 2	09/09/1917	09/09/1917
Operation(al) Order(s)	Operation Order No. 48 By Lieut. Colonel J.D. Scott, Commanding 2nd Bn. The Royal Irish Regt. App 3	15/09/1917	15/09/1917
Operation(al) Order(s)	Operation Order No. 49 By Lieut. Colonel J.D. Scott, Commanding 2nd Bn. The Royal Irish Regt. App 4	27/09/1917	27/09/1917
Miscellaneous	49th Inf. Bde. No. B.M.C. XII/8	29/09/1917	29/09/1917
Heading	War Diary For Month Of October 1917. 2nd Btn. R. Irish Regt. Vol 31		
War Diary	Right Sub Section Left Section	01/10/1917	04/10/1917
War Diary	Croisilles	05/10/1917	10/10/1917
War Diary	Hamelincourt	10/10/1917	21/10/1917
War Diary	Trenches	22/10/1917	28/10/1917
War Diary	Support Croisilles	29/10/1917	31/10/1917
War Diary	Line	30/10/1917	30/10/1917
Operation(al) Order(s)	Operation Order No. 80 App I	03/10/1917	03/10/1917
Operation(al) Order(s)	49th Inf. Bde. Order No. 168	04/10/1917	04/10/1917
Operation(al) Order(s)	Operation Order No. 51 By Lieut. Colonel J.D. Scott. Commanding. 2nd Bn. The. Royal Irish Regiments App3	09/10/1917	09/10/1917
Operation(al) Order(s)	Operation Order No. 52 By Lieut. Colonel J.D. Scott. Commanding. 2nd Bn. The. Royal Irish Regiments App4	20/10/1917	20/10/1917
Operation(al) Order(s)	49th Infantry Brigade Order No. 171	24/10/1917	24/10/1917
Map	Operation By No 3 Special Coy RE		
Miscellaneous			
Operation(al) Order(s)	Operation Order No. 53 By Lieut. Colonel J.D. Scott. Commanding 2nd. Battalion, The Royal Irish Regiment. App 6	27/10/1917	27/10/1917
Operation(al) Order(s)	49th Infantry Brigade Order No. 173	27/10/1917	27/10/1917
Heading	War Diary For Month Of November, 1917 2nd R. Irish Regiment. Vol 32		

War Diary	Hamelincourt	01/11/1917	07/11/1917
War Diary	Croisilles (left Supp)	08/11/1917	12/11/1917
War Diary	Ervillers	13/11/1917	21/11/1917
War Diary	Front Line	19/11/1917	22/11/1917
War Diary	Hamelincourt	23/11/1917	30/11/1917
Miscellaneous			
Operation(al) Order(s)	48th Infantry Brigade. Operation Order No. 170	06/11/1917	06/11/1917
Operation(al) Order(s)	Operation Order No. 57 by Lieut. Colonel J.D. Commanding 2nd. Battalion, The Royal Irish Regiment.	11/11/1917	11/11/1917
Miscellaneous	16th Div. No. G. 131/17	14/11/1917	14/11/1917
Operation(al) Order(s)	Operation Order No. 58 by Lieut. Colonel. J.D. Scott, Commanding, 2nd. Battalion The Royal Irish Regiment. App 5	17/11/1917	17/11/1917
Operation(al) Order(s)	Operation Order No. 55 by Lieut. Colonel, J.D. Scott, Commanding, 2nd. Battalion The Royal Irish Regiment. App 6	06/11/1917	06/11/1917
Miscellaneous	2nd. Battalion, The Royal Irish Regiment		
Miscellaneous	Additional Instructions No. 2., For An Offensive Action.		
Operation(al) Order(s)	Operation Order No. 8 Lieut Colonel T.D. Commanding, 2nd Battalion, The Royal Irish Regiment.	29/11/1917	29/11/1917
Miscellaneous	Messages Form.		
Map			
Heading	War Diary For Month Of December, 1917. 2nd R. Irish Regiment		
War Diary	Hindenburg Line Croissilles	01/12/1917	01/12/1917
War Diary	Clonmel Camp Hamelincourt	02/12/1917	02/12/1917
War Diary	Barastre	03/12/1917	04/12/1917
War Diary	Tincourt	05/12/1917	06/12/1917
War Diary	Lempire	07/12/1917	16/12/1917
War Diary	Tincourt	17/12/1917	23/12/1917
War Diary	Ronssoy	24/12/1917	30/12/1917
Operation(al) Order(s)	Operation Order No. 63 by Lieut Colonel J.D. Scott, Commanding 2nd. Bn. The Rl. Irish Regt.	22/12/1917	22/12/1917
Heading	War Diary For Month Of January 1918 2nd R. Irish Regiment.		
War Diary		01/01/1918	03/01/1918
War Diary		04/01/1918	09/01/1918
War Diary	Hamel	05/01/1918	15/01/1918
War Diary	Lempire	17/01/1918	28/01/1918
War Diary	Ste Emilie	29/01/1918	31/01/1918
Miscellaneous			
War Diary	Hamel	04/01/1918	21/01/1918
Operation(al) Order(s)	Operation Order No. 65 by Capt. M.C.C. Harrison, Commanding, 2nd. Battalion, The Royal Irish Regiment.	03/01/1918	03/01/1918
Operation(al) Order(s)	Operation Order No. 1 by Major, W.L.C. Moore-Brabazon, Commanding, 2nd. Battalion, The Royal Irish Regiment.	09/01/1918	09/01/1918
Miscellaneous	Army Form W.3125		
Operation(al) Order(s)	Operation Order No. 2 by Major W.L.C. Moore-Brabazon, Commanding. 2nd Battalion, The Royal Irish Regiment.	15/01/1918	15/01/1918
Operation(al) Order(s)	Operation Order No. 3 by Major W.L.C. Moore-Brabazon, Commanding, 2nd Battalion, The Royal Irish Regiment.	21/01/1918	21/01/1918

Operation(al) Order(s)	Operation Order No. 41 by Lieut. Colonel, J.D. Scott, D.S.O., Commanding, 2nd. Battalion, The Royal Irish Regiment.	27/01/1918	27/01/1918
Heading	War Diary. For Month Of February 1918 2nd R. Irish Regiment.		
War Diary	Ste Emilie	01/02/1918	03/02/1918
War Diary	Villers Faucon	03/02/1918	09/02/1918
War Diary	Hamel	09/02/1918	14/02/1918
War Diary	Epehy	18/02/1918	28/02/1918
War Diary	Villers Faucon	28/02/1918	28/02/1918
Operation(al) Order(s)	Operation Order No. 5 by Lieut Colonel, J.D. Scott, D.S.O. Commanding. 2nd. Battalion. The Royal Irish Regiment. Appendix No. 1	02/02/1918	02/02/1918
Operation(al) Order(s)	Operation Order No. 6 by Lieut Colonel, J.D. Scott, D.S.O. Commanding 2nd Battalion The Royal Irish Regiment Appendix No. 2	07/02/1918	07/02/1918
Operation(al) Order(s)	Operation Order No. 7 by Lieut Colonel, J.D. Scott, D.S.O. Commanding 2nd Battalion The Royal Irish Regiment. Appendix No. 3	12/02/1918	12/02/1918
Operation(al) Order(s)	Operation Order No. 8 by Lieut Colonel, J.D. Scott, D.S.O. Commanding. 2nd Battalion The Royal Irish Regiment. Appendix No. 4	17/02/1918	17/02/1918
Operation(al) Order(s)	Operation Order No. 9 by Lieut Colonel, J.D. Scott, D.S.O. Commanding 2nd Battalion The Royal Irish Regiment. Appendix No. 5	21/02/1918	21/02/1918
Heading	16th Division. 49th Brigade. 2nd Battalion Royal Irish Regiment March 1918		
War Diary	Villers Faucon	01/03/1918	01/03/1918
War Diary	Ronssoy	04/03/1918	07/03/1918
War Diary	Basse Boulogne	08/03/1918	16/03/1918
War Diary	Ronssoy	16/03/1918	21/03/1918
War Diary	Villers-Faucon Tincourt	22/03/1918	23/03/1918
War Diary	Tincourt Doingt	23/03/1918	23/03/1918
War Diary	La Chapelette	23/03/1918	23/03/1918
War Diary	Biaches	23/03/1918	23/03/1918
War Diary	Cappy-Bray	24/03/1918	26/03/1918
Miscellaneous	Account Of The Action Of 2/Royal Irish Regiment, 49th Brigade, 16th Division, VII Corps, Fifth Army From 25th March to 3rd April 1918		
Miscellaneous	Copied From Private Diary of Major M.C.C. Harrison, D.S.O., M.C. (at that time with 2/R. Irish R. 49th Bde. 16th Div. VII Corps, Fifth Army).		
Miscellaneous	49th Brigade.		
Miscellaneous	49th Brigade.	07/04/1917	07/04/1917
Heading	War Diary 2nd Battn. The Royal Irish Regiment. April 1918		
War Diary	Saleux	04/04/1918	04/04/1918
War Diary	Vismes-Au-Val	08/04/1918	10/04/1918
War Diary	Wizernes	11/04/1918	11/04/1918
War Diary	Elnes	14/04/1918	18/04/1918
War Diary	Aire Steen Becque	19/04/1918	23/04/1918
War Diary	Raincheval	23/04/1915	25/04/1915

1979/1

2 Battalion Royal Irish Regiment

Oct 1916 - Apr 1918

16TH DIVISION
49TH INFY BDE

2ND BN ROY. IRISH REGT

OCT 1916 - APL 1 918

From 7 Div 22 Bde

To 63 Div 188 Bde

WAR DIARY

MONTH OF OCTOBER, 1916.

VOLUME

2nd Royal Irish Regiment.

2ₒ Apl '18

WAR DIARY
or
INTELLIGENCE SUMMARY.

(Erase heading not required.)

Army Form C. 2118.

Place	Date	Hour	Summary of Events and Information	Remarks and references to Appendices
PAPOT.	Oct. 1st		Battalion in Brigade reserve in huts at PAPOT. New pattern of box respirators issued to the battalion.	J.A.M.
do	2nd		Nothing of importance.	J.A.M.
	3rd		The battalion relieved the 1st Royal Welch Fusiliers in the trenches at PLOEGSTEERT. Lt N. CURRAN. M.C.	Appendix 1.
PLOEGSTEERT.	4th		2 men wounded, 1 missing, and 1 officer killed.	J.A.M.
"	5th		Situation quiet save for occasional Trench Mortar activity on the part of the enemy	J.A.M.
	6th		2 men wounded, one of whom subsequently died.	J.A.M.
	7th		Battalion relieved in the front line trenches by 1st Royal WELCH FUSILIERS and goes into Support line in PLOEGSTEERT WOOD.	Appendix 2
	8th		all quiet.	J.A.M.
	9th		"	J.A.M.
	10th		"	J.A.M.

WAR DIARY or INTELLIGENCE SUMMARY.

Army Form C. 2118.

Place	Date	Hour	Summary of Events and Information	Remarks and references to Appendices
PLOEGSTEERT	Oct 11th		Battalion relieved in PLOEGSTEERT WOOD by 2nd H.A.C. "B" & "D" Coys remain in support to two companies of 2/H.A.C. who hold the front-line trenches of the left sector - "A" & "C" Coys relieved by 2 Coys of 2/H.A.C. and march back to camp near ROMARIN vacated by 2/H.A.C. — A draft of 10 other ranks arrived today	Appendices 3, 4, 4. J.A.N.
	12th		All quiet -	J.A.N.
	13th	12 M.d.	"B" & "D" Coys of 2/ROYAL IRISH relieved by 2 Coys of 2/H.A.C. and rejoin rest of the battalion in Camp near ROMARIN.	Appendix 4.
	14th	9 a.m.	Battalion marched to join the 49th Infantry Brigade of the 16th Division - Billeted at KEMMEL Shelters.	Appendices 5, 4, 6. & 7.
KEMMEL SHELTERS	15th		Organization of the battalion broken up - The personnel of 5 Coys (one being the Grenade Coy) rejoin the Grenade Coy respective Coys -	J.A.N.

Army Form C. 2118.

WAR DIARY
or
INTELLIGENCE SUMMARY.
(Erase heading not required.)

Instructions regarding War Diaries and Intelligence Summaries are contained in F. S. Regs., Part II. and the Staff Manual respectively. Title pages will be prepared in manuscript.

Place	Date Oct	Hour	Summary of Events and Information	Remarks and references to Appendices
KEMMEL	16th		All quiet. Arrival of a draft of 14 other ranks - 9 men awarded the Military Medal for gallantry in the field (on the SOMME).	I A.N.
"	17th		The Battalion relieved the 8/ Royal Irish FUSILIERS in the left sub-section - for disposition vide 1 man wounded.	Appendix 8. I A.N.
	18th		Our Trench Mortars & Stokes Guns displayed great activity 1 man wounded.	Appendix 9. I A.N.
	19th		All quiet -	I A.N.
	20th		The Battalion is relieved by 7/8th The ROYAL IRISH FUSILIERS and moves into Brigade Reserve at KEMMEL SHELTERS.	Appendices 10, 11, 12.
	21st		All quiet - Arrival of a draft of 8 other ranks	I A.N.
	22nd		" "	I A.N.
	23rd		" "	I A.N.

Army Form C. 2118.

WAR DIARY
or
INTELLIGENCE SUMMARY.

(Erase heading not required.)

Instructions regarding War Diaries and Intelligence Summaries are contained in F. S. Regs., Part II. and the Staff Manual respectively. Title pages will be prepared in manuscript.

Place	Date	Hour	Summary of Events and Information	Remarks and references to Appendices
	Oct. 24		All quiet - Capt. & Adjutant T. A. LOWE proceeded to ENGLAND and is officer at the strength -	J.A.N. authority A.G.A/17045
	25.		All quiet.	J.A.N.
	26.		The Battalion relieved the 7/8th Battalion the ROYAL IRISH FUSILIERS in the left sub-sector of the front line -	Appendix
	27th.		All quiet - 6 officers and 5 other ranks arrived as reinforcements - one other rank accidentally wounded - Capt. H. J. CONSIDINE (Maxim Gun) killed in action by Trench Mortar	
	28th.		Capt. H. J. Considine was awarded, posthumous, the Military Cross for gallantry on the SOMME. 1 man wounded -	J.A.V.
	29th. 5.30 p.m.		A successful raid was carried out on the German trenches - Promart 2/Lt. J. P. CORCORAN wounded missing 2/Lt. J. J. LITTLE wounded	Appendix No 14, 15.

Army Form C. 2118.

WAR DIARY
or
INTELLIGENCE SUMMARY.
(Erase heading not required.)

Place	Date	Hour	Summary of Events and Information	Remarks and references to Appendices
	29th		2 other ranks killed in action 2 " " wounded + missing 13 " " wounded - For report on raid and map of the area vide	F.B.N. Appendices 15, 16, 17, 20
	30th		Major E. ROCHE-KELLY proceeded to assume command of the 6th ROYAL IRISH Regt.	J.A.M.
	31st		The battalion was relieved by the 7/8th The ROYAL IRISH FUSILIERS in the left-sub-sector	Appendices 18, 19 -

Relief of 1st R.W. Fusiliers

Appendix II
Operation Order
by Lt. Col. Gregorie

2nd. BATTALION, THE ROYAL IRISH REGIMENT.
OPERATION ORDER NO. 35.

Copy No. 1

Reference Map
ST. YVES.

The Field.
2/10/16.

1. The Battalion will relieve the 1/Royal Welch Fusiliers in the trenches tomorrow.

2. Coys. will be disposed as follows and will march off at the undermentioned times.

   "A" Coy.   Right Sector   1 p.m.
   "C" ,,   Left Sector   1-15 p.m.
   "B" ,,   Right Support   1-30 p.m.
   "D" ,,   Left Support   1-45 p.m.

   Route - via the STRAND.
   H.Q., Lewis Gunners, Signallers /and Grenade Coy.
   Scouts will march off at 12-45 p.m. and will take over as before.

3. Officers trench kits to be dumped outside H.Q.Mess at 11 a.m. All valises and surplus stores to be dumped outside old Q.M. Stores at 11-30 a.m. The Transport Officer will arrange to move these as previously.

4. Dinners 12 noon.

5. Battalion H.Q. will close at LA ROMARIN Camp at 2 p.m. and will reopen at PLOEGSTEERT WOOD at the same hour.

Issued at 6-30 p.m.

(Sd.) T. A. Lowe, Captain & Adjutant,
2nd. Battalion, The Royal Irish Regiment.

Copy No. 1. Wardiary.
       2. 22nd. Brigade H.Q.
          (for information.)
       3. O. C. "A" Coy.
       4. O. C. "B" ,,
       5. O. C. "C" ,,
       6. O. C. "D" ,,
       7. O. C. Grenade Coy.

No. 8. Lewis Gun Officer.
    9. Medical Officer.
   10. Transport Officer.
   11. Quartermaster.
   12. 1/Royal Welch Fusiliers.
       (for information.)
   13. R. S. M.
   14. Signalling Sergeant.

Appendix 2.
RELIEF of Trenches.

2ND. BATTALION, THE ROYAL IRISH REGIMENT.
Reference Map   OPERATION ORDER NO. 36.
ST. YVES.

Copy No. 1
The Field.
6/10/16.

1. The Battalion will be relieved in the trenches tomorrow by the 1/Royal Welch Fusiliers.

2. Upon relief Coys. will march to support line as under (REGENT STREET is not to be used).
   "D" Coy. to HUNTERS AVENUE from DEAD HORSE CORNER to REGENTS FORT inclusive.
   "B" Coy. to HUNTERS AVENUE from REGENTS FORT (exclusive) to READING FORT (inclusive).
   "A" Coy. to HUNTERSTOWN and hutments SOUTH of the STRAND.
        Coy. H.Q. at PLOEGSTEERT HALL.
   "C" Coy. to MARLBOROUGH HOUSE and hutments NORTH of the STRAND.
   The Grenade Coy. will be equally divided between "B" and "D" Coys. in HUNTERS AVENUE.
   Lewis Gunners will be attached to "A" Coy. at HUNTERS TOWN.

3. Officers trench kits and stores must be carried back to support line under Coy. arrangements. Officers who want their valises must communicate direct with the Quartermaster.
   Rations for "B" and "A" Coys. will be dumped at NORTH BRITISH RAILWAY dump and for "C" and "D" Coys. at the CANADIAN PACIFIC dump. Ration parties to report to C.Q.M.S's. at 3-30 p.m.

4. Battalion H.Q. will close at PLOEGSTEERT WOOD at 3 p.m. and reopen at CRESLOW FARM at the same hour.

                                 (Sd.) T. A. Lowe, Captain & Adjutant,
                                   2nd. Battalion, The Royal Irish Regiment.

Issued at 9 p.m.

Copy No. 1. War Diary.   No. 7. Lewis Gun Officer.
       2. O. C. "A" Coy.   8. Medical Officer.
       3. O. C. "B" ,,   9. Transport Officer.
       4. O. C. "C" ,,   10. Quartermaster.
       5. O. C. "D" ,,   11. R. S. M.
       6. O. C. Grenade Coy.   12. Signalling Serjeant.

Appendix 3.

2nd R.I.R. relieved by 2/H.A.C

2ND. BATTALION, THE ROYAL IRISH REGIMENT.
OPERATION ORDER NO. 37.

Reference Map: ST. YVES.

Copy No. 1.

The Field.
9/10/16.

1. The Battalion will be relieved in PLOEGSTEERT WOOD by the 2/H.A.C. and will leave the 7th. Division on the 14th. inst. to join the 16th. Division.

2. On the 11th. inst. a semi-relief will be carried out as follows:-
    "B" Coy. will relieve a company of the 1/R.W.F. in ROTTEN ROW.
    "D" Coy. will relieve a company of the 1/R.W.F. in ST. ANDREW'S DRIVE.
    Both these companies will remain in close support to 2 companies of the 2/H.A.C. who will be holding the front line trenches of the Left Sector. They will furnish working parties as before. On the 13th. they will be relieved by 2 companies 2/H.A.C. and will march to camp near ROMARIN.
    On the 11th. "A" and "C" Coys. will be relieved by 2 companies of the 2/H.A.C. in the WOOD and will march back to camp near ROMARIN vacated by the 2/H.A.C.

3. For instructional purposes the following Officers and N.C.O's. will be attached to the Battalion 2/H.A.C. relieving the front line on 11th. inst. They will report to the Adjutant, 2/H.A.C. at 3 p.m.
    Right Company 2/H.A.C.
        2/Lieut. L. A. Hayden.   "B" Coy.
        7575 Sgt. Hanrahan,   M.   "A" ,,
        8297 Cpl. Woods,   W.   "A" ,,
        9494 ,, Kavanagh,   W.   "A" ,,
        7467 ,, Mc.Carthy,   J.   "A" ,,
    Left Company 2/H.A.C.
        2/Lieut. S. B. Griffin.   "C" Coy.
        8253 Sgt. Hunt,   A.   "C" ,,
        8308 ,, Bergin,   J.   "C" ,,
        9475 Cpl. Chester,   J.   "C" ,,
        10481 ,, Murphy,   J.   "C" ,,
    Above will be rationed by 2/H.A.C. and relieved on instructions from the Adjutant, 2/R.I.Regt.

4. The Commanding Officer and Adjutant, 2/R.I.Regt., will remain at Battalion H.Qrs., 2/H.A.C., to give any assistance required.
    Senior Major and Assistant Adjutant will establish Battalion H.Qrs. at camp near ROMARIN at 3 p.m. on the 11th. inst.

App: 3 (contd)

8. Instructions re baggage and transport will be issued later.

(Sd.) T. A. Lowe, Captain & Adjutant,
2nd. Battalion, The Royal Irish Regiment.

Issued at 6 p.m.

Copy No. 1. War Diary.
2. 22nd. Infantry Brigade.
  (For information.)
3. 1/Royal Welch Fusiliers.
  (For information.)
4. 2/H.L.I.
  (For information.)
5. O.C. "A" Coy.
6. O.C. "B" "

No. 7. O.C. "C" Coy.
8. O.C. "D" "
9. O.C. Grenade Coy.
10. Lewis Gun Officer.
11. Medical Officer.
12. Transport Officer.
13. Quartermaster.
14. R. S. M.
15. Signalling Sergeant.

Appendix 4.

SECRET.

Officer Commanding.
2nd. R. Irish Rgt.
~~1st. R.W. Fusiliers.~~
2nd. H.A.C.

The relief of the 2nd. R. Irish Rgt. by the 2nd. H.A.C. will be carried out as follows :-

1. On the afternoon of the 11th. inst., 2 Companies 2nd. H.A.C. will relieve the 2 Companies 1st. R.W. Fusiliers holding the front trenches of the Left Sub-sector.
Officer Commanding 2nd. R. Irish Rgt. will attach 1 Officer to each Company 2nd. H.A.C., and 1 N.C.O. to each Platoon.
2 Companies 2nd. R. Irish Rgt. will relieve 2 Companies 1st. R.W. Fusiliers in support to the left Sub-sector.

2. The 1st. R.W. Fusiliers on relief will withdraw to PAPOT.
The 2 Companies 2nd. R. Irish Rgt. not already detailed for the trenches, will take over the billets vacated by 2nd. H.A.C.

3. Officer Commanding 2nd. H.A.C. will assume command of the Left Sub-sector on completion of the relief.
The details of relief will be arranged by Commanding Officers concerned.
2nd. H.A.C. will take over from 2nd. R. Irish Rgt. the Code Calls, Code Books, and Trench Maps at present in their possession.

4. Officer Commanding 2nd. R. Irish Rgt. or his Adjutant, or both if possible, will remain at the Headquarters 2nd. H.A.C. to give any information or assistance required.
The Battalion Intelligence and Lewis Gun Officers will similarly give every assistance in their power.

5. On the 13th. inst., the 2 Companies 2nd. H.A.C. from rest billets, will relieve the 2 Companies 2nd. R. Irish Rgt. in support to the left Sub-sector. This relief will be completed by 12 noon.
The 2 Companies 2nd. H.A.C. already in the front trenches, will remain there till the completion of their tour in the trenches.
On relief, 2 Companies 2nd. R. Irish Rgt., and details will take over billets vacated by 2 Companies 2nd. H.A.C.

6. ACKNOWLEDGE. ✓

8th. October 1916.   J.E. Chads   Captain,
                             Brigade Major 22nd. Infantry Brigade.

Appendix 5.
Transfer of 2 R.I. to 16th Division

2ND. BATTALION, THE ROYAL IRISH REGIMENT. Copy No. 1
Reference Map OPERATION ORDER NO. 38. The Field.
Sheet 28. S.W. 13/10/16.

1. The Battalion will march at 9 a.m. on the 14th. inst. to join the 49th. Infantry Brigade, 16th. Division.
   The Battalion on arrival in new area will be billetted in KEMMEL SHELTERS.

2. *Route.* Starting Point :- Road Junction S.30.c.9.5. - WESTHOF FARM - Road Junction S.18.b.2.2. - DRANOUTRE - Road Junction N.24.d.4.7. - KEMMEL.

3. Order of March. Companies will march in the following order :-
   "A" Coy.
   "B" ,,
   "C" ,,
   "D" ,,
   Grenade Coy.
   Drums and Headquarter Party.

   An interval of ¼ mile will be maintained between Coys. Leading company will pass the starting point at 9 a.m.

4. A billetting party consisting of the 4 C.Q.M.S's., C.Q.M.S. Haynes and A.S.S. Ingram will report to the Q.M. at the camp at 6-15 a.m. tomorrow. This party will ride bicycles.

5. Officers' valises, stores, etc, will be dumped in the space opposite the Bn. H.Q. Guard before 8 a.m. ready for loading.

6. DRESS. Steel helmets will be worn on the march and not carried.

(sd.) W.C.V.Galwey, 2/Lieut. & A/Adjutant,
Hour of issue 1 p.m. 2nd. Battn. The Royal Irish Regiment.
Copy No. 1. War Diary. No. 7. Lewis Gun Officer.
2. O. C. "A" Coy. 8. Medical Officer.
3. O. C. "B" ,, 9. Transport Officer.
4. O. C. "C" ,, 10. Quartermaster.
5. O. C. "D" ,, 11. R. S. M.
6. O. C. Grenade Coy. 12. Signalling Sergeant.
13. H.Q. 2nd Infy. Bde.
(for information)

SECRET

Appendix 6.
Transfer of 2 R.I. to
16th Division

Officer Commanding.
2nd. R.Irish Regt.

1. The 2nd. Battalion the Royal Irish Regiment will march at 9 a.m. on the 14th. inst., to join 49th. Infantry Brigade of the 16th. Division.

Battalion on arrival in new area will be billeted in KEMMEL Chateau. SHELTERS

2. Route to be followed :-

Road Junction S.30.c.10.5.- WESTHOF FME.

Road Junction S.18.b.2.2.- DRANCOTRE.

Road Junction M.24.d.4.7.- Kemmel.

3. Billeting party to report to Headquarters 49th. Infantry Brigade, KEMMEL.

4. Battalion will be rationed by 7th. Division for 15th. instant.

5. Application for any extra transport required to reach Divisional Headquarters by 12 noon, 13th. inst.

6. Train wagons of R.Irish Regt. will return to 7th. Divisional Train on the 15th. instant.

13th. October 1916.

JHF Chads Captain,
Brigade Major 22nd. Infantry Brigade.

Appendix 7

SECRET.   Copy No....5....

49th. Infantry Brigade Order No. 64 - 12/10/16.

1. The 2nd. Royal Irish Regiment will join the 49th. Brigade on or about the 14th. August.

2. The 7th. and 8th. Battalions R. Irish Fusiliers will be amalgamated and will be called the 7th/8th. Battalion Royal Irish Fusiliers from the 15th. October.

3. The following moves will take place on the 14th. inst.

Right Sub-Section.

7th. R. Inniskilling Fus. will relieve the 8th. R. Irish Fus. Guides will be at Brigade Headquarters at 1 PM.
On relief the 8th. R. Irish Fus. will move into Doncaster Huts, LOCRE.

Left Sub-Section.

8th. R. Inniskilling Fus. will relieve the 7th. R. Irish Fus. Guides will be at KEMMEL CHATEAU at 2 PM.
On relief the 7th. R. Irish Fus. will move to Doncaster Huts, LOCRE.

4. Billeting Parties of the 7th. & 8th. R. Irish Fusiliers will report at the Headquarters of the 8th. R. Inniskilling Fus. at 12 noon on the 14th. inst.

5. On arrival the 2nd. R. Irish Regt. will be accommodated in KEMMEL Shelters. Billeting Parties will report at Brigade H.Q. N.20.d.3.3.

6. Trench Store Lists will be sent to Brigade H.Q.

7. Completion of all reliefs will be reported in 2nd. Army Code to Brigade Headquarters.

W.W.Willem Captain,
Brigade Major, 49th. Infantry Brigade.

Issued through Signals :
Copy No. 1 to 7th. R. Innis. Fus.
  "   2 " 8th. R. Innis. Fus.
  "   3 " 7th. R. Irish Fus.
  "   4 " 8th. R. Irish Fus.
  "   5 " 2nd. R. Irish Regt.
  "   6 " 49th. M.G. Company.
  "   7 " 49th. T.M. Battery.
  "   8 " 48th. Infantry Brigade.
  "   9 " 109th. Infantry Brigade.
  "   10 " 16th. Division (G).
  "   11 " 16th. Division (Q).
  "   12 " A.D.M.S. 16th. Division.
  "   13 " Staff Captain.
  "   14 " Bde. Signal Officer.
  "   15 " 157th. Fd. Coy. R.E.
  "   16 " 144th. Coy. A.S.C.
  "   17 " 113th. Fd. Ambce.
  "   18 " Bde. Supply Officer.
  "   19 " Bde. Transport Officer.
  "   20 " 171st. Tunnelling Coy. R.E.
  "   21 " 250th.   "   "
  "   22 " O.C. Right Group Artillery.
  "   23 - 24 War Diary.
  "   25 " File.

Appendix 8.

2ND. BATTALION, THE ROYAL IRISH REGIMENT.
OPERATION ORDER NO. 39.

Reference Maps
WYTSCHAETE & Sheet 28 S.W.

Copy No. ....
The Field.
16/10/16.

The Battalion will relieve the 8/Royal Innis. Fusiliers in the left sub-section tomorrow, the 17th. inst. and will also take over 5 fire bays from 7/Royal Innis. Fusiliers (Trench N.29.3.)

Companies will be disposed as follows and will march off at the times stated below :-

"A" Coy.	Front Line	1-30 p.m.
"B" "	Right Support	1-40 p.m.
"C" "	Left Support	1-50 p.m.
"D" "	KEMMEL CHATEAU	2 p.m.
H.Q. and Scouts	KEMMEL CHATEAU	2-10 p.m.

On reaching Bde. H.Q. (N.29.d.3.3.) an interval of 200 yards will be maintained between platoons. Guides will be at KEMMEL CHATEAU at 2 p.m.

The Lewis Gun Officer will arrange to attach 2 extra Lewis Guns to "A" Coy.

Officers valises, stores, etc. will be stacked at Battn. H.Q., KEMMEL SHELTERS BY 12 NOON THE 17TH. INST.

The Drums will march to the Transport and will remain there while the Battalion is in the trenches.

Dinners - 12 noon.

Battalion H.Q. will close in KEMMEL SHELTERS at 2 p.m. and will re-open at KEMMEL CHATEAU at the same hour.

Arrangements r. rations will be issued later.

(Sd.) W. C. V. Galway, 2/Lieut. & A/Adjutant,
2nd. Battalion, The Royal Irish Regiment.

Hour of issue 4 p.m.
Copy No. 1. Wardiary
2. H.Q. 49th. Infy. Bde.
   (for information.)
3. 7/R. Innis. Fusiliers.
   (for information.)
4. 8/R. Innis. Fusiliers.
   (for information.)
5. O. C. "A" Coy.
6. O. C. "B" "
7. O. C. "C" "
No. 8. O. C. "D" Coy.
9. Lewis Gun Officer.
10. Bn. Bombing Officer.
11. Medical Officer.
12. Transport Officer.
13. Quartermaster.
14. R. S. M.
15. Scout Sergeant.
16. Signalling Sergeant.
17. Drums.

Appendix 9

SECRET.   Copy No... 1

Ref. Map 28 S.W.   17th. October 1916.
1/20,000.

49th. INFANTRY BRIGADE OPERATION ORDER No. 66.

-:-:-:-:-:-:-:-:-

1.   A Ten minutes Trench Mortar Bombardment will take place on the Brigade Front on Wednesday 18th. October 16. commencing at 9 a.m.

2. TARGETS.

   Stokes Guns :-

   No. 1.   N.30.a.2.0.   to   N.30.a.3.2½.
   No. 2.   N.30.a.3.2½.   to   N.30.a.5.5.
   No. 3.   N.30.a.5.5.   to   N.30.a.4.8.
   No. 4.   N.30.a.4.8.   to   N.30.a.6.9.

   2" T.Ms.

   No. 1.   N.30.a.2.0.   Junction of C.T. with Front Line.
   No. 2.   N.30.a.5.5.   Junction of C.T. with Front Line.

   After end of bombardment 2" T.Ms. will be ready to retaliate if enemy commence.

   RATE OF FIRE for T.Ms.

   Stokes 10 per minute.

   2" T.Ms. as fast as possible.

   Machine Guns will, starting from Zero, give bursts of Indirect fire on selected points.

   Rifle Grenade Batteries will keep up a fire on the enemy's front trench along the front.

   The Right Group Artillery will give covering fire on lines of Communication and Support Trenches and any known O.Ps.

   Watches to be synchronised at 7.30 a.m.

                                    Brimson Gower   Brig. General,
                                    Commanding : 49th. Infantry Brigade.

Issued through Signals :
Copy No. 1 to 2nd. R. Irish Regt.
   ..   2 .. 7th. R. Innis. Fus.
   ..   3 .. 49th M.G. Company
   ..   4 .. 49th T.M. Battery
   ..   5 .. 48th. Infantry Brigade.
   ..   6 .. 109th. Infantry Brigade.
   ..   7 .. 16th. Division (G).
   ..   8 .. 157th. Fd. Coy. R.E.
   ..   9 .. 171st. Tunnelling Coy. R.E.
   ..   10 .. 250th. Tunnelling Coy. R.E.
   ..   11 .. O.C. Right Group Artillery.
   ..   12 - 13 War Diary.
   ..   14 .. File.

Appendix 10.

2ND. BATTALION, THE ROYAL IRISH REGIMENT.
OPERATION ORDER NO. 40.

Reference Map
WYTSCHAETE & Sheet 28 S.W.

The Field,
19/10/16.

1. The Battalion will be relieved by the 7/8th. Battn., The Royal Irish Fusiliers on the 20th. October 1916.

2. O's.C. "A", "B" & "C" Coys. will detail 1 guide per platoon. Guides to be at KEMMEL CHATEAU at 2 p.m.

3. On relief the Battalion will move into Brigade Reserve at KEMMEL SHELTERS.

4. The Quartermaster, the 4 Coy. Q.M.Sgts. and C.Q.M.S. Haynes will report to H.Q., 7/8th. Battn., The Royal Irish Fusiliers at 12 noon and will take over billets.

5. Previous orders re movement east of LOCRE and east of Bde. H.Qrs. will be observed.

6. All working parties, schemes of work and intelligence will be carefully handed over to relieving unit.

7. Trench store lists will be rendered to this H.Q. by 12 noon 20th. inst.

8. Officers' trench kits, mess stores, etc., will be dumped at this H.Q. by 12 noon tomorrow.

(Sd.) W.C. Galwey, 2/Lieut. & A/Adjutant,
2nd. Battn., The Royal Irish Regiment.

Hour of issue 5 p.m.

Copy No. 1. War Diary.
2. H.Qrs., 49th. Inf. Bde.
   (for information.)
3. 7/8th. R. Irish Fusiliers.
   (for information.)
4. O. C. "A" Coy.
5. O. C. "B" ,,
6. O. C. "C" ,,
7. O. C. "D" ,,

No. 8. Assistant Adjutant.
9. Lewis Gun Officer.
10. Bn. Bombing Officer.
11. Medical Officer.
12. Transport Officer.
13. Quartermaster.
14. R. S. M.
15. Scout Sergeant.
16. Signalling Sergeant.

Appendix 11.

Operation Orders no 2.   Copy No. 11
by
Captain. J.J. O'Donnell. M.C. Commanding
7/8th Bn Royal Irish Fusiliers.   19-10-16

This Battn will relieve the 2nd Royal Irish Regt in the left Subsection on the 20th October 1916. Guides 1 per platoon will be at KEMMEL. CHATEAU. at. 2 pm.

The dividing line between Subsection has been adjusted and now is :- Trench N. 293. Bay 6. (this point is distinguished by a board with a black cross on a yellow background) Junction of Reserve Trench with Lindenhock Road. Junction of YOUNG Street with Queens Gate. – thence in a straight line to N. 27. b. 2.5. Defence Schemes should be adjusted accordingly.

An advance party, consisting of 2nd in Command of each Coy and 1. N.C.O. per Coy. Lewis Gunners and Signallers will be at KEMMEL CHATEAU at 12. noon.

A billetting party of 2nd R. Irish Regt will arrive here to take over huts at 12. noon. Huts should be thoroughly clean by this hour.

Coys will move to KEMMEL. CHATEAU in following order :-
 A, B, C, D. by platoons in file at 200 yds interval.
All Schemes of Work will be handed over to relieving unit.
Officers Kits will be piled by Coys, outside Coy Lines. Bundles to be brought up at night, will be piled separately, & Q.M. Sgts. concerned notified. Each Coy will detail 2. O.R. to look after these Stores which will be removed by the Transport.

Men will take pack and blanket into line.

(Continued).

(Sheet 2)

Transport Officer will detail 2 limbers + maltese cart, to be at Orderly Room at 1.pm. to take Orderly Room boxes etc. to KEMMEL CHATEAU.

Sgt. Cook and 1. Cook per Coy. will remain at QM Stores

Cookers of A.B.C.D. Coys & Water carts will be taken back to transport lines.

Quartermaster will arrange for D. Coy. Cooker to be sent to KEMMEL CHATEAU as soon as it is dark.

Water will be sent up each night in petrol cans. Empty cans must be taken to respective ration dumps and sent down each night.

Trench Store lists etc. to be sent to Orderly Room as soon as possible.

Relief to be reported by 2nd Army Code.

Acknowledge.

7th R. Irish Fus.
A Coy will relieve Coy of R.I.Rgt. in front line
B " — do — — do — in YOUNG STREET.
Two platoons C " — do — 2 platoons — in S.P. 10.
Two platoons C " — do — 2 " — in FORT REGINA.
D " — do — Coy — in KEMMEL CHATEAU

A. Still
Captain & Adjutant
7th Bn. Royal Irish Fusiliers.

Copy to 1. A Coy.   Copy to 7. Transport Officer.
     2. B "   8. Signals.
     3. C "   9. L.G.O.
     4. D "   10. R.S.M.
     5. M.O   2/R. Irish Regt.
     6. Q.M   File Copy

SECRET.   Appendix 12   Copy No. 1

49th. Infantry Brigade Order No. 67 - 19/10/16.

1. The following reliefs will take place on the 20th. and 21st. instant.

2. **Left Sub-Section.**

    The 7th/8th. Bn. R. Irish Fus. will relieve the 2nd. R. Irish Regt. on the 20th. October. Guides will be at KEMMEL CHATEAU at 2 p.m.

3. On relief the 2nd. R. Irish Regt. will move into Brigade Reserve at KEMMEL SHELTERS.
    Billeting parties to report at H.Q. 7/8th. Bn. R. Irish Fus. at 12 noon.

4. **Right Sub-Section.**

    The 8th. R. Inniskilling Fus. will relieve the 7th. R. Inniskilling Fus. on 21st. October. Guides will be at Brigade Headquarters at 2 p.m.

5. On relief 7th. R. Inniskilling Fus. will move into Divnl. Reserve at LOCRE.
    Billeting parties will report at H.Q. 8th. R. Inniskilling Fus. at 12 noon.

6. The usual orders re movement East of LOCRE and East of Brigade Headquarters will be observed.

7. All working parties and schemes of work will be carefully handed over to relieving Units.

8. Trench Store Lists will be rendered to Brigade H.Q. by 6 p.m. 22nd.

9. Completion of all reliefs will be reported by wire in code to Brigade Headquarters.

                                          Captain,
                        Brigade Major, 49th. Infantry Brigade.

Issued through Signals :
Copy No. 1 to 2nd. R. Irish Regt.   Copy No. 22 - Z/16 T.M. Bty.
   "   2 .. 7th. R. Innis. Fus.   "   23 - 24 War Diary.
   "   3 .. 8th. R. Innis. Fus.   "   25 - File.
   "   4 .. 7/8th. R. Irish Fus.
   "   5 .. 49th. M.G. Company.
   "   6 .. 49th. T.M. Battery.
   "   7 .. 48th. Infantry Brigade.
   "   8 .. 109th. Infantry Brigade.
   "   9 .. 16th. Division (G).
   "   10 .. 16th. Division (Q).
   "   11 .. A.D.M.S. 16th. Division.
   "   12 .. Staff Captain.
   "   13 .. Bde. Signal Officer.
   "   14 .. 157th. Fd. Coy. R.E.
   "   15 .. 144th. Coy. A.S.C.
   "   16 .. 113th. Fd. Ambulance.
   "   17 .. Bde. Supply Officer.
   "   18 .. Bde. Transport Officer.
   "   19 .. 171st. Tunnelling Coy. R.E.
   "   20 .. 250th.   "   "
   "   21 .. O.C. Right Group Artillery.

2nd. Battalion, The Royal Irish Regiment.   Copy No.

Reference Map.   Operation Order No. 41.   The Field
WYTSCHAETE and Sheet 28 S.W.   25-10-16.
                       Appendix 13

1. The Battalion will relieve the 7/8th Battalion, The Royal Irish Fusiliers in the left sub-section tomorrow, the 26th. inst.

2. Companies will be disposed as follows and will march off at the times stated below:—

   "B" Coy.   Front line   2.30 p.m.
   "C" "   Right Support   2.40 p.m.
   "A" "   Left Support   2.50 p.m.
   "D" "   KEMMEL CHATEAU   3 p.m.
   Headquarters
   and Scouts   KEMMEL CHATEAU   3.10 p.m.

   Guides will be at KEMMEL CHATEAU at 3 p.m.
   The Lewis Gun Officer will arrange to attach 3 extra Lewis Guns to "B" Coy.

3. Previous orders re movement east of LOCRE and east of Brigade Headquarters will be observed.

4. Officers' valises, stores, etc. will be stacked at Battalion Headquarters, KEMMEL SHELTERS, by 12 noon, 26th. inst. Officers trench kits, mess stores &c will be stacked in space opposite Bn. H.Q. Guard tent by 2 pm.

5. Dinners 12.30 p.m.

6. Trench store lists will be rendered to Orderly Room by 9 am. 27th. inst.

7. Battalion Headquarters will close in KEMMEL SHELTERS at 3 pm. and reopen in KEMMEL CHATEAU at the same hour.

                (Sd.) W. C. V. Galwey, 2/Lieut & A/Adjutant,
Hour of issue 5 p.m.   2nd. Battalion, The Royal Irish Regiment.

Copy No. 1. War Diary.   No. 8. Assistant Adjutant.
        2. H.Qrs. 49th. Inf. Bde.   9. Lewis Gun Officer.
           (for information)   10. Bn. Bombing Officer.
        3. 7/8th. Roy. Irish Fusiliers. 11. Medical Officer.
           (for information)   12. Transport Officer.
        4. O. C. "A" Coy.   13. Quartermaster.
        5. O. C. "B" "   14. R. S. M.
        6. O. C. "C" "   15. Scout Sergeant.
        7. O. C. "D" "   16. Signalling Sergeant.

Appendix 14

Orders for Raid on the 49th Infty. Brigade front

1. The raid will take place at   on

Organisation 2. Organisation of raiding parties:—
Right Party: 1 Company 2nd Bn. the R. Irish Regt. under Major Rocke-Kelly
Left Party: 1 Company 8th Bn. The Royal Dublin Fusiliers under Capt. Hunt D.S.O.

Action of Raiding Parties 3. Action 2nd Bn. the Royal Irish Regt:—
The 2nd. Bn. the Royal Irish Regt. will raid from N.30.a.4.8 to N.24.c.6.0
No.1 Party will leave our trench at Zero hour
Nos. 2, 3 & 4 Parties will leave at −2 minutes and will creep forward until level with No.1 Party when all will move forward

Each Stop Gap Party will carry a small white flag which will be fixed in the gaps in the wire.

The Signallers of Nos. 1 and 4 Parties will lay out a line of telephone cable each connected with Company HQrs.

All parties will assemble on return at their points of exit and report by runner to Company HQrs.

All prisoners, material etc, will be passed to Company HQrs. as soon as possible after capture.

Company HQrs will be at the head of KETCHEN AVENUE (about N.24.c.2.2)

The 8th Bn. The Royal Dublin Fusiliers will raid from N.24.c.7.1 to N.24.c.9.5 both inclusive, moving in 4 columns.

The columns will leave our trenches at −2 minutes.

Telephone cable lines will be laid out to connect raiding parties with Company HQrs.

All parties will assemble on return at their points of exit and report by runner to Company HQrs.

Prisoners, material etc, will be passed to Company HQrs and thence to the HQrs. of O.C. Raid at S.P.11.

The C.R.E. will provide a party for the purpose of demolishing suspected Trench Mortars, to accompany this party.

Detail of above parties is shewn in the appendix.

O.C. Raid 4. Throughout the operations the O.C. Raid (Lieut.-Colonel H.G. Gregorie, 2/the Roy. Irish) will be at S.P. 11.

Prisoners and captured material 5. All prisoners and captured material will be passed as quickly as possible to S.P. 11, where prisoners will be examined by a representative of the 49th Infantry Brigade Staff and then sent on to 49th Infantry Brigade HQrs under arrangements made by the O.C. Raid.

Medical 6. Stretcher Bearers with one stretcher will accompany each raiding party.

Casualties will be conveyed by these parties to the fire trench where an equal number of stretcher bearers will take them over and convey them to the Aid Post at BEAVER HAT. Here a number of stretcher bearers (R.A.M.C.) will be in waiting to convey them via VIA GELLIA to the dressing station at KEMMEL.

The M.O., 8th The Royal Dublin Fusiliers will remain at the Aid Post at BEAVER HAT.

The M.O., 2nd Bn The Royal Irish Regt. will remain at the top of KETCHEN AVENUE on the extreme left of the line held by the 2nd Bn. The Royal Irish Regt.

Time 7. Watches will be synchronised at — 4 hrs. and again at — 1 hour.

Box Respirator 8. Box Respirators will be worn by all troops in the line at the alert position during the operations.

Communications 9. Arrangements are being made for communications by the 49th. Infantry Brigade Signalling Officer.

Signal for Withdrawal   10. The Signal for withdrawal will be given by the OS. C. Raiding Companies in conjunction one with another.

         The signal will be golden rain rockets.

Code Word   11. The code word for use by troops when in the enemy's trenches will be :- "ASTHORE"

12. The raiding companies will move to positions from which they are going to deliver the assault at -2 hours.

     From that time VIA GELLIA and KETCHEN AVE. will be used only for UP traffic.

     PELL MELL will be used for DOWN traffic in so far as the 2/ Royal Irish are concerned.

     At zero hour this order will be reversed. KETCHEN AVENUE and VIA GELLIA will be used for DOWN traffic and PELL MELL for UP traffic.

     The Royal Irish will arrange to police these AVENUES.

     After zero hour the returning stretcher bearers and runners will be the only persons permitted to use KETCHEN AVENUE for UP traffic.

                         H.P. Pyne
                         Lieut. Colonel
         Commanding 2/ The Royal Irish

APPENDIX A

Personnel 8/R.D.Fus.

RIGHT COLUMN   1 OFFICER
                           1 N.C.O.
        RAIDING   2 BAYONET MEN
        PARTY   4 BOMBERS
                           2 CARRIERS
                           2 WIRE CUTTERS

                           1 N.C.O.
        BLOCKING   1 BAYONET MAN
        PARTY   3 BOMBERS
                           2 CARRIERS

                           1 N.C.O
        COVERING   4 BAYONETS   O. N.C.Os. OR
        PARTY   2 STRETCHER BEARERS   1   3   22

RIGHT CENTRE   1 OFFICER
COLUMN   1 N.C.O.
    1ST. RAIDING PTY.   2 BAYONET MEN
                           3 BOMBERS
                           2 CARRIERS
                           2 WIRE CUTTERS

                           1 N.C.O.
    2ND RAIDING PTY.   2 BAYONET MEN
                           3 BOMBERS
                           2 CARRIERS
                           2 WIRE CUTTERS

    COVERING PTY.   1 N.C.O and 4 MEN
                           2 STRETCHER BEARERS   1   3   24

LEFT CENTRE   1 OFFICER
COLUMN   1 N.C.O.
                           4 BAYONETS
        RAIDING PARTY   4 BOMBERS
                           2 CARRIERS
                           2 WIRE CUTTERS

                           1 N.C.O. and 6 men
                           2 STRETCHER BEARERS   1   2   20

LEFT COLUMN   1 OFFICER
                           2 N.C.O'S.
        RAIDING   4 BAYONETS
        PARTY   4 BOMBERS
                           2 CARRIERS
                           4 WIRE CUTTERS

        BLOCKING   1 N.C.O. and 3 MEN - BOMBERS
        PARTY   1 BAYONET MAN
                           2 CARRIERS

                           1 N.C.O.
                           4 LEWIS GUNNERS
                           4 BAYONETS
                           2 STRETCHER BEARERS   1   4   30

                                               4 - 12 - 96

               (Sd) J.P. HUNT   CAPTAIN,
               O.C. 8 th. ROYAL DUB. FUS.

APPENDIX B

COMPOSITION OF RAIDING PARTIES, 2/ RF Rgt ????

No. 1 PARTY   2/LT. LITTLE and 1 Runner

RIGHT GROUP
- 1 Group Leader
- 2 Bayonet men
- 2 Bombers
- 2 Carriers

LEFT GROUP
- 1 Group Leader
- 2 Bayonet men
- 2 Bombers
- 2 Carriers

EXPLORING GROUP
- 1 Group Leader
- 2 Bayonet men
- 2 Bombers
- 2 Carriers

STOP GAP PARTY
- 1 N.C.O.
- 1 Bayonet man
- 2 Bombers
- 2 Carriers
- 2 Stretcher Bearers
- 2 Signallers

O.   O.R.
1   32

No. 2 PARTY   2/LT. CORCORAN and 1 Runner

RIGHT GROUP
- 1 Group Leader
- 2 Bayonet men
- 2 Bombers
- 2 Carriers

LEFT GROUP
- 1 Group Leader
- 2 Bayonet men
- 2 Bombers
- 2 Carriers

EXPLORING GROUP
- 1 Group Leader
- 2 Bayonet men
- 2 Bombers
- 2 Carriers

STOP GAP PARTY
- 1 N.C.O.
- 1 Bayonet man
- 2 Bombers
- 2 Carriers
- 2 Stretcher Bearers

1   30

No. 3 PARTY   SERGT. PUGH and 1 Runner

LEFT GROUP
- 1 Group Leader
- 2 Bayonet men
- 2 Bombers
- 2 Carriers

EXPLORING GROUP
- 1 Group Leader
- 2 Bayonet men
- 2 Bombers
- 2 Carriers

- 1 N.C.O.
- 1 Bayonet man
- 2 Bombers
- 2 Carriers
- 1 Stretcher Bearer

   26

APPENDIX B continued

No. 4 PARTY — 2/Lt. ROCHE and 1 Runner

RIGHT GROUP
- 1 Group Leader
- 2 Bayonet men
- 2 Bombers
- 2 Carriers

LEFT GROUP
- 1 Group Leader
- 2 Bayonet men
- 2 Bombers
- 2 Carriers

EXPLORING GROUP
- 1 Group Leader
- 2 Bayonet men
- 2 Bombers
- 2 Carriers

- 1 N.C.O
- 1 Bayonet man
- 2 Bombers
- 2 Carriers
- 2 Stretcher Bearers
- 2 Signallers   1 — 32

COY. HDQr. PARTY — MAJ. ROCHE-KELLY
C.S.M.
- 2 Runners
- 2 Signallers   1 — 5

RIGHT RESERVE
- 1 N.C.O.
- 4 O. Ranks
- 2 Stretcher Bearers   . 12

LEFT RESERVE
- 1 N.C.O.
- 8 O. Ranks
- 2 Stretcher Bearers   . 11

                            4 . 146

APPENDIX C
MATERIALS

Bomb Satchels	74
Bomb Buckets	28
Mats	8
Shillelaghs	60
Large Wirecutters	8
Electric	30
"P" Bombs	36
Revolvers	12
Sandbags	
Blocking Parties	
Strong rope, yards	
Knobkerry	16

Appendix 15.

Report on Raid carried out on night of 29th/30th

16th Division.
16th Div. Artillery.
2nd R. Irish Regt.
47th Infy Brigade.
48th Infy Brigade.

49th Infy Bde No. S.O. 828/5 - 30-10-16-

Attached are Reports on Raid, Orders for which were forwarded under this Office No. S.O. 828/4 dated 28-10-16.

J. M. ...
Captain,
a/Brigade Major, 49th Infantry Brigade.

O.C. 2/R.Ir.

For information. Return herewith for no action by Lieut. named to this office.

Field Mary
2/Royal Irish

Return
31-10-16

Headquarters,

16th. Division.

49th. Inf. Bde. S.O. 828/5 d/ 30.10.16.

Attached is a report from O.C. Raid on the operation.

With reference to the failure in good synchronisation of watches, this was due to making the last hour of synchronisation too close to Zero hour.

Other points worth noticing :-

(1) Either more guns should have been in action on the front raided or the bombardment should have lasted longer.

(2) Two Stokes Mortars and emplacements were knocked out the evening before and difficulty was found in getting mortars to replace these,
(Spare Stokes Mortars should be in hands of Brigade to replace casualties)
and when finally received, and put in temporary emplacements failed to keep up fire because they sank into the ground.
Some easily placed foundation must be at hand made up ready to be put in anywhere, when a Stokes or 2 " Trench Mortar is required.

(3) A Creeping Barrage is very successful as it mitigates the dangers of a late start by the raiders from our lines.

(4) Points of the enemy's line near our lines require very careful arrangements for bombardment. Artillery cannot bombard them effectively and Stokes Mortars cannot fire under 130 yards, and as the bombardment lifts our men have to get over the parapet through our wire and form up, whereas if the enemy's line is far off they can get out before Zero and form up in the open and be ready to advance quickly.

(5) Telephones can be successfully taken with raiders, but a definite final point must be arranged carefully arranged, with a responsible person detailed, whose sole duty is to make reports.
2 D.3. cables twisted together to give metallic circuits, on a D.1 drum mounted on parapet, and pulled out tied round operator's waist was successfully used.

(6) It is now reported that the concrete M.G. emplacements about N.24.b.9.5. mentioned by O.C. Raid were blown up by the R.E. party and only one party returned with their charge.

CASUALTIES
The total casualties suffered by the raiding party (250) are as follows :-
Officers :- 1 wounded & missing believed killed, 2 slightly wounded.
Other Ranks :- 2 missing, 18 slightly wounded, 3 wounded at duty.

[signature] Brigadier-General,

Commanding 49th. Infantry Brigade.

S E C R E T.

Headquarters,

    49th Infantry Brigade.

8/R.Dublin Fus.

    I beg to submit report on the raid carried out last night, in continuation of the previous report rendered by me.

    Captain Hunt, 8th R. Dublin Fus reports that 2/Lt Whitty, in command of No. 3 party, became separated from his party while crossing over from our trenches, and entered the German line alone. He was shot in the chest by a German whom he states he killed. He confirms other reports that the German trenches are in good condition and wood revetted, with good floor boards well laid. In a few places he found the parapet or parados blown in, but no damage to the trench. He saw two well made shelters fitted with doors.

    2/Lieut Clarkes' party took two prisoners out of a shelter, and then destroyed it with bombs.

    The R.E. party (1 L/CPL and 3 men) with explosives, did not accomplish anything, and returned to our lines with their explosives.

2/ R. Irish Regt.

    Lieut Murphy reports :-

    The extreme right party met with considerable opposition ; it seems evident that a number of the enemy crowded into the salient at PECKHAM during the bombardment.

    Other parties entered the German trenches without great difficulty, and carried out their allotted tasks.

    All reports show that the German trenches are in good repair and well revetted, and quite dry, and not affected by Artillery fire. The front line trench is deep and rather narrow, with two fire steps.

    2/Lieut Roches found several small dugouts, all well constructed. He states he also saw several bomb stores, but unfortunately he did not destroy these.

PRISONERS.

    A total of 4 prisoners were brought in - one of them badly wounded. They all belong to the 120th Regt (WURTEMBURG). It seems certain that a fifth prisoner was captured, but in the confusion, succeeded in getting away.

War Material.

    The 8th R. Dublin Fus brought back 1 box Machine Gun ammunition and belts. The 2/ R. Irish brought back two rifles.

Time.

    There seems to have been a considerable amount of confusion over synchronizing of watches.

Artillery and T.M. Action.

    The Royal Artillery and T.M. Batteries carried out their programme excellently. At the beginning of the bombardment a few rounds fell short, but it is recognised that this was almost unavoidable.

CASUALTIES.

-2-

Casualties.

The Royal Irish report 18 casualties of whom 3 are missing, and almost certainly were killed in the German trenches; one of these was 2/Lieut Corcoran, who fell while on the German parapet. Of the other casualties, the great majority are only slightly wounded.

The Royal Dublin Fusiliers report 7 casualties, of whom none are missing.

Communications.

In spite of the excellent arrangements made, communications were disjointed, owing to our line between H.Q. and the Companies being cut by trench mortars. Connections between Raid H.Q. and Brigade was good.

Duration of Raid.

The raid lasted about 42 minutes.

The artillery were asked to go on firing for about 25 minutes after the signal to withdraw, in order to allow the infantry ample time to get clear.

The golden rain rockets were used very successfully as the signal for withdrawal.

Remarks.

The raid succeeded in achieving its object. The German line was penetrated, prisoners taken and identification established. More perhaps might have been done but for the inexperience of some of the group leaders, who let opportunities slip, as for instance - failing to destroy by bombing or some means, munitions which it was not possible to take away.

The artillery bombardment was of scarcely long enough duration for the purposes of a raid on such a large scale.

I should like to pay special tribute to the great assistance rendered by the O.C. 8th R. Dublin Fus and to the excellent arrangements made by Captain Hunt, D.S.O.

(sd) H.G. Gregorie, Lieut Col.,

O. C. Raid.

30-10-16.

SECRET.

Head-Quarters,
49th Infantry Brigade.

I beg to report the results of the Raid so far as known to me at present:-
Captain HUNT. D.S.O.. 8th R.D.F. has reported as follows:-
The 8/R.D.F Party went out at the correct hour.
Heavy and medium Trench Mortars opened on KETCHEN AVENUE at 3 mins., and also along the front line held by R.D.F.. Many of these burst in the air.
Aerial Torpedoes were also observed at about 5 mins.
Nos.I, 2 and 4 Parties reported their return at 6.42 p.m..
Reports from all parties say that enemy trenches are very good, well drained and revetted. The traverses are curved and not square like ours.
I Officer and his party came across a Machine Gun Emplacement - the pivot on which the gun worked was there but the gun had been removed. This machine gun emplacement is apparently in the exact locality where a Machine Gun had previouslt been reported (about N.24.b.9.5). They captured a box of ammunition and belts and bombed two dug-outs where they suspected the gun might be hidden.
I Officer reports that he met opposition.
Lieut. Murphy, 2nd R. Irish Regt. reports :-
The raiders left our trenches at the correct time.
The right hand party met with considerable opposition - bombing and Machine Gun Fire - and failed to reach the enemy trenches. 2nd Lt. Little who had charge of the party was wounded.
The left party at first appear to have run into our own barrage and withdrew.
After a short pause they went forward again and penetrated the enemy's line, and did a certain amount of damage, but I have no accurate details to hand.
I regret to report that 2nd Lt. CORCORAN is missing.
To my knowledge four prisoners have been captured more have been reported but I have no authentic proof that this is the case.
The I20 Regt. WURTEMBERGERS have been unmistakeably identified on our front.
Our Artillery and Trench Mortar Action so far as I can judge at present was quite excellent, and exactly according to schedule.
I will render a fuller report as soon as fuller details are to hand.

10.30 PM.
29/I0/I6.

(Sd) H.G.GREGORIE, Lt. Colonel.
O.C., Raid.

SECRET.   Appendix 18.   Copy No......1....

49th Infantry Brigade Order No. 69 - 30-10-16.

-*-*- Relief -*-*-

1. The following reliefs will take place on the 1st instant.

2. **Right Sub-Section.**
   The 8th R. Innis Fus will relieve the 7th R. Innis Fus. Guides will be at Brigade Headquarters at 2 p.m.
   The 7th R. Innis Fus, on relief, will move into Divisional Reserve at LOCRE. Billeting party will report to H.Q. 8th R. Innis Fus at 12 noon.

3. **Left Sub-Section.**
   The 7/8th R. Irish Fus will relieve the 2nd R. Irish Regt. Guides will be at KEMMEL CHATEAU at 3 p.m. The 2nd R. Irish Regt will, on relief, move into Brigade Reserve at KEMMEL SHELTERS. Billeting party will report to H.Q. 7/8th R. Irish Fus at 12 noon, to take over huts, &c.

4. All details will be arranged between C.O's concerned.

5. Previous orders re movement East of LOCRE and East of Brigade Headquarters will be observed, except that Transport is now allowed into KEMMEL in daylight at 200 yards interval.

6. All working parties and schemes of work will be handed over to relieving units.

7. Trench Store Lists will be rendered to Brigade H.Q. by 6 p.m. 2nd.

8. Completion of reliefs to be wired to Brigade H.Q. in 2nd Army Code.

L. B. Brawley
Captain,
a/Brigade Major, 49th Infantry Brigade.

Issued through Signals.

Copy No. 1 to 2nd R. Irish Regt.   Copy No. 22 - Z/16 T. M. B.
"   2   7th R. Innis Fus.   "   23 - 24 War Diary.
"   3   8th R. Innis Fus   "   24 - File.
"   4   7/8th R. Irish Fus
"   5   49th M.G. Company.
"   6   49th T. M. B.
"   7   48th Infy Brigade.
"   8   109th Infy Brigade.
"   9   O.C. Right Group.
"   10   16th Division (G)
"   11   16th Division (Q)
"   12   Staff Captain
"   13   A.D.M.S. 16th Division.
"   14   157th Field Company
"   15   Bde Signal Officer.
"   16   113th Field Ambulance.
"   17   144th Coy A.S.C.
"   18   Bde Supply Officer
"   19   Bde Transport Officer
"   20   171st Tunnelling Coy R.E.
"   21   250th   do

2nd. Battalion, The Royal Irish Regiment.   Copy no 1.
            Operation Order No. 43.
Reference map.   Appendix 19.   The Field.
WYTSCHAETE and Sheet 28 S.W.   Relief   31-10-16.

1. The Battalion will be relieved by the 7/8th. Battalion, The Royal Irish Fusiliers in the left sub-section tomorrow, 1st. prox.
    On being relieved the Battalion will move into Brigade Reserve at KEMMEL SHELTERS.

2. Guides from platoons will be at KEMMEL CHATEAU at 3 p.m.

3. A billeting party under the Quartermaster will report to Headquarters, 7/8th. Battalion, The Royal Irish ~~Regiment~~ Fusiliers at 12 noon to take over huts, etc.

4. Previous orders re movement east of LOCRE and east of Brigade Headquarters will be observed, except that transport is now allowed into KEMMEL by daylight at 200 yards interval.

5. Officers' trench kits, etc. will be dumped at this Headquarters by 2 pm.

6. Officers Commanding Companies will hand over any work and intelligence reports to relieving units.

7. Trench store lists will be rendered to Battalion Headquarters by 9am. on the 2nd. prox.

                        (Sd.) W. C. V. Galwey, 2/Lieut & A/Adjutant,
Hour of issue 5 pm.   2nd. Battalion, The Royal Irish Regiment.

Copy no. 1. War Diary.   No. 7. O. C. "D" Coy.
       2. H.Q. 49th. Infy. Bde.   8. Lewis Gun Officer.
          (for information)   9. Bn. Bombing Officer.
       3. 7/8th. Bn. The R. I. Fus.   10. Medical Officer
          (for information)   11. Quartermaster
       4. O. C. "A" Coy.   12. Transport Officer.
       5. O. C. "B" "   13. A/R. S. M.
       6. O. C. "C" "   14. Signalling Sergeant.

Appendix 20.

SECRET.

REPORT ON RAID

carried out by 49th Inf. Bde. on

the 29th October, 1916.

16th Div.No. A.S.1239/4/2

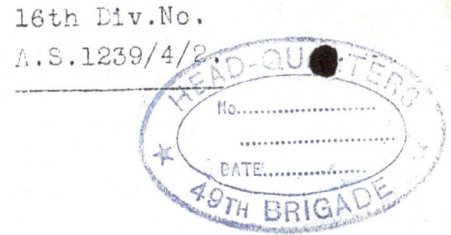

1. On the 29th October a raid against the enemy's Front and communication trenches and farm buildings between N.30.a.5.7. (PECKHAM) and N.24.c.9.5.(MAEDELSTEDE Farm), was carried out by the 49th Inf. Bde with the object of securing identifications, capturing machine guns and trench mortars.
In conjunction with this raid, feint attacks were made at N.30.c.1.7. (SPANBROEKMOLEN) and from N.24.a.8.7. to N.18.c.9.1. (PETIT BOIS SALIENT). (See Map C.)

2. The raiding parties were under command of the Officer Commanding 2nd Royal Irish Regiment, and consisted of:-

<u>Strength.</u>

One company 2nd Royal Irish Regiment, 4 Officers, 146 O.R.
One company 8th R. Dublin Fusiliers, 4 Officers, 108 O.R.

Each company was divided into four parties, each party having a distinct task assigned to it.
The raid was covered by the 16th Divisional Artillery.
The Trench Mortar batteries of the 48th and 49th Inf.Bdes., and the Medium Trench Mortar batteries of the Division co-operated.

3. The feint attack against the PETIT BOIS SALIENT was carried out by the 47th and 48th Inf. Bdes.,assisted by 1-18-pdr.battery, 16th Divisional Artillery and 2-18-pdr.batteries, and one 4.5" How. Battery of the 4th Australian Divisional Artillery.
The feint attack against the SPANBROEKMOLEN was carried out by the 49th Inf.Bde.,assisted by 2 batteries of 18-pdrs. of 36th Divisional Artillery.

4. Zero hour was fixed for 5.45.p.m.
This hour was selected as it was considered it would be sufficiently dark to cover the advance, while there would be sufficient light to enable the parties to avoid falling into shell holes.

5. For the three days previous to the raid, the Medium Trench Mortars had been engaged in cutting gaps in the enemy's wire opposite the front to be assualted, as also opposite the SPANBROEKMOLEN and PETIT BOIS Salient.
These gaps were kept open at night by the fire of machine guns and Stokes Mortars.
On the 29th the 18-pdr. batteries and Medium Trench Mortars at 5.45.p.m. carried out an intense bombardment of the enemy's front line between N.24.c.9.5. and N.30.a.5.3.
This lasted for two minutes.
The artillery then lifted 50 yards, and a creeping barrage was maintained at the rate of 50 yards a minute until the line of the stationary barrage was reached.
The 4.5" and 6" Howitzers blocked communication trenches.
The 60-pdrs. and 4.7" guns searched communication trenches, but were prepared to switch off for counter-battery work if required.
The artillery barrages are shewn on Map B.

-2-

6. (a) <u>RIGHT COMPANY.</u> (2nd R. Irish Regt.) (See Map A).

Under cover of our artillery barrage Nos. 2, 3 & 4 parties advanced at 5.41.p.m. and No. 1. party on the right at 5.45.p.m.

No. 1. party met with considerable opposition, from bombing and machine gun fire directed against it by a number of the enemy who had crowded into the PECKHAM Salient during the bombardment.

The Officer in command of this party was wounded, and the party failed to reach the enemy's trenches.

No. 4. party at first ran into our artillery barrage and withdrew. Subsequently this party again went forward and penetrated into the German trenches.

The remaining two parties successfully entered the hostile trenches without difficulty.

One prisoner and two rifles were taken.

(b) <u>LEFT COMPANY.</u> (8th R. Dublin Fusiliers)(See Map A)

The four parties left their trenches at 5.39.p.m. under cover of our artillery fire, and succeeded in entering the German trenches. Little opposition was met with.

One party secured two prisoners from a shelter, and then destroyed the shelter with bombs.

A concrete machine gun emplacement, from which the gun had been removed, was demolished by the R.E. party

Two dugouts in which it was thought the gun might be hidden were bombed, and a box of ammunition and belts were secured.

A third prisoner was brought back by this company.

(c) The raiding parties remained in the enemy's trenches 42 minutes.

7. Except in the PECKHAM Salient, the hostile trenches were lightly held.

The enemy's retaliation for our bombardment was slight.

There was practically no artillery, rifle or machine gun fire, but considerable Trench Mortar fire on KETCHEN AVENUE, which was badly damaged, and on the front line held by the 8th R. Dublin Fusiliers. Very few rockets or Very lights were seen. NO MANS LAND was swept with searchlights from the direct of PETIT BOIS and GRAND BOIS.

8. The total casualties sustained were as follows:-

	Officers	Other Ranks
Missing (believed killed)	1	-
Wounded	2	21
Missing	-	2
Total	3	23

9. Reports state that the hostile trenches were in good repair, dry and well revetted, with good floor boards well laid.

Shelters were well constructed.

The front line trench was deep and narrow with a step up to the firestep.

The traverses were rounded and not rectangular.

During the time that the raiding parties spent in the enemy trenches a large amount of damage was done to parapets revetments, floorboards etc.

A search was made for hostile machine guns but none could be found, nor were any M.G. emplacements found, except the one mentioned in para. 6 (b).

NOTES.

(a)   A creeping barrage is useful as it mitigates the dangers if, through any cause, parties are late in starting from their trenches.

(b)   Very careful arrangements are necessary if it is intended to assault any portion of the hostile line which is in close proximity to our own trenches.

Artillery cannot carry out a bombardment effectively, and Stokes Mortars cannot fire under 130 yards, and as the bombardment lifts the assaulting parties have to get over the parapet, get through their own wire and form up.

If the enemy's lines are some distance from our own these difficulties do not arise, and the assaulting parties can get out of their trenches and form up before Zero and be ready to rush forward immediately the barrage lifts.

The PECKHAM Salient in under 100 yards from our front trenches.

(c)   2.D.3. cables twisted together to give metallic circuits on a D.1.drum mounted on the parapet and pulled out tied round the operators waist was successfully used.

If telephones are taken out by raiding parties, a definite point must be carefully arranged with a responsible person detailed, whose sole duty is to make reports.

(d)   Spare Stokes Mortars should be available to replace casualties, and some easily placed foundations should be at hand

Two Stokes Mortars and emplacements were put out of action on the evening previous to the raid. Spare Mortars when finally received and put in temporary emplacements failed to keep up their fire, owing to the ground being too soft to support them.

1st Nov. 1916.

S.S.
(20 sheets)

WAR DIARY.

FOR

MONTH OF NOVEMBER, 1916.

VOLUME

2nd. R. Irish Regiment

Vol 21

WAR DIARY
or
INTELLIGENCE SUMMARY.

(Erase heading not required.)

Army Form C. 2118.

2nd R. Irish Regt.

Place	Date Nov.	Hour	Summary of Events and Information	Remarks and references to Appendices
KEMMEL	1.		Major F. ROCHE-KELLY proceeded to assume command of the 6th Battalion The Royal Irish Regt. The Battalion was relieved by the 7/8th Batt. The Royal Irish Fusiliers and moved into Brigade Reserve at KEMMEL SHELTERS.	JAN. 1 Appendix 1.
	2. 3. 4. 5.		Nothing to report	JAN. Jan Appendix 2.
	6. 7.		The Battalion was inspected by the G.O.C. 49th Infantry Brigade. The Battalion relieved the 7/8th The ROYAL IRISH FUSILIERS in the left subsector.	
	8.		Nonapsy HANNERY joined the battalion – 1 Other Rank	JAN.
	9. 10.		Nothing to report. 1 Other Rank died of wounds	
	11.		Under authority granted by H.M. the King, the G.O.C. ii C has awarded the Military Cross to Lieut. H. HARRISON. Lt. L. MURPHY promoted Captain	JAN.

WAR DIARY
or
INTELLIGENCE SUMMARY.
(Erase heading not required.)

Army Form C. 2118.

Place	Date	Hour	Summary of Events and Information	Remarks and references to Appendices
	13th		The Battalion was relieved by the 9/18th Batt: the ROYAL IRISH FUSILIERS and moved into Brigade Reserve at KEMMEL SHELTERS. 2/Lieut E.O. HUMPHREYS wounded - 2/Lt. C. A. BARRY joined the battalion -	Appendix 3, 7 #AN.
	14th		17 other Ranks joined the battalion	#AN.
	15th 16th		Nothing to report -	#AN.
	17th		Military Medals have been awarded to the following. No 6718 Sgt. P. DUFFY - No 11675 L.Cpl. E. SKELLY	#AN.
	18th		Nothing to report.	#AN.
	19th		The Battalion relieves the 9/18th The ROYAL IRISH FUSILIERS in the left subsector.	Appendix 4.

WAR DIARY
or
INTELLIGENCE SUMMARY.

Army Form C. 2118.

Place	Date	Hour	Summary of Events and Information	Remarks and references to Appendices
	19th		The following decorations have been awarded :- Military Medal No 9343 Sgt R. CRUMP. No 9268 Sgt H. SHIELS - 5667 " T. DWYER. - 6810 Pte J. BLACKMORE No 10791. L/C. J. COADY. No 8616 Pte W. SHORT. Meritorious Service Medal - No 6332 Sgt J. FLETCHER. 13 Other Ranks joined the Battalion	J.A.N.
	20th 21st		Nothing to report. 2/Lt. M. J. HIGGINS was transferred to 49th Trench Mortar Battery.	J.A.N.
	23rd		A dummy raid took place at 6 p.m. The enemy seems to have been considerably alarmed and was very nervous throughout the night.	Appendices 5 & 7
	24th		The Battalion was relieved by the 7/8th Battalion the ROYAL IRISH FUSILIERS in the left subsector - moved into Brigade Reserve - Capt. L. Kingston MURPHY awarded the Military Cross -	Appendix 6. J.A.N.
	25th 27th		Nothing to report.	J.A.N.

Army Form C. 2118.

WAR DIARY
or
INTELLIGENCE SUMMARY.
(Erase heading not required.)

Place	Date	Hour	Summary of Events and Information	Remarks and references to Appendices
	28th		Nothing to report.	$AN.
	29th		The Battalion relieved the 118th Battalion the ROYAL IRISH FUSILIERS in the left sub-sector.	Appendix B.
	30th			

H. Pepinster
Comdg. 2nd/5th The Royal West Regt

Appendix T

2nd Battalion, The Royal Irish Regiment Copy No.
Operation Order No. 33

Reference map.   The Field.
1/10000ETE and Sheet 28 S.W.   31-10-16.

1. The Battalion will be relieved by the 7/8th Battalion, The Royal Irish Fusiliers in the left sub-section tomorrow, 1st prox.
   On being relieved the Battalion will move into Brigade Reserve at KEMMEL SHELTERS.

2. Guides from platoons will be at KEMMEL CHATEAU at 3 p.m.

3. A billeting party under the Quartermaster will report to Headquarters, 7/8th Battalion, The Royal Irish Fusiliers at 12 noon to take over huts, etc.

4. Previous orders re movement east of LOCRE and east of Brigade Headquarters will be observed, except that transport is now allowed into KEMMEL by daylight at 200 yards interval.

5. Officers' trench kits, etc. will be dumped at this Headquarters by 2 pm.

6. Officers Commanding Companies will hand over any work and intelligence reports to relieving units.

7. Trench store lists will be rendered to Battalion Headquarters by 9 am. on the 2nd. prox.

(Sd.) W. C. V. Galwey, 2/Lieut. & Adjutant,
2nd Battalion The Royal Irish Regiment.

Hour of issue 5 pm.

Copy No. 1. War Diary.   No. 7. O. C. "D" Coy.
         2. HQ. 49th Infy. Bde.   8. Lewis Gun Officer.
            (for information)   9. Bn. Bombing Officer.
         3. 7/8th Bn. The R. I. Fus.   10. Medical Officer
            (for information)   11. Quartermaster
         4. O. C. "A" Coy.   12. Transport Officer.
         5. O. C. "B" "   13. A/R. S. M.
         6. O. C. "C" "   14. Signalling Sergeant.

Appendix 2

2nd. Battalion, The Royal Irish Regiment.   Copy No. 1

Reference Map   Operation Order No.   In the Field
WYTSCHAETE – Sheet 28 SW.   6-11-

---

1. The Battalion will relieve the 7th Battalion, The Royal Irish Fusiliers, in the left subsection tomorrow, the 7th inst.

2. Companies will be disposed as under and will march off at the times stated:

    "D" Coy.   Front Line   1.30 pm.
    "A" "   Right Support   1.40 pm.
    "B" "   Left Support   1.50 pm.
    "C" "   KEMMEL CHATEAU   2. pm.
    H.Qrs. & Scouts &   KEMMEL CHATEAU   2.10 pm.

3. Guides will be at KEMMEL CHATEAU at 2 pm.

4. Previous orders re movement east of LOCRE and east of Brigade Headquarters will be observed.

5. The Lewis Gun Officer will arrange to attach 2 Lewis guns to "D" Coy.

6. An advance party consisting of 1 officer and 1 N.C.O. per Coy. will meet guides of 7/8th Battalion, The Royal Irish Fusiliers at KEMMEL CHATEAU at 12 noon.

7. Officers' valises, stores, etc. will be stacked at Battalion Headquarters, KEMMEL SHELTERS by 12 noon on 7th. inst.

8. Officers' linen kits, mess stores, etc. will be stacked by companies in the usual barn by 1.15 pm. O.C. Coys. will detail 1 servant per Coy to be in charge of the Coy. Kits.

9. Dinners 12 noon.

10. Trench stores lists will be sent to Battalion Headquarters by 9 am. on the 7th. inst.

11. Battalion Headquarters will close in KEMMEL SHELTERS at 2 pm. and will reopen at KEMMEL CHATEAU at the same hour.

                                    H. Gabbett
                                    2/Lieut & A/Adjutant,
Hour of issue 5pm.   2nd. Battalion, The Royal Irish Regiment.

Copy No 1. War Diary.   No. 7. O.C. "D" Coy.
       2. H.Qrs. 49th. Inf. Bde.   8. Lewis Gun Officer.
          (for information)   9. Bn. Bombing Officer.
       3. 7/8th. Bn. The Roy. Ir. Fus.   10. Medical Officer.
          for information   11. Quartermaster.
       4. O.C. "A" Coy.   12. Transport Officer.
       5. O.C. "B" "   13. R.S.M.
       6. O.C. "C" "   14. Signalling Sergeant.
                       15. Cook Sergeant.

Appendix (5)

OPERATION ORDER NO. 45,
by
MAJOR L. L. FARMER, COMMANDING,
2nd. Battalion, THE ROYAL IRISH REGIMENT.

Reference Map
WYTSCHAETE & Sheet 28 S.W.

The Field.
12/11/16.

1. The Battalion will be relieved by the 7/8th. Battalion, The Royal Irish Fusiliers in the left sub-section tomorrow, the 13th. inst. On being relieved the Battalion will move into Brigade Reserve at KEMMEL SHELTERS.
2. Guides from platoons will be at KEMMEL CHATEAU at 1-30 p.m.
3. A billetting party under the Quartermaster will report to Head Quarters, 7/8th. Battalion, The Royal Irish Fusiliers at 12noon, the 13th. inst., to take over huts, etc.
4. The usual orders re movement east of LOCRE and east of Brigade Headquarters will be observed.
5. Officers' trench kits, etc., will be dumped at this Headquarters by 12-45 p.m.
6. Officers Commanding Companies will hand over all work and intelligence reports to relieving unit.
7. Trench store lists will be rendered to Orderly Room by 9 a.m. on 14th. inst.
8. Completion of relief will be reported in Second Army Code.

2/Lieut. & A/Adjutant,
2nd. Battalion, The Royal Irish Regiment.

Hour of issue 3 p.m.

Copy No. 1. War Diary.
2. H.Qrs., 49th. Inf. Bde. (for information.)
3. 7/8th. Bn. The R. I. Fus. (for information.)
4. O. C. "A" Coy.
5. O. C. "B" ,,
6. O. C. "C" ,,

No. 7. O. C. "D" Coy.
8. Lewis Gun Officer.
9. Bn. Bombing Officer.
10. Medical Officer.
11. Quartermaster.
12. Transport Officer.
13. R. S. M.
14. Signalling Sergeant.

No. 15. Cook Sergeant.

Appendix 4.

OPERATION ORDER NO. 46.   Copy No.

by

LIEUT-COLONEL H. G. GORIE, COMMANDING,
2nd. Battalion, THE ROYAL IRISH REGIMENT.

Reference Map   The Field
WYTSCHAETE & Sheet 28 S.W.   18/11/16.

1. The Battalion will relieve the 7/8th. Battalion, The Royal Irish Fusiliers in the Left Subsection tomorrow, the 19th. inst.
2. Companies will be disposed as under and will march off at the times stated.

   "B" Coy.   Front Line   1 p.m.
   "C" ,,   Right Support   1-10 p.m.
   "D" ,,   Left Support   1-20 p.m.
   "A" ,,   KEMMEL CHATEAU   1-30 p.m.
   H.Qrs. and
   Scouts   KEMMEL CHATEAU   1-40 p.m.

3. Guides will be at KEMMEL CHATEAU at 1-30 p.m.
4. Previous orders re movement east of LOCRE and east of Brigade Headquarters will be observed.
5. The Lewis Gun Officer will arrange to attach 2 extra guns to "B" Coy.
6. An advance party consisting of 1 Officer and 1 N.C.O. per Coy. will meet guides of the 7/8th. Battalion, The Royal Irish Fusiliers at KEMMEL CHATEAU at 11-30 a.m.
7. Officers' valises, stores, etc., will be stacked at Battalion Headquarters, KEMMEL SHELTERS, by 11-30 a.m. on the 19th. inst.
8. Officers' trench kits, stores, etc., will be stacked by Coys. in the usual place by 12-45 p.m. O's. C. Coys. will detail 1 servant per company to be in charge of the Coy. kits.
9. Dinners 11-30 a.m.
10. Trench store lists will be sent to Battalion Headquarters by 9 a.m. on the 20th. inst.
11. Battalion Headquarters will close in KEMMEL SHELTERS at 2 p.m. and will reopen at KEMMEL CHATEAU at the same hour.

                                        2/Lieut. & A/Adjutant,
Hour of issue 3 p.m.   2nd. Battalion, The Royal Irish Regiment.

Copy No. 1. War Diary.   No. 7. O. C. "D" Coy.
        2. H.Qrs., 49th. Inf. Bde.   8. Lewis Gun Officer.
           (for information.)   9. Bn. Bombing Officer.
        3. 7/8th. Bn. The R. I. Fus.   10. Medical Officer.
           (for information.)   11. Quartermaster.
        4. O. C. "A" Coy.   12. Transport Officer.
        5. O. C. "B" ,,   13. R. S. M.
        6. O. C. "C" ,,   14. Signalling Sergeant.
                        15. Cook Sergeant.

TACTICAL PROGRESS REPORT.

49th INFANTRY BRIGADE No.B.M.C.IX/2773.

OPERATIONS.

Appendix 5

DUMMY RAID.

A Dummy Raid took place at 6 p.m. last night. Our Artillery opened with an intense barrage from 18 prs and 4.5" Howitzers on the enemy's front line from SPANBROEKMOLEN to PECKHAM. After two minutes, the barrage lifted to the enemy's support line for a period of five minutes, and then back to the front line again for two minutes. Three minutes before Zero Smoke Bombs, Lachrymatory Grenades and 2" Bombs were thrown into NO MAN'S LAND between N.29.b.8.2 and N.30.a.2.7 with the intention of making the enemy believe that gas was being sent over and that a raid was taking place under cover of the gas. The Smoke Cloud went over successfully. Immediately the Smoke Cloud appeared the enemy sent up Green and Red Lights and a great number of ordinary Very Lights. A big Orange Flare went up just outside the enemy's parapet, probably an Anti-Gas measure.

Together with the Artillery Barrage our Stokes Guns and 2" Trench Mortars opened rapid fire. Our Stokes guns fired 120 rounds on SPANBROEKMOLEN and PECKHAM between the hours of six and six fifteen p.m.. Our 2" Trench Mortars at the same time fired ten rounds on front and support lines of the enemy at SPANBROEKMOLEN, ten rounds on front and support lines at PECKHAM and ten rounds at ANNA. The enemy replied by sending over a few Trench Mortars, heavy and medium, some rifle grenades and a shrapnel barrage in NO MAN'S LAND. He also swept our parapets with intense Machine Gun Fire and xx seems to have been considerably alarmed. Our Vickers Guns co-operated in these operations.

T.M. ACTIVITY.

At 11.45 a.m. FRAU fired 4 rounds and EVE 7 rounds. No damage was done, they fell well behind our front line. Our Stokes Guns replied by firing 20 rounds on enemy's front line opposite FRAU and 19 on enemy's Reserve Line. Between the hours of 11 a.m. and 1 p.m. the enemy fired 20 Trench Mortars and about 30 Rifle Grenades, also about 25 77m.m. shells. Slight damage was done to our parapet at N.30.3. Our Artillery fired intermittently until the enemy's Trench Mortars and Artillery ceased to fire. At 12 noon our 2" Trench Mortars fired 14 rounds on SPANBROEKMOLEN and PECKHAM.

```
No. of rounds fired by 2" T.M............44
No. of rounds fired by Stokes Guns.......212
```

VICKERS GUNS.

Our Vickers Guns fired on enemy's Trench Railways and particularly on:-
  N.30.b.3.8   to PECKHAM
  O.25.a.3.3   to   O.19.c.8.2.
  On crossing at N.30.d.0.9 and Junction at N.30.d.7½.7.
Total rounds fired   12,250.

Our Lewis Guns were very active throughout the night. The enemy's Machine Guns were particularly active last night.

INFORMATION.

The enemy was very nervous throughout the night after the Dummy Raid. About 11.15 a.m. to-day a German Officer was observed examining the GLORY HOLE (N.30.3) with a pair of Field Glasses. Smoke was observed coming from the direction of N.30.a.65.80 just behind his front line. A lot of timber was sent up in the air in enemy's line about N.30.c.45.35 when our artillery was shelling our front.

2nd Lieut,
for Brigade Major 49th Inf. Bde.

Appendix 6.

SECRET.   Operation Order No. 47.   Copy No. 1.
              by
              Lieut-Colonel H. G. Gregorie, Commanding,
              2nd. Battalion, The Royal Irish Regiment.

Reference Map.   The Field.
WYTSCHAETE & Sheet 28 S.W.   23-11-1916.

---

1. The Battalion will be relieved by the 7/8th. Battalion, The Royal Irish Fusiliers in the left subsection tomorrow, the 24th. inst. Relief to commence at 2.30 pm.
    On relief the Battalion will move into Brigade Reserve at KEMMEL SHELTERS.

2. A billeting party under the Quartermaster will report to Headquarters, 7/8th. Battalion, The Royal Irish Fusiliers at 12 noon, the 24th. inst., to take over hutments, etc.

3. The usual orders re movement east of LOCRE and east of Brigade Headquarters will be observed.

4. Officers' trench kits, etc., will be dumped at Battalion Headquarters, KEMMEL CHATEAU, by 1 pm, the 24th. inst.

5. Officers commanding companies will hand over all work and intelligence reports to the relieving unit.

6. Trench Store lists will be rendered to Orderly Room by 9 am., 25th. inst.

7. Completion of relief to be reported to Battalion Headquarters in Second Army Code.

                              P. Mulvey
                              2/Lieut. A/Adjutant.
                    2nd. Battalion, The Royal Irish Regiment.

Hour of issue 4 pm.

Copy No. 1. War Diary.   No. 7. O. C. "D" Coy.
        2. H.Q. 49th. Inf. Bde.   8. Lewis Gun Officer.
            (for information)   9. Bn. Bombing Officer.
        3. 7/8th. Bn. The Roy. Ir. Fus. 10. Medical Officer.
            (for information)   11. Quartermaster.
        4. O. C. "A" Coy.   12. Transport Officer.
        5. O. C. "B" "   13. R. S. M.
        6. O. C. "C" "   14. Signalling Sergeant.
                    15. Cook Sergeant.

O.C.
2nd R. Irish Regt

Appendix

Ref Dummy Raid 1m/16D.

Will you please arrange to send up 4 Red Very lights at ZERO+2 & 4 Green V.L. at ZERO +7. These lights should be fired from about the "Glory Hole"

L.R. Manley
Bn.
A/Lt. Major
29 Bde.

22.11.16

Appendix 7.

TO.
2nd R. Irish Regt.
7th R. Innis. Fus.
Right Group.
49th T.M. Bty.
49th M.G. Coy.
Signals (For information).

49th Inf. Bde. No.B.O. 74/6, dated 22/11/16.

Reference attached:-

Watches will be synchronised at 1 p.m. and 3 p.m. to-day, 22nd inst:.

Captain,
a/Brigade Major,
49th Infantry Brigade.

22/11/16.

SECRET

```
H.Q. 16th. Division. (G)        2nd. R. Irish Regt.
H.Q. 16th. Division. (Q)        7th. R. Innis. Fus.
H.Q. 16th. Divisional Arty.     49th. M.G.Coy.
O.C. Right Group.               49th. T.M.Battery.
H.Q. 47th. Inf. Bde.            157th. Field Coy. R.E.
H.Q. 48th. Inf. Bde.            171st. Tunnelling. Coy. R.E.
H.Q. 109th. Inf. Bde.
```

49th. Inf. Bde. No. B.O. 74/5. - 22/11/16.

Ref. 49th. Inf. Bde. Order No. 74 dated 18/11/16.

The Dummy Raid will be carried out to-night 22nd. Inst.

All details remain the same

L.B.Brayley
Captain.

a/Brigade Major. 49th. Inf. Bde.

SECRET.   Copy No... 8

49th. Infantry Brigade Operation Order No.74. –18/11/16.

1. A Dummy Raid will take place on night Nov. 21/22nd. 1916.
   Zero hour... 6 p.m.

2. Points of attack.
   N.30.c.1.6. to N.30.a.35.25.

3. Object
   To inflict casualties and alarm the enemy.

4. Preparation.
   2" T.M's to cut wire on Brigade front on 20th. and 21st.
   Right Gun to cut wire on the front to be attacked.
   Artillery to register on front and support lines.

5. Method of Attack and Time-Table.

Time	
Zero –3 minutes to Zero + 1 minute.	If wind is favourable smoke candles will will be lit, and P bombs thrown along front of attack.
Zero to + 1 minute.	2" T.M's & Stokes Mortars, and Artillery will open a short vigorous fire on enemy's front line on front of attack.
Zero + 2 minute to Zero + 7 minutes.	Barrage to lift to support line, when a steady rate of fire will be maintained.
Zero + 7 minutes to Zero + 10 minutes.	Barrage to return to front line, and a severe fire to be kept up for two minutes. Stokes guns to arrange to extend their fire for 100 yards on either flank of points of attack.

   Vickers Guns.
   Vickers guns will open at Zero on communication trenches roads, etc.

   Lewis Guns.
   Lewis guns will sweep enemy's parapet either side of front of attack from Zero to Zero + 8 minutes.
        Zero + 8 minutes to Zero + 10 minutes will sweep front of attack.

   Lights.
   Coloured lights will be sent up at Zero to Zero + 2 minutes over enemy's lines.

6. ACKNOWLEDGE.

                                              P. B. Brierley
                                                 Captain.
                                   Brigade Major, 49th. Infantry Brigade.

Copy No. 1 to H.Q.16th. Division (G)   No. 8 to 2nd. R. Irish Regt.
    "   2   "   "   "   (Q)   9   7th. R. Innis Fus.
    "   3   "   "   "   Arty.   10   49th. M.G.Coy.
    "   4 O.C. Right Group.   11   49th. T.M.Batty.
    "   5 47th. Infy. Brigade.   12   157th. Field Coy.
    "   6 48th. Infy. Brigade.   13   171st. Tunnelling Cy.
    "   7 109th. Infy. Brigade.

Appendix IV -
Congratulations on Raid

Lt. Col. H. G. Gregorie
Cmdg. 2⁰ Batt -
The Royal Irish Regt.

W.B. Hickie

My dear Gregorie;

Will you accept & please convey to the Officers & N.C.O's & men who took part in last nights successful raid my appreciation of the spirit and dash that has been shown by all ranks, and of the careful planning, and good arrangement that were everywhere evident. I am very sorry for your losses. The Army Commander came to see me today, and was much pleased. I may take this opportunity of telling you again how pleased I am that your battalion has joined the Division, and that I notice with much satisfaction how smart your Officers and men are.

Yours very truly,
W. B. Hickie

SECRET.

16th. Division.(G)	2nd. R. Irish Regt.
16th. Division.(Q)	7th. R. Innis. Fus.
13th. Divisional Arty.	49th. M.G.Coy.
O.C. Right Group.	49th. T.M.Batty.
47th. Infantry Brigade.	157th. Fd.Coy. R.E.
48th. Infantry Brigade.	171st. Tunnelling Coy.
109th. Infantry Brigade.	

49th. Inf. Bde. Order No. 74/1. - 19/11/16.

The following amendments are made in 49th. Inf. Bde. Order No. 74. dated 18/11/16.

Para. 5.   Time Table.   line 5.

for Zero to read Zero to
    + 1 minute   + 2 minutes.

for Zero + 1 minute read Zero + 2 minutes
    to   to
    Zero + 8 minutes   Zero + 7 minutes.

for Zero + 3 minutes read Zero + 7 minutes.
    to   to
    Zero + 10 minutes.   Zero + 9 minutes.

Para. 5.   Lewis Guns

Line 2 for Zero to Zero + 8 minutes.
       read Zero to Zero + 7 minutes.

Line 3 for Zero + 8 minutes to Zero + 10 minutes.
       read Zero + 7 minutes to Zero + 9 minutes.

ACKNOWLEDGE.

L. B. Brunley
Captain.

a/Brigade Major, 49th. Inf. Bde.

2nd R. Irish Regt.
7th R. Innis. Fus.
Staff Captain.   (For information).

49th Inf. Bde. No.B.O.74/2, dated 20/11/16.

    With reference to Dummy Raid (B.O. 74, dated 18/11/16) Officers Commanding Sub=Sections will arrange to thin their line as much as possible between N.29.d.80.65 and N.29.b.80.20, from Zero - 5 minutes until artillery cease fire at Zero + 9 minutes.

    They will also arrange for their Lewis Guns to fire according to scheme.

    If wind is favourable, a few men will be detailed to light Smoke Candles and throw P Bombs opposite PECKHAM and on the front of attack. These Smoke Candles &c. will be sent to Battalion Head-Quarters on Monday evening 20th or early Tuesday morning 21st inst:.

Captain,
a/Brigade Major, 49th Inf. Bde.

2nd. R. Irish Regt.
7th. R. Innis. Fus.
O.C. Right Group.
49th. T.M. Battery.

49th. Inf. Bde. No. B.O. 74/3 - 20/11/16.

    Ref. Dummy Raid. -(49th. Inf. Bde. Order No. 74 dated 18/11/16.)

    Watches will be synchronized at 1 p.m. and 3 p.m. to-morrow 21st. Instant.

                                                 Captain.

                a/Brigade Major, 49th. Inf. Bde.

Appendix 8

OPERATION ORDER NO. 48.   Copy No. _____

by

Captain W. L. Moore-Brabazon, Commanding,
2nd. Battalion, The Royal Irish Regiment.

Reference Map   The Field.
WYTSCHAETE & Sheet 28 S.W.   29/11/16.

1. The Battalion will relieve the 7/8th. Battalion, The Royal Irish Fusiliers in the left sub-section tomorrow, the 30th. inst.

2. Companies will be disposed as under and will march off at the times stated.

"A" Coy.	Front Line.	1-30 p.m.
"D" "	Right Support.	1-40 p.m.
"C" "	Left Support.	1-50 p.m.
"B" "	KEMMEL CHATEAU.	2 p.m.
H.Qrs. & Scouts.	KEMMEL CHATEAU.	2-10 p.m.

3. Previous orders re movement east of LOCRE and east of Brigade Headquarters will be observed.

4. The Lewis Gun Officer will arrange to attach 2 extra guns to "A" Coy.

5. An advance party consisting of 1 Officer and 1 N.C.O. per Coy. will leave KEMMEL SHELTERS at 11-50 a.m. to take over trench stores, etc.

6. Officers' valises, stores, etc., will be stacked at Battalion Headquarters, KEMMEL SHELTERS, by 12 noon on the 30th. inst.

7. Officers' trench kits, mess stores, etc., will be stacked by Coys. in the usual place by 1-15 p.m. O's. C. Coys. will detail 1 servant per Coy. to be in charge of the Coy. kits.

8. Dinners 12 noon.

9. Trench Store Lists will be sent to Battalion Headquarters by 9 a.m. on 1st. December.

10. Battalion Headquarters will close in KEMMEL SHELTERS at 2 p.m. and will reopen at KEMMEL CHATEAU at the same hour.

                                    2/Lieut. & A/Adjutant,
                              2nd. Battalion, The Royal Irish Regiment.

Hour of issue 3-30 p.m.
Copy No. 1. War Diary.   No. 7. O. C. "D" Coy.
        2. H.Qrs., 49th. Inf. Bde.   8. Lewis Gun Officer.
           (for information.)   9. Bn. Bombing Officer.
        3. 7/8th. Bn. The R. I. Fus.   10. Medical Officer.
           (for information.)   11. Quartermaster.
        4. O. C. "A" Coy.   12. Transport Officer.
        5. O. C. "B" "   13. R. S. M.
        6. O. C. "C" "   14. Signalling Sergeant.
                        15. Cook Sergeant.

WAR DIARY FOR MONTH OF DECEMBER, 1916.

VOLUME

2nd Royal Irish Regiment

WAR DIARY 2nd BATTALION The ROYAL IRISH REGIMENT
INTELLIGENCE SUMMARY

Army Form C. 2118.

Instructions regarding War Diaries and Intelligence Summaries are contained in F.S. Regs., Part II. and the Staff Manual respectively. Title pages will be prepared in manuscript.

(Erase heading not required.)

Place	Date	Hour	Summary of Events and Information	Remarks and references to Appendices
	1st		The Battalion was in the line.	Jan
	2nd		2 Other ranks joined as reinforcements 2 other ranks wounded 1 " " killed	Jan
	4th		The Battalion extended its line to the left - and took over part of the line hitherto held by the 9th Bn. The ROYAL DUBLIN FUSILIERS. 3 other ranks joined the battalion.	Appendices 1, 2, 3, 4. Jan
	6th		The Battalion was relieved by the 9/10th The ROYAL IRISH FUSILIERS and moved into Brigade Reserve at KEMMEL SHELTERS	App. 5
	10th		The following officers joined the Battalion today. Capt. P.J.G. GORDON RALPH. " R.A.B. BELMORE. " B.D. de A. BORCHERDS " R.H. FRANKENBERG Lieut. W. TOD. 2/Lieut. P.J. GODFREY. " D.J. KELLEHER " C.F. FREEMAN Capt. P.J.G. GORDON-RALPH took over command of C Coy.	Jan

Army Form C. 2118.

WAR DIARY
or
INTELLIGENCE SUMMARY.
(Erase heading not required.)

Place	Date	Hour	Summary of Events and Information	Remarks and references to Appendices
KEMMEL.	11th		Capt. D.B. de A BORCHERDS proceeded to join the 6th. Bn. The ROYAL IRISH Regt.	JAN.
	12th		The Battalion relieved the 7/8th. Batt. The ROYAL IRISH FUSILIERS in the left sector of the Brigade front.	Appendix 6.
	13th		Lieut. W. TOD appointed Battalion Scout Officer.	
	14th	7pm -12pm	The whole of the enemy front line opposite our sector was patrolled during the night with the object of ascertaining the enemy's movements and intentions. The patrols on returning reported enemy quiet.	Appendix 7.
	16th		As retaliation for the Trench Mortar Bombardment carried out by the 36th Division (on our RIGHT) on the 15th instant, the enemy's trench mortars were very active against our front between the hours of 11.15 am & 12.30 pm. During the afternoon he shelled our trenches intermittently with heavy artillery.	Appendix 8. JAN.
			1 other rank was killed.	JAN.
	17th		1 other rank wounded.	JAN.

Army Form C. 2118.

WAR DIARY
or
INTELLIGENCE SUMMARY.
(Erase heading not required.)

Instructions regarding War Diaries and Intelligence
Summaries are contained in F. S. Regs., Part II.
and the Staff Manual respectively. Title pages
will be prepared in manuscript.

Place	Date	Hour	Summary of Events and Information	Remarks and references to Appendices
	18th		The Battalion was relieved by the 7/8th Batt. The ROYAL IRISH FUSILIERS in the left subsector and moved into Divisional Reserve at DONCASTER HUTS -	Appendix 9
	20th		71 other ranks joined the battalion from the BORDER Regt. -	7AM
			The Battalion was inspected by the C. in C., who expressed pleasure in their appearance -	Appendix 10.
	21st		H.M. the KING of Montenegro graciously awarded the Medal of Kmil to No 9037 R.Q.M.S. J. HOPKINS. No 8577 Sgt. DALTON awarded a bar to his Military Medal.	7AM
	23rd		5 other ranks joined the Battalion.	7AM
	24th		The Battalion relieved the 7/8th The ROYAL IRISH FUSILIERS in the left sub sector	Appendix 11.
	27th		The enemy front line was extensively bombarded by trench mortars cooperating with artillery from 2.15 p.m. to 5.30 p.m. During the bombardment, the enemy retaliation was very weak and caused no casualties among our troops. It was observed that the enemy front line and wire suffered severely -	Appendix N. 13.

Army Form C. 2118.

WAR DIARY
or
INTELLIGENCE SUMMARY.
(Erase heading not required.)

Instructions regarding War Diaries and Intelligence Summaries are contained in F.S. Regs., Part II. and the Staff Manual respectively. Title pages will be prepared in manuscript.

Place	Date	Hour	Summary of Events and Information	Remarks and references to Appendices
	27th (cont.)		During the night of the 27th to the 28th the following night seemed to be in great apprehension of a raid on his trenches. Had his Very lights were thrown from his support trenches into his own front line, and his machine guns were very active against our parapet.	App.
	28th		At 9 pm. the enemy front line and wire which were bombarded yesterday were again injured shells for 5 minutes - It is believed that there were many casualties amongst the enemy, as cries were heard from the German line.	Appendix 17
	30th		The Battalion was relieved by the 7/8th The ROYAL IRISH FUSILIERS in the left subsector and on relief moved into Divisional reserve at DONCASTER HUTS.	App. x No. 15.
			2/Lieuts L.A. HAYDEN & C. HUGHES joined the battalion. O. CROSBIE. H. SANDERSON. G.C. POLSON. H.W. CONWAY.	App.

Appendix I

SECRET. OPERATION ORDER. NO. 49.   Copy No. _____

by

LIEUT-COLONEL ▇▇ GREGORIE, COMMANDING,
2nd. Battalion, THE ROYAL IRISH REGIMENT.

Reference Map   The Field.
Sheet 28. S.W. 2.   3/12/16.

1. The Battalion will extend its line to the left and take over tomorrow, the 4th. inst., part of the line at present held by the 9th. Battalion, The Royal Dublin Fusiliers.

   The 7th. Battalion, The Royal Inniskilling Fusiliers will take over that part of the present Battalion-front south of 2" Trench Mortar in SUICIDE ROAD (GLORY HOLE dip - N.30.a.00.70.).

   The Battalion frontage will then be as follows :-
   ASH LANE - N.30.a.00.70.

   The new boundry between Sub-sections will be SUICIDE ROAD, inclusive to Left Sub-section, except that YONGE STREET, as far South as entrance to C.P. 10 (including YONGE STREET DUGOUTS) will belong to Left Sub-section.

2. Disposition.

   Companies will be disposed as under :-

   "B" Coy.   Front Line - ASH LANE exclusive - Head of VIA GELLIA exclusive.

   "D" Coy.   Front Line - Head of VIA GELLIA inclusive - N.30.a.00.70 exclusive.

   "A" Coy.   3 Platoons ALBERTA DUGOUTS.
              1 Platoon FORT REGINA.

   "C" Coy.   The Company less 1 N.C.O. and 6 men YONGE STREET DUGOUTS.
              1 N.C.O. and 6 men FORT SASKATCHEWAN.

3. Advance Parties.

   Advance parties will consist of 1 Officer per company and 1 N.C.O. per platoon.

   "A" Coy. Advance party for ALBERTA DUGOUTS will be at VIA GELLIA end of YONGE STREET at 10 a.m.

   "B" Coy. Advance party to be at DOCTOR'S HOUSE at 10 a.m.

   "D" Coy. Advance party to be at Headquarters, "A" Company, 9th. Battalion, The Royal Dublin Fusiliers, at 10 a.m.

4. Relief.

   "B" Coy. will be met at DOCTOR'S HOUSE by guides from 9th. Battalion, The Royal Irish Fusiliers, at 2 p.m.

   Platoons to march at 10 minutes interval.

   "A" Coy. will be met by guides from 9th. Battalion, The Royal Dublin Fusiliers, at the VIA GELLIA end of YONGE STREET at 2 p.m.

   "D" Coy. On relief by the 7th. Battalion, The Royal Inniskilling Fusiliers, the 2 Right Platoons of "D" Coy. will move via the front line and relieve the 2 Platoons of "A" Coy., 9th. Battalion, The Royal Dublin Fusiliers, holding from Head of KETCHEN AVENUE to VIA GELLIA. This will not take place before 3-30 p.m.

   O. C. "C" Coy. will arrange to relieve FORT SASKATCHEWAN at 2 p.m.

5. Lewis Guns.

   Guides from 9th. Battalion, The Royal Dublin Fusiliers will be at the VIA GELLIA end of YONGE STREET at 10 a.m.

Appendix I (contd).

6. Companies will take over all trench stores with the exception of the following :-
   Gum Boots, Primus Stoves, Soyers Stoves, Lewis Gun Magazines, Carriers and Periscopes.
   All trench stores will be taken over by an Officer.
7. Completion of relief to be reported to Battalion Headquarters in Second Army Code.
8. Battalion Headquarters will close in KEMMEL CHATEAU at 3 p.m. and will reopen at DOCTOR'S HOUSE at the same hour.
9. ACKNOWLEDGE.

2/Lieut. & A/Adjutant,
2nd. Battalion, The Royal Irish Regiment.

Hour of issue 9.30 p.m.

Copy No. 1. War Diary.
2. H.Qrs., 49th. Inf. Bde.
3. 1st. Bn. The R. Munst. Fus.
4. 9th. Bn. The R. Dublin Fus.
5. O. C. "A" Coy.
6. O. C. "B" ,,
7. O. C. "C" ,,
8. O. C. "D" Coy.
   No. 17. Cook Sergeant.

No. 9. Lewis Gun Officer.
10. Bn. Bombing Officer.
11. Medical Officer.
12. Quartermaster.
13. Transport Officer.
14. Regtl. Sergt Major.
15. Signalling Sergeant.
16. Scout Sergeant.

SECRET. Appendix 2   Copy No. 1

49th Infantry Brigade Order No. 77 - 3-12-16.

Ref Sheet 28.S.W. 2.
 1/10000.

1.   The IX Corps Front is being reorganized with the result that the 16th Division is taking over the SPANBROEK Section from the 36th Division on the night of the 5/6th December, and the frontages at present allotted to Brigades will be modified.

2.   As the result of above, the following relief will take place, on the 4th instant :-
   The 49th Infantry Brigade will take over from the 48th Infantry Brigade the portion of the line from KETCHEN AVENUE to ASH LANE (exclusive). The new boundary between the 48th and 49th Brigades is shown on attached table.
   Headquarters, 49th Infantry Brigade remains at LITTLE KEMMEL.

3.   In order to affect the above relief -
   (a) The 7th R. Innis Fus will take over from the 2nd R. Irish Regt the portion of the front line up to the 2" T.M. Emplacement, N.30.a.00.70 (exclusive)
   .... Battalion Headquarters will remain at FORT VICTORIA.
   (b) The 2nd R. Irish Regt will take over from the 9th R. Dublin Fus as far as ASH LANE (exclusive). The 48th Brigade will retain Company Headquarters in LEEMING LANE, N.24.d.1¼.9¾.
   Battalion Headquarters will be at LA POLKA (Doctor's House).

The new boundary between Sub-sections will be SUICIDE ROAD, inclusive to Left Sub-section, except that YONGE STREET, as far South as entrance to S.P. 10 (including YONGE STREET DUGOUTS) will belong to Left Sub-section.

4.   The 49th Machine Gun Company will relieve Guns of 48th Machine Gun Company in the new area on the 4th instant, under arrangements to be made between O.C's concerned.

5.   The 49th Trench Mortar Battery will relieve Guns of 48th Trench Mortar Battery in the new area on the 4th instant, under arrangements to be made between O.C's concerned.

6.   (a) All further details to be arranged between O.C. Battalions concerned.
            (b) Incoming battalions will take over all trench stores, maps, &c, with the exception of the following:-
Gun Boots, Primer's Stoves, Soyer's Stoves, Lewis Gun Magazines, Carriers,   Periscopes.
Officers Commanding will arrange that Lists of Trench Stores taken over are signed and countersigned by an officer.
            (c) On completion of reliefs, reports will be sent in to Brigade Headquarters in Code, and command will pass to the incoming unit.

7.   The Battalions in Brigade and Divisional Reserve will remain as at present.

8.   ACKNOWLEDGE.

                                     R.B. Brunley
                                         Captain,

               a/Brigade Major, 49th Infantry Brigade.

                                              P.T.O.

Issued through Signals.

Copy No. 1 to 2nd R. Irish Regt.
" 2   7th R. Innis Fus.
" 3   8th R. Innis Fus.
" 4   7/8th R. Irish Fus.
" 5   49th M.G. Company.
" 6   49th T. M. B.
" 7   48th Infantry Brigade.
" 8   109th Infantry Brigade.
" 9   O.C. Right Group.
" 10   16th Division (G)
" 11   16th Division (Q)
" 12   Staff Captain,
" 13   Bde Signal Officer.
" 14   Bde Transport Officer.
" 15   A.D.M.S. 16th Division.
" 16   113th Field Ambulance.
" 17   157th Field Company, R.E.
" 18   144th Coy, A.S.C.
" 19   Bde Supply Officer.
" 20   Z/16 T.M.B.
" 21   250th Tunnelling Coy.
" 22-23 War Diary.
" 24   FILE.

SECRET.

TABLE SHOWING BOUNDARIES OF BRIGADE AREA. TO ACCOMPANY 49TH INFANTRY BRIGADE ORDER NO. 77 DATED 3/12/16.

SECTION	FRONT LINE	BOUNDARIES	REMARKS
WYTSCHAETE.	5th bay North of PICCADILLY (exclusive) about N.29.d.82.62 to ASH LANE (exclusive)	(a) SOUTHERN. As at Present between 16th and 36th Divisions i.e. - PICCADILLY - VIGO STREET and REGENT STREET - REGENT DUGOUTS and FORT VICTORIA to 49th Infantry Brigade..Trence to LINDENHOEK Cross Roads. (b) NORTHERN. ASH LANE (exclusive) as far as junction with OAK TRENCH thence in a straight line to junction of PARK AVENUE and PARK LANE, LEEMING LANE (inclusive): thence in a straight line to point where tramway crosses HARINGHEBEEK at N.23.a.20.35 (BANFF DUGOUTS and IRISH HOUSE (exclusive): tramway line (exclusive) as far as YORK ROAD, thence in a straight line to N.19 central.	(i) The allotment of all existing back billets, horse standings, etc, will remain as at present. (ii) The billeting accommodation in KEMMEL will be allotted under arrangements to be issued later.

Appendix 3.

48th INFANTRY BRIGADE

OPERATION ORDERs 83

Reference sheet 28.S.W.
1/20,000

1.	Reorganisation of the IX Corps Front in will involve the extension of the 16th Division Front Southward to DURHAM ROAD (N.36.c.9.8½)

2.	The readjustment of Brigade Fronts thus necessary will take place on the nights of 4/5th, 5th/6th December

3.	(a) 49th Infantry Brigade will take over from 48th Infantry Brigade the portion of the Front Line from KETCHEN AVENUE to ASH LANE (exclusive).
	The new boundaries between Infantry Brigades will be as shown in attached tables.
	(b) The 48th Infantry Brigade will take over the present LEFT SECTION from the 47th Infantry Brigade; the new Front line to be held by the 48th Infantry Brigade will thus extend from ASH LANE (inclusive) to the VIERSTRAAT - WYTSCHAETE Road.(exclusive).
	(c) ROSSIGNOL ROAD - VAN WAY - LARK LANE: all inclusive to new RIGHT sub-section, will form boundary between RIGHT and LEFT Sub-sections in new LEFT SECTION.
	(d) Head Quarters 48th Infantry Brigade will remain at BRULOOZE.

4.	In accordance with above, the following reliefs will take place on December 4th.

5.	2nd ROYAL IRISH REGIMENT will relieve 9th ROYAL DUBLIN FUSILIERS in present RIGHT Sub-section.(KETCHEN AVENUE exclusive to ASH LANE exclusive)
	On relief 9th ROYAL DUBLIN FUSILIERS will withdraw to Billets at BIRR BARRACKS, LOCRE and become Battalion in Divisional Reserve at 4 hours notice.

6.	7th ROYAL IRISH RIFLES relieve 2nd ROYAL DUBLIN FUSILIERS in new RIGHT Sub-section, (ASH LANE inclusive to LARK LANE inclusive)
	On relief 2nd ROYAL DUBLIN FUSILIERS will withdraw to Billets in KEMMEL, with Headquarters at PRIEST'S HOUSE, and become Battalion in Brigade Reserve.

7.	8th ROYAL DUBLIN FUSILIERS will relieve 1st ROYAL MUNSTER FUSILIERS in LEFT SECTION (LARK LANE exclusive to VIERSTRAAT - WYTSCHAETE ROAD exclusive.

8.	All details for reliefs will be arranged direct/between Commanding Officers concerned.

9th	Units concerned will detail an officer per company to go into the line in advance to take over Trench Stores.

10.	Lists of Stores handed over to 49th Infantry Brigade, and of Stores handed over by 47th Infantry Brigade will be forwarded to Brigade Headquarters on attached "pro forma", A, B, and C,. These forms signed and countersigned must reach Brigade Headquarters by 6 p.m. on December 5th.

11.	The customary consolidated returns will be furnished to Brigade Headquarters for all Stores taken over by 7th ROYAL IRISH RIFLES from 2nd ROYAL DUBLIN FUSILIERS..

Operation Orders 83 Continued:-

12.   The following Stores will NOT be handed over:-

GUM BOOTS, PRIMUS STOVES, SOYERS STOVES, LEWIS GUN MAGAZINE CARRIERS, PERISCOPES, DIXIES. (except as between 7th ROYAL IRISH RIFLES and 2nd ROYAL DUBLIN FUSILIERS.

13.   No's 1 of LEWIS GUN TEAMS, and SNIPERS will go into the line not less than FOUR HOURS in advance on day of relief.

14.   Relief of 47th T. M. BATTERY by 48th T. M. BATTERY, and of Guns of 48th T. M. Battery now in act of being taken over by 49th Infan- Brigade, will be arranged direct between O. C., T. M. Batteries concerned.

Reliefs to take place on the 4th December.

15.   Separate orders will be issued for relief of VICKER'S GUNS.

16.   Usual precautions as regards movement by Platoons at 200 yards distance will be observed.

17.   Billeting parties to report to Headquarters of Battalions concerned at 11 a. m. on the 4th December.

18.   Completion of relief to be notified in code by wire to Brigade Headquarters.

T. B. Brady.
Captain.
Brigade Major, 48th Infantry Brigade.

3rd December 1916.

Copies to:-
1 and 2 War Diary
3 Filed
4 G.O.C.
5 7th Royal Irish Rifles
6 2nd Royal Dublin Fusiliers
7 8th Royal Dublin Fusiliers
8 9th Royal Dublin Fusiliers
9 48th M. Gun Company
10 48th T.M.Battery
11 47th T.M.Battery
12 Staff Captain
13 48th Brigade Signals
14 48th Brigade Transport Officer
15 48th Brigade Supply Officer

16 155th Field Co,.R.E.
17 1st Royal Munster Fusiliers
18 2nd Royal Irish Regiment.
19 16th Division
20 16th Division Artillery
21 Centre Group 16th D.A.
22 16th Division "Q"
23 47th Infantry Brigade
24 49th Infantry Brigade
25 250th Tunnelling Co,.R.E.
26 Y.16.T.Mortar Battery
27 A.D.M.S. 16th Division
28 145th Company. A.S.C.

SECRET.

TABLE SHOWING BOUNDARIES OF BRIGADE AREAS. TO ACCOMPANY 48TH INFANTRY BRIGADE ORDER No 83 DATED 3RD DECEMBER 1916.

SECTION	FRONT LINE	BOUNDARIES	REMARKS
SPANBROEK. (47th Inf.Bde.)	DURHAM ROAD (exclusive) to 5th Bay north of PICCADILLY (inclusive) about N.29.d.82.62.	(a) SOUTHERN. DURHAM ROAD (exclusive) - N.35.d.10.00 - T.4.a.90.20.- G.H.Q. 2nd Line at N.33.d.80.40. (b) NORTHERN. As at present between 16th and 36th Divisions but 47th Inf.Bde retains GURARH CAMP and present horse standings.	NOTES. (i) Except as shown in this order, the allotment of all existing back billet horse standings etc., will remain as at present. (ii) The exact administrative boundary with 36th Div. west of G.H.Q. 2nd Line will be notified later It remains practically the same as at present, except
WYTSCHAETE. (49th Inf.Bde.)	5th bay north of PICCADILLY (exclusive) about N.29.d.82.62.- to ASH LANE (exclusive)	(a) SOUTHERN. (see above) (b) NORTHERN ASH LANE (exclusive) as far as junction with OAK TRENCH; thence in a straight line to junction of PARK AVENUE & PARK LANE, LEEMING LANE (inclusive); thence in a straight line to point where tramway crosses HARINGHEBEEK at N.23.a.20.35. (BANFF DUGOUTS and IRISH HOUSE exclusive);tramway line (exclusive) as far as YORK ROAD, thence in a straight line to H.19 central.	that DERRY HUTS and Inf.Bd H.Q. at DRANOUTRE are handed over to 16th Div. (iii) The billeting accomodation in KEMMEL will be allotted under arrangements to be made by "Q" 16th DIV. (iv) DERRY HUTS will become finally available for 47th Inf.Bde on Dec 6th. The billeting accomodation in KEMMEL will be finally adjusted on the same date.
VIERSTRAAT. (48th Inf.Bde.)	ASH LANE (inclusive) to VIERSTRAAT-WYTSCHAETE ROAD (exclusive)	(a) SOUTHERN.(see above) (b) NORTHERN. As at present between 16th & 41st Divisions.	

SECRET   Copy No. 9

Appendix 4

7TH. (S) BATTALION ROYAL INNISKILLING FUSILIERS OPERATION ORDER No. 67

1. The Battalion will take over from the 2nd. Battn. Royal Irish Regiment at 3 p.m. to-morrow 4th. inst. the portion of the front line up to the 2" T.M. emplacement R.30.A 0.0.70.(exclusive).

2. Boundaries for the Battalion front will then be from fifth Bay north of Picadilly (exclusive) to 2" T.M. emplacement R.30.A 0.0.70.(exclusive).

3. The Companies will take over line as follows:-

    "C" Coy. Five Bays North of Picadilly (exclusive) to present Left Coy. Headquarters (Approximate)

    "D" Coy. from present Coy. Hdqrs.(Approximate) to 2" T.M. emplacement R.30.A 0.0.70. (Suicide Road).

    "A" Coy. will take over Strong Point 10.

    "B" Coy. will remain at Regent Street Dug-Outs.

    Battalion Headquarters will remain at FORT VICTORIA.

    "D" Coy. will take over Trench Stores from 2nd. Battn. Royal Irish Regiment with the exception of the following:- Gum Boots, Primus Stoves, Soyers Stoves, Lewis Gun Magazines, Carriers and Periscopes, and will bring such of these articles as are in their possession with them.

    A similar procedure will be adopted by "C" Coy. in taking over from "D" Coy.

4. Lists of Trench Stores taken over must be signed and counter-signed by an Officer, and rendered to Battalion Headquarters by 9 a.m. 5th. inst.

5. On completion of reliefs reports will be sent to Battalion Headquarters in CODE.

6. The Lewis Gun Officer will arrange that six Lewis Guns are placed in the Battalion front.

7. All work in progress will be carefully taken over.

8. Acknowledge.

                    (Signed) A. A. Seward, Lieut. & A/Adjutant,

                    7th. (S) Battalion Royal Inniskilling Fusiliers.

ISSUED THROUGH SIGNALLERS:-

                    Copy 1. File
                         2. "A" Coy.
                         3. "B" "
                         4. "C" "
                         5. "D" "
                         6. Lewis Gun Officer.
                         7. Commanding Officer
                         8. Brigade Headquarters.
                         9. 2nd. Battn. Roy. Irish Regt.

3.12.16.

Appendix 5

OPERATION ORDER NO. 50.
by
LIEUT-COLONEL H. G. GREGORIE, COMMANDING,
2nd. Battalion, THE ROYAL IRISH REGIMENT.

Reference Map.
WYTSCHAETE & Sheet. 28 S.W.

The Field.
6/12/15.

1. The Battalion will be relieved by the 7/8th. Battalion, The Royal Irish Fusiliers in the left sub-section tomorrow, The 6th. inst. Relief to commence at 2 p.m. On relief the Battalion will move into Brigade Reserve at KEMMEL SHELTERS.
2. The usual orders re movement east of LOCRE and east of Brigade Headquarters will be observed.
3. All work, intelligence reports, etc., will be carefully handed over to incoming unit.
4. A billeting party under the Quartermaster will report to Headquarters, 7/8th. Battalion, The Royal Irish Fusiliers at 12-30 p.m. to take over hutments, etc.
5. Officers' trench kits, etc., will be dumped at KEMMEL CHATEAU by 1-30 p.m.
6. Trench Store lists will be rendered to Orderly Room by 9 a.m. on the 7th. inst.
7. Completion of relief to be reported to Battalion Headquarters in Second Army Code.

2/Lieut. & A/Adjutant,
2nd. Battalion, The Royal Irish Regiment.

Hour of issue. 7 p.m.
Copy No. 1. War Diary.
    2. H.Q'rs., 49th. Inf. Bde.
       (for information.)
    3. 7/8th. Bn. The R. I. Fus.
       (for information.)
    4. O. C. "A" Coy.
    5. O. C. "B" "
    6. O. C. "C" "

No. 7. O. C. "D" Coy.
    8. Lewis Gun Officer.
    9. Bn. Bombing Officer.
   10. Medical Officer.
   11. Quartermaster.
   12. Transport Officer.
   13. Regtl. Sergt. Major.
   14. Signalling Sergeant.

No. 15. Cook Sergeant.

Appendix 6.

OPERATION ORDER NO. 51.   Copy No. 1
by
LIEUT-COLONEL H. G. GREGORIE, COMMANDING,
2nd. Battalion, THE ROYAL IRISH REGIMENT.

Reference Map   The Field.
WYTSCHAETE & Sheet 28 S.W.   11/12/16.

1. The Battalion will relieve the 7/8th. Battalion, The Royal Irish Fusiliers in the Left Sub-section tomorrow, the 12th. inst.

2. Companies will be disposed as under and will march off at the times stated:-

    "B" Coy.   Right Front Line.   12-30 p.m.
    "D" ,,   Left Front Line.   12-40 p.m.
    "C" ,,   Right Support.   12-50 p.m.
    "A" ,,   Left Support.   1 p.m.
    H.Qrs.   DOCTOR'S HOUSE.   1-10 p.m.

3. Previous orders re movement east of LOCRE and east of Brigade Headquarters will be observed.

4. The Lewis Gun Officer and the Scout Officer will make their own arrangements re relief.

5. An advance party consisting of 1 Officer and 1 N.C.O. per Coy. will leave KEMMEL SHELTERS at 11 a.m. to take over trench stores etc.

6. Officers' valises, stores, etc., will be stacked at Battalion Headquarters, KEMMEL SHELTERS, by 11 a.m. on the 12th. inst.

7. Officers' trench kits, mess stores, etc., will be stacked by Coys. in the usual place by 12-15 p.m. O's. C. Coys. will detail 1 servant per Coy. to be in charge of the company kits.

8. Dinners 11-30 a.m.

9. Trench Store Lists will be sent to Battalion Headquarters by 9 a.m. on the 13th. inst.

10. Battalion Headquarters will close in KEMMEL SHELTERS at 1 p.m. and will reopen at DOCTOR'S HOUSE at the same hour.

                                                          Lieut. & A/Adjutant,
                                 2nd. Battalion, The Royal Irish Regiment.

Hour of issue 6 p.m.

Copy No. 1. War Diary.   No. 9. Scout Officer.
    2. H.Qrs., 49th. Inf. Bde.   10. Bn. Bombing Officer.
    3. 7/8th. Bn. The Roy. Ir. Fus.   11. Medical Officer.
    4. O. C. "A" Coy.   12. Quartermaster.
    5. O. C. "B" ,,   13. Transport Officer.
    6. O. C. "C" ,,   14. Regtl. Sergt. Major.
    7. O. C. "D" ,,   15. Signalling Sergeant.
    8. Lewis Gun Officer.   16. Cook Sergeant.

Appendix Y

SECRET

O.C. B Coy
    D Coy.

Patrols will be carried out on the whole Battalion front to-night.
The method to be adopted will be as follows:-

Each Company will send out 4 patrols on its front at intervals of 2 hours each — starting at 7 p.m. Each patrol will in fact be an advanced listening post & their orders will be to go out and lie as near the German wire as possible and listen for any movement. On return they will render a written report as soon as possible. These reports will be collected and forwarded to Battalion H.Q as soon as possible.

Company Commanders will select a point from which each patrol will depart from our line and will give definite instructions as to where they are to go to.

It is to be understood that it is required to listen along the whole German line opposite our front and the object of these patrols is to ascertain if anything can be heard at various points.

Patrols will go out in sequence from the Left starting with D Coys left patrol, which will go out at 7 p.m and return at 8 p.m

B Coys left patrol will go out at 8 p.m and return at 9 p.m etc.

Please warn Battalions on either flank.

14/12/16

Plaisted Lieut
    Adjt
2nd The Royal Irish Regt

Appendix 8.

Right Battalion.   S E C R E T.
Left Battalion.
49th M.G. Company.
49th T. M. B.

49th Inf'y Bde No. S.O.904 — 14-12-16.

A combined Trench Mortar Bombardment will be carried out by the 36th Division at 10-30 a.m. on the 18th December, against the salient in the enemy's front line trenches south of LA PETITE DOUVE FME. (U.8.a & b).

ACKNOWLEDGE.

[signature]
Captain,
Brigade Major, 49th Infantry Brigade.

SECRET. Operation Order No 52. Copy No 1
Appendix 9.
Lieut Colonel R.G. Frijou, Commanding
2nd Battalion The Royal Irish Regiment

Reference Map:
WHYTSCHAETE & Sheet 28 SW.

the Field
17-12-16.

1. The Battalion will be relieved by the 7/8th Battalion the Royal Irish Fusiliers in the left Sub-section tomorrow, the 18th inst. Relief to commence at 11-30 a.m. On relief the Battalion will move into Divisional Reserve at DONCASTER HUTS, LOCRE.

2. The usual orders re movement east of LOCRE and east of Brigade Headquarters will be observed.

3. All work, intelligence reports, etc. will be carefully handed over to incoming unit.

4. A billeting party under the Quartermaster will report to Headquarters, 8th Battalion The Royal Inniskilling Fusiliers at 12 noon, to take over hutments etc.

5. Officers' trench kits, etc., will be dumped outside 113th Field Ambulance, KEMMEL, by 10 a.m.

6. Trench Store lists will be rendered to Orderly Room by 9 a.m. on 19th inst.

7. The Cook Sergeant will make arrangements that Coys. get their dinners immediately on arrival in LOCRE.

8. Completion of relief to be reported to Battalion Headquarters in "B.A.B" Code.

Gulvey
Lieut & Adjt
2nd. Battalion The Royal Irish Regiment

Hour of Issue 4 p.m.
Copy No 1. War Diary.
    2. H.Qrs 49th Inf. Bde.
    3. 7/8. Battn. The R.I. Fusrs
    4. 8th Battn. The R. Innis. Fusrs
    5. O.C. "A" Coy
    6. O.C. "B" "
    7. O.C. "C" "
    8. O.C. "D" "
    9. Lewis Gun Officer.
    10. Battn Bombing Officer
    11. Medical Officer
    12. Quartermaster
    13. Transport Officer
    14. Regtl Sergt Major
    15. Signalling Sergeant
    16. Cook Sergeant

SECRET.　　　　　　　　　　　Appendix 10.
　　　　　　　　　　　　　49th. I.Bde. S.C.C.VIII/365.

O.C.

　　2nd. R.Irish Regt.

　　　　　　　　　　　　For your information and necessary
action.

　　　　　　　　　　　　　　　　[signature]　　　Captain,
19.12.16.　　　　　　　for Staff Captain, 49th. Inf. Bde.

SECRET

16th. Div. Art.	"G.S."	)
48th. Inf. Bde.	A.P.M., 16th.Div.	)
49th. Inf. Bde.	IX. Corps.	) For information.
16th. Div. Engrs.		)
Senior Chaplain, R.C.	No.4. D.S.C.	)
Lieut-Col. Jameson.	113th. Fld. Amb.	)

16th. Division No. A/174. 19th. December 1916.

1. The following detail of Troops will parade for inspection by the Commander-in-Chief on Wednesday, 20th. instant, at 2-45p.m.

 (i) <u>2nd. Bn. R. Dublin Fusiliers</u> - will be drawn up in line facing South on the BIRR BARRACKS Road. The right of the line will rest on M.29.a.7.7. Regtl. Band on Right of the line.

 (ii) <u>2nd. Bn. R. Irish Regt.</u> - will be drawn up in line facing South, on the continuation of the BIRR BARRACKS Road to the HOSPICE. The Right of the line will rest on M.29.b.2½.9½. Regtl. Band on the Left of the Line.

2. <u>DRESS</u>:- Infantry Fighting Order, without packs. Steel helmets. If wet, great coats will be worn.

3. Brigadiers and Brigade Majors will be on the outer flanks of their respective Units.

4. <u>Royal Artillery</u> - will parade on the road opposite the Baths, facing East. Their left will be exactly opposite the South end of the Baths.

5. The Corner of the triangle formed by the junction of the BIRR BARRACKS and HOSPICE Roads, and the LOCRE and HOSPICE Road, will be left clear.

6. The following Staff Officers will attend, and will be drawn up at the triangle in line, dismounted :-

 C.R.A.
 G.S.O.1.
 A.A. & Q.M.G.
 C.R.E.
 Senior R.C. Chaplain.
 Lt-Col. Jameson, (attached.)

7. DRESS FOR ALL OFFICERS, other than Regimental Officers, will be Drill Order.

8. It is not known on which flank the C-in-C. will arrive, but he will be received with the General Salute (bayonets fixed), by each Company as he approaches it.

9. ACKNOWLEDGE. *GaCWebb* Lieut-Colonel,
 A.A. & Q.M.G., 16th. Division.

Appendix 11

SECRET.   OPERATION ORDER NO. 54.   Copy No. 1.
by
LIEUT-COLONEL E. G. GREGORIE, COMMANDING,
2nd. Battalion, THE ROYAL IRISH REGIMENT.

Reference Map   The Field.
WYTSCHAETE & Sheet 28 S.W.   23/12/16.

1. The Battalion will relieve the 7/8th. Battalion, The Royal Irish Fusiliers in the left sub-section tomorrow, the 24th. inst.

2. Companies will be disposed as under and will march off at times stated.

   "A" Coy.   Left Front Line.   9-30 a.m.
   "C"   ,,   Right Front Line.   9-40 a.m.
   "B"   ,,   Left Support.   9-50 a.m.
   "D"   ,,   Right Support.   10 a.m.

3. Previous orders re movement east of LOCRE and east of Brigade Headquarters will be observed.

4. An advance party consisting of 1 Officer and 1 N.C.O. per Coy. will leave DONCASTER HUTS at 8 a.m. to take over trench stores, etc.

5. Officers' valises, packs, blankets, etc. will be dumped in Coy. lines by 8-30 a.m.

6. Trench Store lists will be rendered to Orderly Room by 9 a.m. on 25th. inst.

7. Battalion Headquarters will close in DONCASTER HUTS at 12-30 p.m. and will reopen at DOCTOR'S HOUSE at the same hour.

8. The Cook Sergeant will make the necessary arrangements re dinners.

                                                    Lieut. & A/Adjutant,
                                        2nd. Battalion, The Royal Irish Regiment.

Hour of issue 6-30 p.m.
Copy No. 1. War Diary.   No. 9. Bn. Bombing Officer.
        2. H.Qrs., 49th. Inf. Bde.   10. Medical Officer.
        3. 7/8th. Bn. The R. Ir. Fus.   11. Quartermaster.
        4. O. C. "A" Coy.   12. Transport Officer.
        5. O. C. "B" ,,   13. Regtl. Sergt. Major.
        6. O. C. "C" ,,   14. Signalling Sergeant.
        7. O. C. "D" ,,   15. Scout Sergeant.
        8. Lewis Gun Officer.   16. Cook Sergeant.

Appendix 12

SECRET. OPERATION ORDER NO. 53.   Copy No. 9
by
LIEUT-COLONEL H. G. GREGORIE, COMMANDING,
2nd. Battalion, THE ROYAL IRISH REGIMENT.

Reference Map
WYTSCHAETE & Sheet 28 S.W.

The Field
23/12/16.

1. A Trench Mortar Bombardment will take place on 27th. December.

2. OBJECT.

To damage or destroy the enemy's front line system, especially his wire.

3. POINTS OF ATTACK.

"A" Group T.M's..... N.30.c.10.80. to N.30.a.30.15.
"B" Group T.M's..... N.30.a.30.15. to N.30.a.50.48.
"C" Group T.M's..... N.30.a.50.48. to N.30.a.65.85.
"D" Group T.M's..... N.30.a.65.85. to N.24.b.80.20.
"E" Group T.M's..... N.24.c.80.20. to N.24.c.85.54.

4. TIME TABLE.

Zero = 2-15 p.m.

Zero to Zero + 30 minutes.	Fire by 2" T.M's. as fast as possible. Stokes to fire 100 rounds in bursts.
Zero + 30 minutes to Zero + 45 minutes.	Rest.
Zero + 45 minutes to Zero + 75 minutes.	Fire as before.

5. At - 60 minutes the O. C. Right Company will withdraw his company via VIA GELLIA to YONGE STREET Dugouts, leaving 2 sentry groups at points selected by himself.

At - 60 minutes the O. C. Right Support Company will withdraw his company to FORT REGINA.

At - 45 minutes the O. C. Left Company will withdraw via VIA GELLIA to ALBERTA DUGOUTS and S. P. 11, leaving 2 sentry groups in the front line.

At - 45 minutes the O. C. Left Support Company will withdraw to FORT SASKATCHEWAN.

(2)

At conclusion of Bombardment companies will reoccupy the front line as early as enemy's possible retaliation will permit.

It is obviously impossible to lay down a fixed hour for reoccupation of the line and Company Commanders must use their discretion, but the line must be reoccupied, at the latest, by + 3 hours.

6. The Lewis Guns in the front line will remain in position throughout the operation.

7. Signal for commencement of Bombardment :-
 1 RED ROCKET fired from Reserve Trench near Barricade, SUICIDE ROAD.

8. Watches will be synchronised on 27th inst. with Battalion Headquarters at 8 a.m. and 12 noon.

9. The Medical Officer will make arrangements for First Aid for the front line.

Lieut-Colonel,
Commanding, 2nd. Battalion, The Royal Irish Regt.

Hour of issue 1 p.m.

Copy No. 1. War Diary.
     2. H.Q., 49th. Inf. Bde.
     3. O. C. "A" Coy.
     4. O. C. "B" ,,

No. 5. O. C. "C" Coy.
     6. O. C. "D" ,,
     7. Lewis Gun Officer.
     8. Medical Officer.

2nd R. Irish Regt.   S E C R E T.
7th R. Innis Fus.
8th R. Innis Fus.
7/8th R. Irish Fus.
49th M.G. Company.
49th T. M. B.
2/16 T. M. B.
O.C. Centre Group.
16th Division.
157th Field Coy, R.E.
47th Infy Brigade.
48th Infy Brigade.

49th Infy Bde No. B.O.81/1 - 21-12-16.

Acknowledged 21/12/16 9.50 pm

    Reference 49th Infantry Brigade Order No. 81 of 20-12-16, para 8 is now cancelled.

    Watches will be synchronised on 26th instant with Brigade Headquarters at 8 a.m. and 12 a.m.

    ACKNOWLEDGE.

                                         Captain,

        Brigade Major, 49th Infantry Brigade.

Appendix 13

2nd R. Irish Regt.
7th R. Innis Fus.
8th R. Innis Fus.
7/8th R. Irish Fus.
49th M.G. Company.
49th T. M. B.
Z/16 T. M. B.
O.C. Centre Group.
16th Division.
157th Field Coy, R.E.
47th Inf. Bde.
48th Inf. Bde.

S E C R E T.

49th Infy Bde No. B.O. 81/2 — 22-12-16.

With reference to 49th Infantry Brigade Order No. 81 dated 20-12-16.

The Bombardment has been postponed until 27th December. All other details remain the same.

ACKNOWLEDGE.

[signature] Captain,
Brigade Major, 49th Infantry Brigade.

"C" Form (Duplicate).
MESSAGES AND SIGNALS.

Army Form C. 2123.
(In books of 50's in duplicate.)
No. of Message..................

Service Instructions. 1 BAP 19 FF4 Sgt...

Charges to Pay. £ s. d.

Office Stamp. FK2

Handed in at......FF4......Office......m. Received......m.

TO ......FF3......

Sender's Number	Day of Month	In reply to Number	A A A
	30	9/L	
	a	time	12 am should

FROM PLACE & TIME: FF4 9:10 P.m.

S E C R E T.   Copy No..............

49th Infantry Brigade Order No. 81 - 20-12-16.
****

1. A Trench Mortar Bombardment will take place on 26th December.

2. OBJECT.
   To damage or destroy the enemy's front line system, especially his wire.

3. POINTS OF ATTACK.

   "A" Group T.M's.....N.30.c.10.80 to N.30.a.30.15.
   "B" Group T.M's.....N.30.a.30.15 to N.30.a.50.48.
   "C" Group T.M's.....N.30.a.50.48 to N.30.a.65.85.
   "D" Group T.M's.....N.30.a.65.85 to N.24.c.80.20.
   "E" Group T.M's.....N.24.c.80.20 to N.24.c.85.54.

4. TIME TABLE.

                 Zero = . . 2-15 p.m.

   Zero to   Fire by 2" T.M's as fast as
   Zero + 30 minutes   possible. Stokes to fire 100
                              rounds in bursts.

   Zero + 30 minutes.
   to Zero + 45   Rest.
   minutes.

   Zero + 45 minutes
        to   Fire as before.
   Zero + 75 minutes.

5. Troops will be withdrawn from front line only leaving some Lewis Guns, and a few groups of sentries.
   The troops withdrawn will withdraw to Reserve Line, REGENT STREET & YONGE STREET DUGOUTS, who will replace a corresponding number withdrawn to FORT VICTORIA, FORT REGINA and FORT SASKATCHEWAN.

6. A Report Officer on telephone will be stationed at S.P.10 and S.P.11 to report on operations and enemy's fire direct to Brigade Headquarters.

7. Divisional Artillery to co-operate by firing on O.P's and enemys T.M.emplacements. Heavy Artillery to counter-battery if the enemy's Artillery open fire, and engage strong observation points.

8. Signal for commencement of Bombardment:-

      1 RED ROCKET fired from Reserve Trench near Barricade, SUICIDE ROAD.

                                      Stevens Gower
                                              Brigadier General,
               Commanding 49th Infantry Brigade.
Issued through Signals.
   Copy No. 1 to 8th R. Innis Fus.   6 to O.C. Centre Group.
        "   2   7/8th R. Irish Fus. 7   16th Division.
        "   3   49th M.G. Coy   8   157th Field Coy, R.E.
        "   4   49th T.M.B.   9   47th Inf. Bde.
        "   5   7/16 T.M.B.   10   48th Inf. Bde.
                                     11   2nd Roy Irish Regt.
                                     12   7th Roy Innis Fus

Appendix B.

16th Division.
Centre Group.
O.C. Left Subsection.   S E C R E T.
O.C. Right Subsection.
49th T. M. B.
Z/16 T. M. B.
49th M.G. Company.
47th Infy Bde.
48th Infy Bde.
157th Field Company, R.E.

49th Infy Bde No. H.M. B.0 84/1 - 28-12-16.

Reference this Office Order No. 84 of today.

If no ammunition is required for retaliation after the bombardment at 9 p.m., the artillery of Centre Group will again open on enemy's wire and front line trenches at 12 midnight tonight, 28th instant.

Bombardment will last two minutes.

O.C. Right and Left Subsection will please acknowledge.

Captain,

a/Brigade Major, 49th Infantry Brigade.

SECRET.   Copy No...3......

49th Infantry Brigade Order No.84 - 28-12-16.

  A vigorous bombardment of enemy's wire and front line, which was bombarded yesterday, will take place tonight, 28th. instant, and will last 5 minutes.

  Artillery, 2" T.M's, Stokes Guns, Vickers and Lewis Guns will be used.

  18-pdrs will fire on enemy's wire and front line, 4.5" Howitzers or suspected T.M's.

  2" T.M's will fire on junction of Communication Trenches with front line. Stokes Guns will traverse front line.
  Fire to be as fast as possible.

  Lewis Guns will open on enemy's wire immediately signal is fired,

  Vickers will fire on all communications.

  O.C. Left Battalion will arrange to fire a Gold and Silver Rain rocket from the 'GLORY HOLE' at ZERO hour.

  ZERO hour will be 9 p.m.

  Watches will be synchronised at 5 p.m.

  ACKNOWLEDGE.

              F.B.Brinley
                Captain,

   a/Brigade Major, 49th Infantry Brigade.

Issued through Signals.

    Copy No. 1 to 16th Division.
     .. 2 Centre Group.
     .. 3 O.C. Left Subsection.
     .. 4 O.C. Right Subsection.
     .. 5 49th T. M. B.
     .. 6 Z/16 T. M. B.
     .. 7 49th M.G. Company.
     .. 8 47th Infy Bde.
     .. 9 48th Infy Bde.
     .. 10 157th Field Coy, R.E..
     .. 11 250th Tunnelling Coy.
     .. 12-13 War Diary.
     .. 14 File.

Appendix #15

SECRET.   OPERATION ORDER NO. 55.   Copy No. _____

by

MAJOR L. L. FARMER, COMMANDING,

2nd. BATTALION, THE ROYAL IRISH REGIMENT.

Reference Map   The Field.
WYTSCHAETE & Sheet 28 S.W.   29/12/16.

1. The Battalion will be relieved by the 7/8th. Battalion, The Royal Irish Fusiliers in the left sub-section tomorrow, the 30th. inst. On relief the Battalion will move into Divisional Reserve at DONCASTER HUTS LOCRE.

   Zero hour for relief = 11-30 a.m.

2. The usual orders re movement east of LOCRE and east of Brigade Headquarters will be observed.

3. All work, intelligence reports, etc., will be carefully handed over to incoming unit.

4. A billeting party under the Quartermaster will report to Headquarters 7/8th. Battalion, The Royal Irish Fusiliers at - 1 hour 30 minutes.

5. Officers' trench kits, etc., will be dumped outside 113th. Field Ambulance, KEMMEL, by - 1 hour 30 minutes.

6. Trench store lists will be rendered to Orderly Room by + 21½ hours.

7. The Cook Sergeant will make arrangements that Coys. get their dinners immediately on arrival in LOCRE.

8. Completion of relief to be reported to Battalion Headquarters in "B.A.B." Code.

Lieut. & A/Adjutant,

2nd. Battalion, The Royal Irish Regiment.

Hour of issue - 20½ hours.

Copy No. 1. War Diary.
     2. H.Qrs., 49th. Inf. Bde.
     3. 7/8th. Bn., The R. I. Fus.
     4. O. C. "A" Coy.
     5. O. C. "B" ,,
     6. O. C. "C" ,,
     7. O. C. "D" ,,

No. 8. Lewis Gun Officer.
    9. Medical Officer.
   10. Quartermaster.
   11. Transport Officer.
   12. Regtl. Sergt. Major.
   13. Signalling Sergeant.
   14. Cook Sergeant.

WAR DIARY for month of JANUARY, 1917.

VOLUME

2nd. Royal Irish Regiment.

WAR DIARY
or
INTELLIGENCE SUMMARY. The ROYAL IRISH REGIMENT
2nd Battalion

Army Form C. 2118.

(Erase heading not required.)

Place	Date	Hour	Summary of Events and Information	Remarks and references to Appendices
LOCRE	1st - 4th January 1917		The Battalion was in Divisional Reserve at DONCASTER HUTS.	JAN
	5th		The Battalion relieved the 7/8th The ROYAL IRISH FUSILIERS in the left subsector. 1 other rank wounded.	Appendix 1. JAN.
	6th		Enemy wire was bombarded from N 24.C. 81.39 – N 24.C 93.18. The following honours and awards have been conferred on the regiment. To be Brevet Colonel – Bt. Lieut Col (Temp: Brig: Gen) G. F. BOYD. D.S.O. " " (" Maj: Gen) L. J. LIPSETT. C.M.G. To be Brevet Lieut: Colonel. Major (Temp: Brig: Gen) W. J. DUGAN. D.S.O. Distinguished Service Order Major (acting Lt Col) H. G. GREGORIE. D.S.O Major (Temp " ") G. N. GROGAN - Major " R. J. REES - MOGG Capt. (Temp: Lt Col) T. B. VANDELOUR. Capt. F. O. BOWEN. P. R. BUTLER.	Appendices 2. 3.

WAR DIARY
or
INTELLIGENCE SUMMARY.
(Erase heading not required.)

Army Form C. 2118.

Place	Date	Hour	Summary of Events and Information	Remarks and references to Appendices
			Military CROSS	
			Capt. The Hon. H.A.J. PRESTON.	
			Capt. H.J.M. O'REILLY.	
			Capt. V.E.W. SIMPSON	
			No 9120 C.S.M. SMITH-W.A.H.	
			Mentioned in Dispatches	F.A.N
			Lt Col - Fitz.R. E.P. CURZON. Lt J.O. Mc CALL.	
			Maj. (act L Col) H.G. GREGORIE. Temp. Lt H. ROLCOMSON.	
			B Major (temp L Col) W. B. LYONS Temp Lt B.N. FITZGIBBON.	
			Temp Major W. H. K. REDMOND 2/Lt W.C.V. GALWEY.	
			Temp Major (temp L Col) F.O. BOWEN. 2/Lt L.A. HAYDEN.	
			Temp Capt H R LLOYD. 2/Lt F.A. NEWSAM.	
			Lieut (temp Capt) T.W. FITZPATRICK 2/Lt R.E.W. BURKE.	
			No R.Q.M.S. HOPKINS J. No 3648 Pte CARGAN J.	
			No 8352 Sgt - FLETCHER J.H No 3679 Pte ROBB T.	

Army Form C. 2118.

WAR DIARY
or
INTELLIGENCE SUMMARY.
(Erase heading not required.)

Place	Date	Hour	Summary of Events and Information	Remarks and references to Appendices
	8th		Lt. R.F.M. SPRING wounded – Capt. T.A. LOWE returned from Senior Officers Course at ALDERSHOT	Appx.
	10th		2/Lt L.A. HAYDEN was wounded in action + 3 other ranks wounded + died of wounds on the 14th inst.	Appx.
	11th		The Battalion was relieved by the 118th the ROYAL IRISH FUSILIERS + moved into Brigade reserve at KEMMEL SHELTERS	Appendix 4.
	16th		1 other ranks joined the battalion	Appx.
	17th		The battalion relieved the 118th The ROYAL IRISH FUSILIERS in the Left sub sector.	Appendix 5.
	18th		Capt. R.H. FRANKENBURG was transferred to the 6th ROYAL IRISH Regt 2/Lt C.J. KENNY ⎱ joined the battalion today from the 3rd Battn – J. DONOVAN ⎰ – B.H.H. STRATH ⎰ Principal work in the trenches during the period 17th – 23rd patrolling the transverse line, and repairing the parts of the trench damaged by enemy trench mortars. Heavy falls of snow	Appx.
	20th		1 other rank wounded –	
	21		1 other rank wounded –	

Army Form C. 2118.

WAR DIARY
or
INTELLIGENCE SUMMARY.
(Erase heading not required.)

Instructions regarding War Diaries and Intelligence Summaries are contained in F. S. Regs., Part II. and the Staff Manual respectively. Title pages will be prepared in manuscript.

Place	Date	Hour	Summary of Events and Information	Remarks and references to Appendices
	23rd		The Batt. was relieved by the 1/8th Batt. The ROYAL IRISH FUSILIERS & moved into Divisional reserve at DONCASTER HUTS.	Appendix 6
	24th		Lieut: H. HARRISON M.C rejoined the Battalion. Weather very cold - freezing hard.	
	26th		Capt. J. L. COTTER joined the Batt. toar.	
	29th		2/Lt. J. G. ELLISON and 11 other ranks joined to-day. The Battalion remained in Divisional Reserve at LOCRE and for 8 days and underwent a course of training. Attached a programme of work.	Appendix 7.

Appendix I

SECRET. OPERATION ORDER NO. 1. Copy No. ...

by

MAJOR L. L. PAYNE, COMMANDING,
2nd. BATTALION, THE ROYAL IRISH REGIMENT.

Reference Map
WYTSCHAETE & Sheet 28 S.W.

The Field.
4/1/17.

1. The Battalion will relieve the 7/8th. Battalion, The Royal Irish Fusiliers in the Left Sub-section tomorrow, the 5th. inst.
Zero hour for relief = 11.30 a.m.

2. Companies will be disposed as under and will march off at times stated:-

    "D" Coy. Left Front Line   - 2 hours.
    "B" "   Right Front Line   - 1 hour 50 minutes.
    "C" "   Left Support   - 1 hour 40   "
    "A" "   Right Support   - 1 hour 30   "

3. Previous orders re movement east of LOCRE and east of Brigade Headquarters will be observed.

4. An advance party consisting of 1 Officer and 1 N.C.O. per Coy. will leave DONCASTER HUTS at - 3½ hours to take over trench stores, etc.

5. Officers' valises, packs, blankets, etc., will be dumped in Coy. lines by - 2 hours.

6. Advance parties of 7/8th. Battalion, The Royal Irish Fusiliers will will be at DONCASTER HUTS at - 1½ hours.

7. The Cook Sergeant will make necessary arrangements re dinners.
8. Trench store lists will be rendered to Orderly Room by + 2½ hours.
9. Battalion Headquarters will close in DONCASTER HUTS at +1½ hours and will reopen at DOCTORS HOUSE at the same hour.

Hour of issue = 19½ Hours.

Pulvley
Lieut. & A/Adjutant,
2nd. Battalion, The Royal Irish Regiment.

Copy No. 1. War Diary.
    2. H.Qrs., 49th. Inf. Bde.
    3. 7/8th. Bn. The R. Ir. Fus.
    4. O. C. "A" Coy.
    5. O. C. "B" "
    6. O. C. "C" "
    7. O. C. "D" "
    8. Lewis Gun Officer.

No. 9. Bn. Bombing Officer.
    10. Medical Officer.
    11. Quartermaster.
    12. Transport Officer.
    13. Regtl. Sergt. Major.
    14. Signallers.
    15. Scouts.
    16. Cook Sergeant.

Appendix 2

SECRET.   Copy No...........

49th Infantry Brigade Order No.87 - 5-1-17.

Ref. Map 28.S.W.2. Ed. 3.E.
Scale 1/10000.

A Bombardment of enemy's wire N.24.c.81.39 to N.24.c.73.18 will take place on Saturday, 6th January, 1917.

4 2" T.M's and 6 Stokes Guns will be employed.

Artillery will co-operate by firing on O.P's, etc.

ZERO hour will be 2 p.m.

Time Table as follows :-

Zero to Zero + 5   Bombardment.
Zero + 5 to Zero + 10. Rest.
Zero + 10 to Zero + 15. Bombardment.
Zero + 15 to Zero + 20   Rest.
Zero + 20 to Zero + 25   Bombardment.

2" T.M's to fire as fast as possible.

Stokes to fire 200 rounds per gun.

O.C. 49th Trench Mortar Group will make arrangements to place sufficient ammunition in suitable emplacements.

O.C. Left Subsection will arrange to withdraw troops from front line, *leaving* only Lewis Gunners and a few sentry groups.

Watches will be synchronized at 11 a.m. 6th January.

ACKNOWLEDGE.

                                        R.B. Bewley
                                        Captain,
                        a/Brigade Major, 49th Infantry Bde.

Issued through Signals.

```
Copy No. 1  to 16th Division (G)
   ..    2     49th T. M. B.
   ..    3     2/16 T. M. B.
   ..    4     O.C. Right Subsection.
   ..    5     O.C. Left Subsection.
   ..    6     157th Field Coy, R.E.
   ..    7     Centre Group.
   ..    8     47th Infy Brigade.
   ..    9     48th Infy Brigade.
   ..   10     49th M.G. Company.
   ..   11-12  War Diary.
   ..   13     File.
   ..   14     Staff Captain.
```

SECRET. Operation Order No. 2 Copy No. 1
by
Major L. L. Farmer, Commanding,
2nd. Battalion, The Royal Irish Regiment.

Reference Map Appendix 3 The Field
WYTSCHAETE & Sheet 28 S.W. 5-1-17

---

1. A bombardment of enemy's wire from N.24.c.81.39. to N.24.c.73.18. will take place on Saturday, 6th. January, 1916.
2. 4 2" French mortars and 6 Stokes Guns will be employed.
3. Artillery will co-operate by firing on O.P's., etc.
4. Zero hour will be 2 pm.
5. Time Table as follows:-
    Zero   to Zero +5   Bombardment.
    Zero +5   to Zero +10   Rest.
    Zero +10 to Zero +15   Bombardment.
    Zero +15 to Zero +20   Rest.
    Zero +20 to Zero +25   Bombardment.
6. 2" French mortars to fire as fast as possible.
7. Stokes Guns to fire 200 rounds per gun.
8. At - 60 minutes the O.C. Right Coy. will withdraw his company via VIA GELLIA to YONGE STREET Dugouts, leaving 2 sentry groups at points to be selected by himself.
   At - 60 minutes the O.C. Right Support Coy. will withdraw his Coy. to FORT REGINA.
   At - 45 minutes the O.C. Left Coy. will withdraw via VIA GELLIA to ALBERTA DUGOUTS and S.P.11, leaving 2 sentry groups in the front line.
   At - 45 minutes the O.C. Left Support Coy. will withdraw to FORT SASKATCHEWAN.
   At conclusion of bombardment companies will re-occupy the front line as early as possible retaliation will permit.
9. The Lewis Guns in the front line will remain in position throughout the operation.
10. Watches will be synchronised on 6th. inst. with Battalion Headquarters at 11 am.
11. The Medical Officer will make arrangements for First Aid for the front line.
12. ACKNOWLEDGE.

L. Farmer
Major
Commanding, 2nd. Bn. the Royal Irish Regt.

Hour of issue - 19 hours.

Copy No. 1. War Diary.   No. 5. O.C. "C" Coy.
       2. H.Q., 49th. Inf. Bde.   6. O.C. "D" Coy.
       3. O.C. "A" Coy.   7. Lewis Gun Officer.
       4. O.C. "B" Coy.   8. Medical Officer.
          H.Q. File.

SECRET. OPERATION ORDER No. 2. Copy No. ....

of

MAJOR L. L. FARMER, COMMANDING,
2nd. BATTALION, THE ROYAL IRISH REGIMENT.

Reference Map   The Field
BETHUNE & Sheet 28 S.W.   Appendix 4   10/1/17.

1. The Battalion will be relieved by the 7/8th. Battalion, The Royal Irish Fusiliers in the left sub-section tomorrow, the 11th. inst. On relief the Battalion, less "D" Coy., will move into Brigade Reserve at KEMMEL SHELTERS.

    Relief to commence at 11-30 a.m.

2. The usual orders re movement east of LOCRE and east of Brigade Headquarters will be observed.

3. All work, intelligence reports, etc., will be carefully handed over to incoming unit.

4. A billeting party under the Quartermaster will report to H.Qrs., 8th. Battalion, The Royal Irish Fusiliers at 12 noon.

5. Officers' trench kits, etc., will be dumped outside 110th. Field Ambulance, KEMMEL, by 10-30 a.m.

6. "D" Coy., as soon as relieved, will be billeted in KEMMEL CHATEAU and will find all working parties, receiving instructions direct from Brigade.

7. Trench Store Lists will be rendered to the Orderly Room by 9 a.m. on the 12th. inst.

8. The Cook Sergeants will make arrangements that Coys. get their dinners immediately on arrival in KEMMEL SHELTERS.

9. Completion of relief to be reported to Battalion Headquarters in "B.A.B." Code.

                                                        Lowe   Captain & Adjutant,

Hour of issue: 5 p.m.   2nd. Battalion, The Royal Irish Regiment.

Copy Nos: 1. War Diary.   No. 8. O. C. "D" Coy.
         2. H.Qrs., 49th. Infy. Bde.   9. Scout Officer.
         3. 7/8th. Bn. The R.I.Fus.   10. Lewis Gun Officer.
         4. 8th. Bn., The R. Innis. Fus.   11. Medical Officer.
         5. O. C. "A" Coy.   12. Quartermaster.
         6. O. C. "B" "   13. Transport Officer.
         7. O. C. "C" "   14. Regtl. Sergt. Major.
                         15. Signalling Sergeant.

SECRET.   Operation Order No 3.   Copy to:
by
Major L.L. Farmer, Commanding,
2nd. Battalion, The Royal Irish Regiment.

Reference Map.   Appendix 5.   The Field.
WYTSCHAETE + Sheet 28 S.W.   16-1-17.
_____

1.   The Battalion will relieve the 7/8th. Battalion, the Royal Irish
Fusiliers in the left sub-section tomorrow, the 17th. inst.
     Relief to commence at 11.30 am.

2.   Companies will be disposed as under and will march off
at times stated.

   "A" Coy.   Left Front Line   10.30 am.
   "C" "   Right Front Line   10.40 am.
   "B" "   Left Support   10.50 am.
   "D" "   Right Support   11 am.

3.   Previous orders re movement east of LOCRE and east of
Brigade Headquarters will be observed.

4.   An advance party consisting of 1 Officer and 1 N.C.O. per
Coy. will leave KEMMEL SHELTERS at 9.30 am. to take over trench
stores, &c.

5.   Officers' valises, packs, blankets, &c., will be dumped in
Coy. lines by 10 am.

6.   Advance parties of 7/8th. Battalion, the Royal Irish Fusiliers
will be at KEMMEL SHELTERS at 10 am.

7.   Trench Store Lists will be rendered to Orderly Room by
9 am on the 18th inst.

8.   Battalion Headquarters will close in KEMMEL SHELTERS
at 12 noon and will reopen at DOCTOR'S HOUSE at the
same hour.

                              Above. Captain & Adjutant,
                       2nd. Battalion, The Royal Irish Regiment.

Hour of issue 2 pm.
Copy No. 1. War Diary.   9. Scout Officer.
         2. H.Q. 49th. Inf. Bde.   10. Bn. Bombing Officer.
         3. 7/8th Bn. the R.I. Fus. 11. Medical Officer.
         4. O.C. "A" Coy.   12. Quartermaster.
         5. O.C. "B"   13. Transport Officer.
         6. O.C. "C"   14. Regtl. Sergt Major.
         7. O.C. "D"   15. Signallers.
         8. Lewis Gun Officer   16. Cook Sergeant.

Appendix 6.

SECRET.   OPERATION ORDER NO. 4.   Copy No. 1

BY
MAJOR L. L. FARRAR, COMMANDING,
2nd. BATTALION, THE ROYAL IRISH REGIMENT.

Reference Map.   The Field.
WYTSCHAETE & Sheet 28 S.W.   22/1/1917.

1.   The Battalion will be relieved by the 7/8th. Battalion, The Royal Irish Fusiliers in the left sub-section tomorrow, the 23rd. inst. Relief to commence at 11-30 a.m. On relief the Battalion will move into Divisional Reserve at DONCASTER HUTS, LOCRE.

2.   The usual orders re movement east of LOCRE and east of Brigade Headquarters will be observed.

3.   All work, intelligence reports, etc., will be carefully handed over to incoming unit.

4.   A billeting party under the Quartermaster will report to Headquarters 8th. Battalion, The Royal Inniskilling Fusiliers at 12 noon to take over huts, etc.

5.   Officers' trench kits, etc., will be dumped outside 113th. Field Ambulance, KEMMEL, by 10 a.m.

6.   Trench Stores Lists will be rendered to Orderly Room by 9 a.m. on the 23rd. inst.

7.   The Cook Sergeant will make arrangements that Companies get their dinners immediately on arrival in LOCRE.

8.   Completion of relief to be reported to Battalion Headquarters in "L. A. B." Code.

                                                    Captain & Adjutant,
Hour of issue 4 p.m.   2nd. Battalion, The Royal Irish Regiment.

Copy No. 1. War Diary.   No. 9. Scout Officer.
        2. H.Q., 49th. Inf. Bde.   10. Signalling Officer.
        3. 7/8th. Bn., The R.I.Fus.   11. Lewis Gun Officer.
        4. 8th. Bn. The R.Innis.Fus.   12. Medical Officer.
        5. O. C. "A" Coy.   13. Quartermaster.
        6. O. C. "B" ,,   14. Transport Officer.
        7. O. C. "C" ,,   15. Regtl. Sergt. Major.
        8. O. C. "D" ,,   16. Cook Sergeant.

Appendix Y.

Programme of work for week ending 5th Feby. 19

Officers and Sergeants

30th Jany.	9 am to 9.45 am	Extended order drill.
		Visual training and signals.
	10.15 am to 11 am	Bayonet Fighting.
	11.15 am to 12 noon	Lecture on use of ground and cover, for sergeants in preliminary stages of attack.
	3 pm to 2.40 pm	Musketry.
31st Jany.	9 am to 9.45 am	Physical Training.
	10.15 am to 11 am	Extended order drill.
	11.15 am to 12 noon	Fire Control
	2 pm	Visual Training and Judging Distances
1st Feby.	9 am to 9.40 am	Extended order drill and Fire Control.
	10.30 am to 12 noon	Practice Platoon in attack
	2 pm	Lecture on issue of orders to Coy. in firing line. Passing orders &c.
2nd Feby.	9 am to 9.40 am	Physical Training.
	10.30 am to 12 noon	Practice Coy. in attack.
	2 pm	Musketry.
3rd Feby.	9.30 am	Route March.
5th Feby.	9 am to 9.40 am	Swedish Drill.
	10.30 am to 12.15 pm	Battalion attack.

Lieut. & Adjutant
2nd Battalion the Royal Irish Regt.

WAR DIARY.

FOR MONTH OF FEBRUARY, 1917.

VOLUME

UNIT:- 2nd Btn Royal Irish Regiment.

Army Form C. 2118.

WAR DIARY
or
INTELLIGENCE SUMMARY

2nd Battalion The ROYAL IRISH REGIMENT.

(Erase heading not required.)

Instructions regarding War Diaries and Intelligence Summaries are contained in F.S. Regs., Part II. and the Staff Manual respectively. Title pages will be prepared in manuscript.

Hour, Date, Place	Summary of Events and Information	Remarks and references to Appendices
February 1st – 5th 1919.	The Battalion was in billets at DONCASTER Hus.	F.A.N
6th	The Battalion relieved the 1st Battalion The ROYAL MUNSTER FUSILIERS in the right subsection of the Brigade area. 2/Lt F.T.G. ELLISON transferred to 13th R. IRISH RIFLES. 21 other ranks joined today.	Appendices I, II
7th	2 other ranks wounded in action.	
10th	The Battalion was relieved by the 7/8th R. IRISH FUSILIERS and moved into close support – See 1 other rank killed in action. 2/Lieut E.J. WARD transferred to Portugese Division.	Appendices III, IV F.A.N
13th		
14th	The Battalion was relieved in Brigade Support by the 6th Bn The ROYAL IRISH REGt, and on relief, moved into reserve at CURRAGH CAMP. Reorganisation of the Battalion.	Appendices V, VI Appendix VII

WAR DIARY
or
INTELLIGENCE SUMMARY

(Erase heading not required.)

Army Form C. 2118.

Hour, Date, Place	Summary of Events and Information	Remarks and references to Appendices
15th – 22nd	No 9444 Sgt. EAGAR. C. was awarded the MEDAILLE MILITAIRE.	Appendix VIII
15th	The Battalion was in training at CURRAGH CAMP – for programme of work – vide	
16th	6 other ranks joined the battalion.	
19th	29 other ranks joined.	
20th	4 other ranks joined.	
22nd	The Battalion relieved the 6th Bn. The CONNAUGHT RANGERS in support. { 2 other ranks joined the battalion { 1 other rank wounded in action	Appendix IX
24th		NAN
26th	The Battalion relieved the 7/8th ROYAL IRISH FUSILIERS in the right subsector. Capt. R. A. BELMORE rejoined today 1 other rank wounded in action.	Appendix X.

Army Form C. 2118.

WAR DIARY
or
INTELLIGENCE SUMMARY
(Erase heading not required.)

Hour, Date, Place	Summary of Events and Information	Remarks and references to Appendices
26th February – 2nd March '19	The Battalion was in the front line – Everything quiet –	
27th	2 other ranks wounded in action	

A.J. Pepperdine Lt Col
2nd Bn The Royal Irish Regt

Appendix I

Operation Orders
by
**Major L.L. Farmer, Commanding,
2nd. Battalion, The Royal Irish Regiment.**

Reference Map   The Field.
Sheet 28 S.W.   5-2-17.

Copy No 1.

---

1. The Battalion will relieve the 1st. Battalion, The Royal Munster Fusiliers in the right subsection tomorrow, the 6th inst. Relief to commence at 5.30 pm.

2. Companies will be disposed as under and will march off at times stated.

    "A" Coy. 2/R.I. will relieve "Y" Coy. 1/R.M.F. in the right front line and will move off at 2 pm.

    "C" Coy. 2/R.I. will relieve "W" Coy. 1/R.M.F. in the centre front line and will move off at 2.10 pm.

    "B" Coy. 2/R.I. will relieve "Z" Coy. 1/R.M.F. in the left front line and will move off at 2.20 pm.

    "D" Coy. 2/R.I. will relieve "X" Coy. 1/R.M.F. in support and will move off at 2.30 pm.

3. Guides from platoons for "B" and "D" Coys. will be at the bottom of REGENT STREET at 4.30 pm.

    Guides from platoons for "A" and "C" Coys. will be at KINGSWAY at 4.30 pm.

4. The Lewis Gun Coy. will relieve in the morning.

    Guides for left front line and support will be at REGENT STREET at 11 am.

    Guides for right front line and centre front line will be at KINGSWAY at 11 am.

5. Movement east of the LOCRE - DRANOUTRE Road will be by platoons at 300 yards.

6. All work, information, &c. will be carefully taken over from outgoing units.

7. Officers valises, packs, blankets, &c., will be dumped in Coy. lines by 1 pm.

8. Trench store lists will be rendered to Orderly Room by 9 am. on the 7th. inst.

9. Battalion Headquarters will close in DONCASTER HUTS at 5 pm. and will re-open at NEWPORT DUG-OUTS at the same hour.

P. Culverly
Lieut. & Adjt.
2nd. Battalion, The Royal Irish.

Hour of issue 5.30 pm.
Copy No. 1. War Diary.
       2. H.Q. 49th. Inf. Bde.
       3. 1/Roy. Munster Fus.
       4. O.C. "A" Coy.
       5. O.C. "B" Coy.
       6. O.C. "C" "
       7. O.C. "D" "
       No. 8. Lewis Gun Officer.
       9. Signalling Officer.
       10. Scout Officer.
       11. Medical Officer.
       12. Quartermaster.
       13. Transport Officer.
       14. Regtl. Sergt. Major.

Appendix II

SECRET. Copy No. 1

49th Infantry Brigade Order No. 95 – 5-2-17.

1. The Brigade will relieve the 47th Infantry Brigade in the Right (SPANBROEK) Section on the 6th instant.

2. The 2nd R. Irish Regt will relieve the 1st R. Munster Fus. in the Right Subsection.
   Relief to commence at 5-30 p.m.

3. The 7th R. Innis Fus will relieve the 6th R. Irish Regt in the Left Subsection.
   Relief to commence at 4 o'Clock.

4. The 7/8th R. Irish Fus will relieve the 7th Leinster Regt. in support. Relief to commence at 2-30 p.m.
   Os. C. Coys will come under the orders of the Subsection Commanders for tactical purposes immediately relief is complete, and will report to Os.C. Subsections as soon as possible.

5. The 8th R. Innis Fus will relieve the 6th Connaught Rangers in Brigade Reserve, with H.Q. and two Coys at DERRY HUTS and two Coys in KEMMEL.
   Relief to commence at 1-30 p.m.

6. All details for relief will be arranged between Os.C. Battalions concerned. Arrangements should be made to relieve Lewis Guns in the morning if possible.

7. Movement East of LOCRE-DRANOUTRE Road will be by platoons at 300 yards distance.

8. All work, information, etc, will be carefully taken over from outgoing units.

9. (i) All trench stores, maps, etc, will be taken over, lists being signed and counter-signed by an officer.
   (ii) Trench Store Lists will be rendered to Brigade H.Q. by 6 p.m. 7th instant.

10. Bde H.Q. will close at LOCRE at 7 p.m. and will open at LITTLE KEMMEL at the same hour.

11. Completion of all reliefs to be reported in Code to Brigade Headquarters.

12. ACKNOWLEDGE.

F B Brinkley
Captain,
a/Brigade Major, 49th Infantry Brigade.

Issued through Signals.

Copy No.		Copy No.	
1	to 2nd R. Irish Regt.	13	to Staff Captain,
2	7th R. Innis Fus.	14	Bde Signal Officer
3	8th R. Innis Fus.	15	Bde Transport Off.
4	7/8th R. Irish Fus.	16	A.D.M.S. 16th Div.
5	49th M.G. Company.	17	113th Fd. Ambulance
6	49th T.M.B.	18	157th Field Coy. RE
7	2/16 T.M.B.	19	144th Coy, A.S.C,
8	47th Inf. Brigade.	20	Bde Supply Officer
9	48th Inf. Brigade.	21	250th Tunnelling Coy, R.E.
10	Centre Group.		
11	16th Division (G)	22-23	War Diary.
12	16th Division (Q)	24	File.

Secret   Operation Order No. 6   Copy No. 1
                      by
              Major L. L. Farmer, Commanding
              2nd. Bn. The Royal Irish Regt.
Reference Trench Map   The Field, 9th Feb. 1917

1. The Battalion will be relieved by the 7/8th Bn. The R. Irish Fus in the right subsection tomorrow the 10th. inst.

2. Relief to commence at 5.30 pm

3. On relief Os. C. Coys. will come under the orders of subsection commanders for tactical purposes and will report to the Os. C. Sub sections as soon as possible.
   "A" and "C" Coys., 2/R.I. will be in support to the right sub section; "B" and "D" Coys., 2/R.I. to the left sub section.

4. "A" Coy., 2/R.I. will be relieved by "C" Coy, 7/8 R.I.Fus.
   "C" Coy., 2/R.I. will be relieved by "A" Coy, 7/8 R.I.Fus.
   "D" Coy., 2/R.I. will be relieved by "B" Coy, 7/8 R.I.Fus.
   "B" Coy., 2/R.I. will be relieved by "D" Coy, 7/8 R.I.Fus.

5. On moving into support Coys. will be disposed as under:-
   "A" Coy 2/R.I. (who will relieve "C" Coy 7/8 R.IR.F.) —
       HQrs and 2 platoons at COOKER FARM.
       1 platoon at BEEHIVE DUGOUTS
       1 platoon at GALWAY DUGOUTS
   "C" Coy 2/R.I. (who will relieve "A" Coy 7/8 R.IR.F.) —
       HQrs - BEEHIVE DUGOUTS
       4 Platoons - FORT EDWARD
   "D" Coy 2/R.I. (HQrs - YOUNG ST.
       2 platoons (who will relieve 1 platoon 7/8. R.IR.F.) at YOUNG ST.
       1 platoon (who will relieve "B" Coy, 7. R. INNIS. F.) at S.P. 11.
       1 platoon (who will relieve 1 platoon 7/8. R.IR.F.) at S.P. 10.
   "B" Coy 2/R.I. - HQrs at REGENT ST. DUGOUTS
       1 platoon (who will relieve 1 platoon 7/8 R.IR.F.) at S.P. 9
       2 platoons (who will relieve "A" Coy, 7. R. INNIS. F.) at REGENT ST. DUGOUTS.
       1 platoon (who will relieve 1 platoon 7/8. R.IR.F.) at FORT REGINA.

6. One guide per platoon from "A" Coy, 2/R.I. will be at COOKER FARM at 5.30 p.m.
   One guide per platoon from "C" Coy 2/R.I. will be at FORT EDWARD at 5.30 pm
   One guide per platoon from "D" Coy 2/R.I. will be at REGENT ST. DUGOUTS at 5.30 pm.

Army Form B. 2069.

Offence Report (*Field Service only*).

Corps ─────────

Squadron, Troop, Batty, or Company	Regt. No.	Rank	Name	Place and Date of offence	Offence	By whom reported and Names of Witnesses	Initials of Officer Comdg. Company, &c.	Punishment awarded	Signature of Officer by whom ordered and date of award	Date of entry in Conduct Sheet	Remarks

N.B.—A horizontal line should be drawn the whole length of the Return after each day's offences are entered.

– 2 –

3 (contd).

One guide per platoon from "B" Coy, 2/R.I. will be at REGENT ST. DUGOUTS at 6 p.m.

7. <u>Lewis Guns</u>: The relief of the Lewis Guns will take place in the morning under arrangements to be made by the Lewis Gun Officers concerned.

8. Advanced parties consisting of an Officer per coy, and one representative per platoon of "A", "C" and "D" Coys. 2/R.I. will be at H.Qrs. of the coy. of the 7/8 R.IR.F. which they are relieving at 2 pm.

Advanced party from "B" Coy., 2/R.I. will be at H.Qrs. "A" Coy 7. R. INNIS. F. at REGENT ST. DUG OUTS at 2 p.m.

9. The O.C. "B" Coy., 2/R.I. will send 1 platoon to take over REGENT ST. DUGOUTS at 4 p.m.

10. 1 N.C.O. per platoon will accompany advanced parties and will return to their Coys. and act as guides to outgoing platoons.

11. Os. C. Coys. will make their own arrangements for the conveyance of kits, stores etc.

12. All work, information etc., will be carefully handed over to incoming units.

13. Trench Store Lists to be rendered to the Orderly Room by 9 am on the 11th. inst.

14. Completion of relief to be reported to Bn. H.Qrs in B.A.B. Code.

15. Battn. H.Qrs will close at NEWPORT DUGOUTS at 6 pm and will re-open at DOCTOR'S HOUSE at the same hour.

16. ACKNOWLEDGE.

H. Ealwey
Lieutenant
a/Adjt. 2/The Royal Irish. Regt.

Issued at 9 p.m.
Copies to:—

1. WAR DIARY
2. 49th. BDE HQRS.
3. 7. R. INNIS FUS.
4. 8. R. INNIS FUS.
5. RT. SUPPT. COY. 7/8 R.IR.F.
6. LT. SUPPT. COY. 7/8 R.IR.F
7. 7/8 R.IR.F.
8. SEN. NATOR
9. O/C. "A" Coy
10. " "B" "
11. " "C" "
12. " "D" "
13. LEWIS GUN OFFR.
14. Q.MR
15. TRANS. OFFR.
16. MED. OFFR.
17. SIG. OFFR.
19. R.S.M.
20. COOK SGT.
21. N.C.O. i/c SCOUTS.

Offence Report (*Field Service only*).

Army Form B. 2069.

Squadron, Troop, Batty. or Company	Regtl. No.	Rank	Name	Corps	Place and Date of offence	Offence	By whom reported and Names of Witnesses	Initials of Officer Comdg. Company, &c.	Punishment awarded	Signature of Officer by whom ordered and date of award	Date of entry in Conduct Sheet	Remarks

N.B.—A horizontal line should be drawn the whole length of the Return after each day's offences are entered.

Appendix IV

S E C R E T.   Copy No. 1

49th Infantry Brigade Order No. 96 - 8-2-17.

1. The following reliefs will take place on the 10th instant.

2. LEFT SUBSECTION.

   The 8th R. Innis Fus will relieve the 7th R. Innis Fus. Relief to commence at 4. p.m. On relief the 7th R. Innis Fus will move into Brigade Reserve, with H.Q. and 2 Coys at DERRY HUTS and 2 Coys in KEMMEL.

3. RIGHT SUBSECTION.

   The 7/8th R. Irish Fus will relieve the 2nd R. Irish Regt. Relief to commence at 5-30 p.m. On relief, Os. C. Coys, 2nd R. Irish Regt will come under the orders of Subsection Commanders for tactical purposes, and will report to Os. C. Subsections as soon as possible.

4. All details for relief will be arranged between Os.C. Battalions concerned. Arrangements should be made to relieve Lewis Guns in the morning if possible.

5. All work, etc, will be carefully handed over to incoming units.

6. Trench Store Lists to reach Bde H.Q. by 6 p.m. 11th instant.

7. Completion of relief to be reported in Code to Bde H.Q.

8. ACKNOWLEDGE.

                                                    Captain,

a/Brigade Major, 49th Infantry Brigade.

Issued through Signals.

Copy No.	Recipient
1	2nd R. Irish Regt.
2	7th R. Innis Fus.
3	8th R. Innis Fus.
4	7/8th R. Irish Fus.
5	49th M.G. Company.
6	47th M.G. Company.
7	49th T.M.B.
8	47th T.M.B.
9	Z/16 T.M.B.
10	X/16 T.M.B.
11	48th Inf. Brigade.
12	10th Inf. Brigade.
13	Right Group.
14	16th Division (G)
15	16th Division (Q)
16	Staff Captain.
17	Bde Signal Officer.
18	Bde Transport Officer.
19	Bde Supply Officer.
20	A.D.M.S. 16th Division.
21	113th Field Ambulance.
22	144th Coy, A.S.C.
23	157th Field Coy, R.E.
24	250th Tunnelling Coy, R.E.
25-26	War Diary.
27	File.

SECRET Appendix V COPY NO. 1

Operation Order No. 7
by
Major L. L. Flood, Commanding
2/The Royal Irish Regt.

Reference Map 28 S.W.   The Field, 13-2-17.

1. The Brigade will be relieved by the 47th Infantry Brigade in the right (SPANBROEK) section on the 14th inst., and will become the Brigade in Divisional Reserve.

2. The Battalion will be relieved in Brigade Support by the 6th. Bn. The Royal Irish.
   Relief to commence at 2:30 p.m.
   On relief the Battalion will move to CURRAGH CAMP.

3. Platoons will march via KEMMEL-LOCRE route.

4. The Billeting Party under the Quartermaster will take over CURRAGH CAMP at 1 p.m.

5. Officers trench kits, stores, etc., will be dumped outside the 113th. F.A., KEMMEL by 1 p.m.

6. Trench Store Lists will be rendered to the Orderly Room by 9 a.m. the 15th inst.

7. Completion of relief to be reported to Battalion Headquarters in "B.A.B" Code.

P. Galwey, Lieutenant
A/Adjutant 2/The Royal Irish Regt.

Hour of Issue. 4 p.m.

Copy No. 1. War Diary   No. 8 Lewis Gun Officer
     2. H.Qrs 49th I. Bde.   9. Medical Officer
     3. 6/R.I. Regt.   10. Quartermaster
     4. O.C. A Coy   11. Transport Officer
     5. "   B "   12. R.S.M.
     6. "   C "   13. Signalling Sergt.
     7. "   D "   14. Cook Sergt.
           No. 15. N.C.O i/c Scouts.

2nd Bn. The Royal Irish Regt.

............Coy. *(Etc.)*

Duties *from*....................m. to....................m.....................1916.

Detail	Hours ....m. ....m.				Remarks

....................*(Signature)*....................*(Rank)*.

(Date)....................1916. Commanding....................2nd Bn. R. Irish Regt.

SECRET.   Copy No... 1 ......

Appendix VI

49th Infantry Brigade Order No. 98 – 11-2-17.

1. The Brigade will be relieved by the 47th Infantry Brigade in the Right (SPANBROEK) Section on the 14th instant, and will become the Brigade in Divisional Reserve.

2. The 7th R. Innis Fus will be relieved in Brigade Reserve by the 1st R. Munster Fus.
   Relief to commence at 1-30 p.m.
   On relief the 7th R. Innis Fus will move to DONCASTER HUTS.

3. The 2nd R. Irish Regt. will be relieved in Brigade Support by the 6th R. Irish Regt.
   Relief to commence at 2-30 p.m.
   On relief the 2nd R. Irish Regt will move to CURRAGH CAMP.

4. The 8th R. Innis Fus will be relieved in the Left Subsection by the 6th Connaught Rangers.
   Relief to commence at 4 p.m.
   On relief the 8th R. Innis Fus will move to (to be notified later).

5. The 7/8th R. Irish Fus will be relieved in the Right Subsection by the 7th Leinster Regt.
   Relief to commence at 5-30 p.m.
   On relief the 7/8th R. Irish Fus will move to WAKEFIELD and LURGAN CAMPS.

6. All details will be arranged between Os.C Battalions concerned.
   Lewis Guns will be relieved in the morning.

7. The 49th Machine Gun Coy. and 49th T.M. Battery will remain in position.

8. All trench stores, maps, etc, will be handed over to incoming units. Lists, signed and counter-signed by an officer, will be rendered to Bde. H.Q. by 6 p.m. 15th instant.

9. Brigade H.Q. will close at KEMMEL at 7 p.m. and open at LOCRE at the same hour.

10. Completion of Reliefs to be reported to Brigade H.Q. in Code.

11. ACKNOWLEDGE.

P.B. Bu...ley
Captain,
a/Brigade Major, 49th Infantry Brigade.

Issued through Signals.

Copy No.	Unit	Copy No.	Unit
1	2nd R. Irish Regt.	15	to 16th Division (G)
2	7th R. Innis Fus.	16	16th Division (Q)
3	8th R. Innis Fus.	17	Staff Captain.
4	7/8th R. Irish Fus.	18	Bde Signal Officer.
5	49th M.G. Company.	19	Bde Transport "
6	47th M.G. Company.	20	A.D.M.S. 16th Div.
7	47th T.M.B.	21	113th Fld. Ambulance
8	49th T.M.B.	22	157th Field Coy, R.E.
9	X/16 T.M.B.	23	156th Field Coy, R.E.
10	Z/16 T.M.B.	24	144th Coy, A.S.C.
11	47th Inf. Brigade.	25	Bde Supply Officer.
12	48th Inf. Brigade.	26	250th Tun. Coy, R.E.
13	108th Inf. Brigade.	27-28	War Diary.
14	Right Group.	29	File.

O.C. A Coy.
O.C. B Coy.
O.C. C Coy.
O.C. D Coy.
Lewis Gun Officer
Bombing Officer
Regimental Sergeant Major

Appendix VII

O.R. No. 783 - 13-2-17.

With reference to the attached, the Commanding Officer directs that Companies and platoons be formed as laid down.

In the Field
13th Feb. 17

P. Cahrley
Lieutenant
A/Adjutant 2/The Royal Irish.

2nd Bn. The Royal Irish Regt.

............Coy. (Etc.)

Duties from............m. to............m. ....1916.

Detail	Hours			Remarks

(Signature)........................(Rank).................

(Date)............1916. Commanding 2nd Bn. R. Irish Regt.

ORGANISATION OF AN INFANTRY BATTALION

1. After considering the numerous recommendations received regarding the organisation of the Infantry Battalion, the C-in-C has decided generally to adhere to the organisation as it stands, and directs that no fundamental change is to be made in the authorised organisation of an Infantry Bn.

But in order to ensure the necessary degree of uniformity of training and tactical method throughout the Army, it is necessary that there should be similarity of organisation in all Battalions. The following instructions are therefore issued:-

The Battalion. 2. The Battalion will continue to consist of:-

    A   Battalion Headquarters;
    B   4 Companies, consisting of 4 Platoons of 4 sections each.

Battalion Headquarters. 3. In addition to the personnel shewn in War Establishments as forming part of the Battn. HQrs., certain other personnel will be attached. This personnel, which is principally employed on administrative duties, will be temporarily detached from coys. whilst so employed, but will remain on the establishment of the coys for accounting purposes. A HQrs. Coy. as such will not be formed.

The detail of the personnel included in the Battalion HQrs is given in Appendix 1.

The total should not exceed 150 Other Ranks.

The personnel composing the Battalion HQrs., can be conveniently divided into 2 categories, viz., the Fighting portion and the Administrative portion. The former will be grouped into sections each under a Commdr. The strength of the latter should not exceed 80 Other Ranks.

Companies. 4. Each coy. will consist of:-

    A.   Coy. HQrs.
    B.   4 Platoons

............Coy. (Etc.)

2nd Bn. The Royal Irish Regt.

Duties from..............m. to..............m..............1916.

Detail	Hours	Remarks

(Signature)..............(Rank).

(Date)..............1916.

Commanding 2nd Bn. R. Irish Regt.

-2-

Coy H.Qrs., the strength of which should not exceed 14 Other Ranks, will be composed entirely of Fighting troops, and will be formed as a Section under a Commander.

Platoons 5. The platoon, the minimum strength of which should not be allowed to fall below 28 Other Ranks, and the maximum strength of which will normally not exceed 44 Other Ranks, will consist of :-

    A. Platoon H.Qrs..
    B. 4 Sections permanently organised, each with its own leader and an understudy, ~~Platoon H.Qrs.~~,

Platoon Headquarters, the strength of which should not exceed 4 Other Ranks, will be composed entirely of Fighting Troops.

The composition of the Sections will normally be :-

    A. 1 Section Lewis Guns { Lewis Gunners except Nos.1 to carry rifle & bayonet & to be proficient in their use

    B. 1 Section Bombers:
    C. 2 Sections Riflemen, containing a proportion of Rifle Grenadiers.

6. The organisation outlined above is designed to create a fighting machine composed solely of fighting ranks and distinct from the necessary administrative establishment

7. The essence of this organisation is :-

    A. That the platoon should constitute a unit for fighting and training, and should consist of homogenous combination of all the weapons with which the Infantry is now armed:

    B. That Specialists should all be with their platoons, except such as may be required at Battalion & Coy. H.Qrs., either for purposes of fighting or for instructional duties;

    C. That every portion of the Battalion, including the fighting portion of Bn. H.Qrs.

2nd Bn. The Royal Irish Regt.

...........Coy. (Etc.)

Duties from............m. to............m. ....1916.

Detail	Hours			Remarks
	....m.		....m.	

.................(Signature)

.................(Rank).

(Date)............1916. Commanding 2nd Bn. R. Irish Regt.

and Coy. HQrs., should consist of a certain no. of permanently formed units, namely sections, each under its own Commander;

D. That the rifle & bayonet is first, and the hand grenade the second, weapon of every soldier, and that all men in rifle sections must be trained either in the Lewis Gun or the Rifle Grenade, so as to be ready to replace casualties amongst the personnel employed with those weapons;

E. That every man is available for working & carrying parties irrespective of the weapon with which he is armed:

F. One Lewis Gun with its detachment is allotted to each platoon this organisation may be altered in dealing with particular tactical situations.

Para 5, App 17 of "Instructions for the training of Divisions for Offensive Action" will be amended accordingly

8. During active operations such amalgamations of Sections, Platoons & Coys, of the Battalion should be made as to meet the exigencies of the situation.

    x   x   x   x   x

GHQ oS.
7-2-17.

Sd/ L. E. Kiggell
Lieut General
C. G. S.

2nd Bn. The Royal Irish Regt.

............Coy. *(Etc.)* ....1916.

Duties *from*............m. *to*............m. ....1916.

Detail	Hours			Remarks

............*(Signature)*............(Rank).

(Date)............1916. Commanding............2nd Bn. R. Irish Regt.

2/ The Royal Irish.

Appendix 8

Programme of Training for
period 15 – 22/2/17.

Date	Time	Training proposed
15th.	10 a.m.	Conference of all officers. Cleaning of arms, clothing, equipment etc., – haircutting.
16th.	9 a.m.	Parade by companies in new organisation.
	10.30 am to 12 noon	Arm drill etc. Subordinate commanders will practise words of command.
	2 pm.	Musketry.
17th.	9.30 a.m.	Route march. Route to be notified later.
18th.		Divine Services
19th.	9am to 12 noon	Right Half Battn:– Baths
	9am to 10 am.	Left Half Battn:– Bayonet Fighting.
	10.30 am to 11.30 am	Extended Order Drill and Musketry.
	3 pm to 5 pm	Left Half Battn:– Baths
	2 pm to 3.30 pm.	Arm drill; Extended Order drill.
20th.	9.30 am	Small Tactical Scheme.
21st.	9am to 10 am	Arm drill
	10.30 am to 11.30 am	Artillery formations, rapid extensions etc.
	2.30 pm.	Cross Country Run.

14th Feb '17

J. Mawles
Lieutenant
A/Adjutant 2/The Royal Irish

2/The Royal Irish
Programme of Training for Bombers.

Date	Time	Training proposed.
Daily	9.15 am to 10 am	Lecture on Mills Grenades
	10.15 am to 11 am	Throwing dummy Mills
	11.15 am to 12 noon	Lecture on Rifle Grenades
	*2.15 pm to 3 pm	Firing Rifle Grenades
Last day.		Throwing live grenades

14/2/17

P. Enherley, Lieutenant
A/Adjutant 2/The Royal Irish

2/The Royal Irish
Programme of training for Lewis Gunners

Date	Time	Training proposed.
15th.	10 am to 11 am	Lecture on care of Lewis Guns, Magazines and Ammunition
16th.	9.30 am - 10 am	Nomenclature of Parts.
	10 am - 11 am	Mechanism.
	11.15 am - 12 noon	Stoppages.
	2 pm - 3 pm	Gun Drill.
17th.	9 am - 10 am	Stoppages.
	10 11 - 12.15 pm	Range Practice.
	2 pm - 3 pm	Gun drill.
19th.	9 am - 12 noon	Tactical Scheme. Rifle Range
	2 pm - 3 pm	Stripping & Assembling
20th.	9 am - 12 noon	Range Practice. Tact: Scheme
	2 pm - 3 pm	Use of Ground & Cover
21st.	9 am - 11 am	Revision
	11.15 am - 12 noon	Gun drill
	2 pm - 3 pm	Gun drill

14/2/17 P. Enherley - Lieut. & A/Adjt 2/R.I.

SECRET.   Operation Order No. 8   COPY NO. ____
                        by
        Lieut. Colonel H.G. Gregorie D.S.O. Commanding
                2/The Royal Irish.
Reference French Map: The Field, 21st Feb. '17.

1. The Brigade will relieve the 47th Infantry Brigade in the right (SPANBROEK) section on the 22nd inst.

2. The Battalion will relieve the 6/Connaught Rangers in support.

3. On relief Officers Commanding Companies will come under the orders of sub-section commanders for tactical purposes and will report to the Officer Commanding Sub-section as soon as possible.
    "B" and "D" Companies 2/R.I. will be in support to the right sub-section, "A" and "C" to the left subsection.

4. Companies will move off as under:
    "A" Company   at   12 noon
    "B"   "   "   12.10 p.m.
    "C"   "   "   12.20 p.m.
    "D"   "   "   12.30 p.m.

5. On moving into support, Companies will be disposed as under:-
    "A" Company: H.Qrs and 2 Platoons: LA POLKA
                          1 Platoon: FT. SASKATCHEWAN
                          1 Platoon: S. P. 11.
    "C" Company: H.Qrs and 1 Platoon: YONGE ST.
                          1 Platoon: FT. REGINA.
                          1 Platoon: S. P. 9.
                          1 Platoon: S. P. 10.
    "B" Company: H.Qrs   : BEEHIVE DUGOUTS
                 4 Platoons   : FT. EDWARD
    "D" Company: H.Qrs and 2 Platoons : COOKER FARM.
                          1 Platoon : BEEHIVE DUGOUTS
                          1 Platoon : GALWAY DUGOUTS

6. Officers trench kits, stores etc., will be dumped in the open space behind the Guard Room by 11 a.m.

7. Previous orders re movement East of LOCRE will be observed.

8. Completion of relief to be reported to Battalion H.Qrs in B.A.B. Code.

9. Trench Store Lists will be rendered to the Orderly Room by 9 a.m. on the 23rd inst.

10. Battalion H.Qrs. will close at CURRAGH CAMP at 3.p.m. and re-open at DOCTOR'S HO. at the same hour.

                                P. Emley
                                    Lieutenant,
                    A/Adjutant 2/The Royal Irish Regt.

Issued at 5 p.m.

Copy No.1. War Diary   No.8. O/C "D" Coy.   No.15. R.S.M.
     2. H.Q. 49 I.B.   9. Lewis Gun Offr.   16. Cook Sgt.
     3. O.C. 6/C.R.   10. Scout Offr.
     4. Sec-in-Commnd.   11. Medical Offr.
     5. O/C "A" Coy   12. Transport Offr.
     6.   " "B" "   13. Quartermaster
     7.   " "C" "   14. Sig. Offr.

Army Form B. 2069.

Offence Report (*Field Service only*).

Corps _____

Squadron, Troop, Batty, or Company	Regt. No.	Rank	Name	Place and Date of offence	Offence	By whom reported and Names of Witnesses	Init^{ls} of Officer Comdg. Company, &c.	Punishment awarded	Signature of Officer by whom ordered and date of award	Date of entry in Conduct Sheet	Remarks

N.B.—A horizontal line should be drawn the whole length of the Return after each day's offences are entered.

SECRET.

Appendix X

Operation Order No. 9.
by
Lieut. Colonel H. G. Gregorie, D.S.O, Commanding,
2nd. Battalion, the Royal Irish Regiment,

Copy No. 1

Reference Map.
WYTSCHAETE and Sheet 28 S.W.

The Field
25-2-17.

1. The Battalion will relieve the 7/8th. Battalion the Royal Irish Fusiliers in the right subsection tomorrow the 26th. inst.
Relief to commence at 5.30 pm.

2. Companies will be disposed as under:-
   "D" Coy.   Right Front Line.
   "B" "   Centre Front Line.
   "C" "   Left Front Line.
   "A" "   Support.

3. "D" Coy. 2/RI. will relieve "C" Coy. 7/8th. R.I.F. having 2 platoons in Front Line and H.Q. and 2 platoons in SHAMUS DUGOUTS.
   "B" Coy. 2/RI. will relieve "A" Coy. 7/8th. R.I.F. having H.Q. and 2 platoons in S.P.6 and 2 platoons in Front Line.
   "C" Coy. 2/RI. will relieve "B" Coy. 7/8th. R.I.F. having H.Q. and 2 platoons in ULSTER ROAD and 2 platoons in Front Line.
   "A" Coy. 2/RI. will relieve "D" Coy. 7/8th. R.I.F. having H.Q. and 2 platoons in S.P.7 and 2 platoons in S.P.8 and PICCADILLY DUGOUTS.
   The relief of the Lewis Gunners will be carried out under arrangement to be made by C.O.'s concerned. Relief to be complete by 8 pm.

4. Guides. Guides 1 per platoon for right company will be at COOKER FARM at 4.30 pm.
   Guides 1 per platoon for centre company will be at FORT EDWARD at 4.30 pm.
   Guides 1 per platoon for left company will be at Y.M.C.A., REGENT STREET DUGOUTS at 4.30 pm.
   Guides 1 per platoon for support company will be at Y.M.C.A. REGENT STREET DUGOUTS at 5 pm.

5. All work, information, &c., will be carefully taken over from outgoing unit.

6. Companies will make their own arrangements regarding the transport of kits, stores, &c.

7. Trench store lists to be rendered to Bn. H.Q. by 9 am. 27th inst.

8. Completion of relief to be reported to Bn. H.Q. in B.A.B. Code.

9. Battalion Headquarters will close in DOCTOR'S HOUSE at 6 pm. and will reopen at NEWPORT DUGOUTS at the same hour.

10. ACKNOWLEDGE.

V. Kulverley
Lieut. & Adjutant,
2nd Battalion, The Royal Irish Regiment.

Hour of issue 8 pm.

Copy No. 1. War Diary
2. H.Q. 49th Inf. Bde.
3. 7th R. Innis Fus
4. 7/8th R.I. Fus
5. Sec. in Command
6. O.C. "A" Coy

No. 7. O.C. "B" Coy.
8. O.C. "C"
9. O.C. "D"
10. Bombing Offr.
11. L.G. Offr.
12. Scout Offr.

No. 13. Signalling Offr.
14. Medical Offr.
15. Quartermaster.
16. Transport Offr.
17. R.S.M.
18. Cook Sergt.

12.G.
(24 sheets)

WAR DIARY
FOR MONTH OF MARCH, 1917.

VOLUME

UNIT:— 2nd Btn Royal Irish Regt.

Vol 24

WAR DIARY 2nd Batt'n
or The ROYAL IRISH
INTELLIGENCE SUMMARY REGIMENT.

(Erase heading not required.)

Army Form C. 2118.

Hour, Date, Place	Summary of Events and Information	Remarks and references to Appendices
March 18th 1917	The battalion was in the front line – At 7 p.m. Lt L.H. HARRISON and 10 other ranks raided the enemy's line – No prisoners were taken and no casualties were incurred – the raiding party report the enemy line to be full of wire vide 3 other ranks wounded in action	Appendix 1/1
2nd	The battalion was relieved in the right sub-section by the 8th ROYAL MUNSTER FUSILIERS & moved into WAKEFIELD CAMP. Capt. J.D. SCOTT & Lt A.S.AIR joined the battalion	1.A.N. Appendix 11/11 2.A.N.
3rd	2/Lt C.J. KENNY proceeds to M.G. School at GRANTHAM.	3.A.N.
4th	13 other ranks joined. No 10315. Cpl W. MEARA + No 7862 L/Cpl S. BRENNAN awarded the Military Medal – Lt G.H. PALMER + 2/Lt W.G.D. GIFFIN joined the battalion	3.A.N.
5th	1 other rank wounded in action	7.A.N.
6th	The Battalion was inspected by the G.O.C. Comdg the 49th Brigade	6.A.N.
8th	1 other rank wounded in action. The Germans carried out 2 raids on the Divisional front – inflicted over 150 casualties captured 1 Lewis Gun and about 20 men. this sector is getting "lively".	7.A.N.

WAR DIARY
or
INTELLIGENCE SUMMARY

Army Form C. 2118.

(Erase heading not required.)

Hour, Date, Place	Summary of Events and Information	Remarks and references to Appendices
10th	Normally the battalion would have gone into the front line today, but the relief was cancelled. 7 other ranks joined as reinforcements.	App IV
11th	WAKEFIELD CAMP shelled by enemy 4.2" Howitzers - Two duds fell on the huts - no casualties.	App IV
12th - 15th	The battalion was working on the G.H.Q. 2nd and 3rd lines & erecting new wire, and generally repairing trenches.	App IV
13th	2/Lt S.B. GRIFFIN joined today - Capt R. McGRATH proceeded to the 16th Divl Composite Coy - No 8194 Pte HUNT M. awarded the Italian Bronze Medal.	App IV
14th		App IV
15th	3 officers and 18 other ranks were awarded the Parchment certificate of the 16th (IRISH) Division. Lt L. MURPHY proceeded to join the R.F.C., and Lt J.O. McCAUL was struck off the strength of the battalion. 4 other ranks joined.	App IV
17th	The following message was received from Lt Col Randal Viscount French G.C.B. O.E. G.C.V.O etc Greetings to the 2nd Royal IRISH Regt from their colours	
18th	2/Lt G.J. FOGARTY proceeded to the 49th T.M. Battery.	
19th	The battalion relieved the 9th Bn The Royal DUBLIN FUSILIERS in the right subsector	Appendices III & IV
20th	2/Lt H. WILSON was admitted to hospital	

Army Form C. 2118.

WAR DIARY
or
INTELLIGENCE SUMMARY

(Erase heading not required.)

Instructions regarding War Diaries and Intelligence Summaries are contained in F. S. Regs., Part II. and the Staff Manual respectively. Title pages will be prepared in manuscript.

Hour, Date, Place	Summary of Events and Information	Remarks and references to Appendices
22ⁿᵈ 19ᵖ - 25ᵖ	25 other ranks joined today.	£A.iv.
	On the whole a quiet time in the front line. On the night of the 19ᵗʰ an enemy raid was expected, as 3 white flags had been put up in No Man's Land opposite weak points in our wire, and his last raid had been aimed our armed. On the night of the 20ᵗʰ a white tape was observed running from the enemy wire to a trench in our left Coy lines. This was brought in during the night.	
23ʳᵈ	The battalion was relieved by the 7/8ᵗʰ R Irish Fusiliers and moved into Brigade support at ROSSIGNOL-	Appendix V
23ʳᵈ - 29ᵗʰ	Battalion in support. Fairly good weather, occasional very cold. Carrying parties furnished worked parties for the front line.	£A.iv.
28ʳᵈ 24ᵗʰ	1 other rank wounded in action. { 1 " " killed in action { 6 other ranks joined as reinforcements	£A.iv.
25ᵗʰ	1 other rank killed in action	
26ᵗʰ	Capt. C. TAYLOR joined from the 6ᵗʰ battalion	
29ᵗʰ	The battalion relieved the 7/8ᵗʰ R Irish Fusiliers in the night sub-sector of the front line.	Appendices VI, VII

Army Form C. 2118.

WAR DIARY
or
INTELLIGENCE SUMMARY

(Erase heading not required.)

Instructions regarding War Diaries and Intelligence Summaries are contained in F. S. Regs., Part II. and the Staff Manual respectively. Title pages will be prepared in manuscript.

Hour, Date, Place	Summary of Events and Information	Remarks and references to Appendices
29th	2 other ranks wounded in action	JAM.
29 - 31	Fairly quiet. Enemy was occasionally active with 4.2" Howitzers + Trench Mortars, chiefly on our support and communication trenches	JAM.
April 1st	The 49th Brigade was relieved by the 44th Brigade and the battalion moved into KEMMEL SHELTERS -	Appendices VII & VIII

R. J. Fanu Drew
Comdg. 2nd Bn. Phillyg. Irish Regt.

SECRET.   Copy No ....

49th Infantry Brigade Operation Order No. 10 - 28-2-17.
* * * * * * * * * * * * * * * * * *

1. **OBJECT.**

    A minor enterprise will be carried out by a party of 1 Officer and 10 Other Ranks of 2nd R. Irish Regt. at N.36.a.55.75 on the night 1st/2nd March, with the object of capturing a prisoner.

2. **TIME.**

    Zero hour will be 7 p.m.

3. **ARTILLERY.**

    At Zero Hour the O.C. SPANBROEK Group will arrange to bombard the enemy's front line from N.30.c.35.50 to N.36.a.55.60, using intense fire between N.30.c.50.0 and N.36.a.60.50. At Zero plus 5 minutes the barrage will creep back for 3 minutes and will become a stationary box barrage on the line -
    N.30.c.50.0 - N.30.a.90.90 - N.36.b.20.70 - N.36.a.60.50. also keeping the enemy's front line just North of N.30.c.50.0 under enfilade fire.

    The artillery will cease fire at Zero plus 20 minutes, unless the O.C. 2nd R. Irish Regt. asks by telephone or rocket signal, which will be arranged, for the barrage to be continued.

4. The Raiding Party will advance over the parapet at Zero, and will crawl forward, entering the enemy's trench as the Artillery lifts.

5. **TRENCH MORTARS.**

    As per attached Table.

6. **VICKERS GUNS.**

    Vickers Guns will open bursts of fire on the following points from Zero to Zero plus 20 minutes :-

    49th M.G.Company.

    BOGAERT FARM - HOP POINT - BONE POINT.

    47th M.G.Company.

    L'ENFER WOOD - OCCULT AVENUE - OCCUR TRENCH.

7. **LEWIS GUNS.** Will open bursts of fire at Zero on German front line, taking care no fire is directed anywhere near N.36.a.55.75.

8. ACKNOWLEDGE.

                                            JWBWilkin Captain,
                                Brigade Major, 49th Infantry Brigade.

Issued through Signals.
Copy No. 1 to 2nd R. Irish Regt. Copy No. 7 to 49th T.M.B.
  "   2   7th R. Innis Fus.   "   8   47th T.M.B.
  "   3   8th R. Innis Fus.   "   9   SPANBROEK GROUP.
  "   4   7/8th R. Irish Fus.   "   10   16th Div. (G)
  "   5   49th M.G.Company.   "   11   16th Div. Arty.
  "   6   47th M.G.Company.

TRENCH MORTAR TABLE.

Issued with 49th Inf. Bde. O.O. No. 16.

BATTERY.	TIME.	TARGET.	RATE OF FIRE.	REMARKS.
49th T.M.B.	Zero to Zero plus 20 minutes.	N.30.c.37.70.	4 rounds per minute.	Stokes.
"	"	N.30.c.10.90.	"	"
"	"	N.30.c.07.87.	"	"
"	"	N.30.a.20.07.	"	"
"	"	N.30.c.12.65.	1 round per minute.	2" Trench Mortar.
"	"	N.30.a.20.07.	"	"
49th T.M.B.	"	S. of N.36.a.63.30.	3 rounds per gun per minute.	3 Stokes Mortars to be employed. 2" T.M's to co-operate if possible.

COPY No 5.

SECRET.

SPANBROEK OPERATION ORDER No. 12.

by

Lieut-Colonel L. E. S. WARD, D.S.O., R.F.A.

1.3.17.

Ref. Map WYTSCHAETE Edition 4 a 1/10,000.

1. A minor enterprise is being carried out by a party of one Officer and 10 other ranks 2nd. ROYAL IRISH Regt. at N.36.a.55.75. on the night 1st. 2nd. March.

2. A table of battery tasks is attached.

3. Zero hour will be 7.0. p.m.

4. Watches will be synchronized at 6.30. p.m. under arrangements to be made by the Adjutant 180th. Bde. R.F.A.

5. After the completion of the bombardment table, batteries will stand by to render further assistance if required.

   The signal for this action will be the code word "RESUME" sent from Group Headquarters.

   On the receipt of this message batteries will re-open fire on the last tasks shown on the attached table (box barrage) at a rate of fire of 2 rounds per gun per minute until further orders.

6. ACKNOWLEDGE.

L. E. S. Ward.
Lt-Col. R.F.A.
Commdg. SPANBROEK GROUP.

Copies to ;-

1. A/180
2. B/180
3. C/180
4. D/180
5. 49th. Inf. Bde. ✓
6. 16th. D.A.
7. Vierstraat Group
8. Left Group 36th. D.A.
9. War Diary
10. File.

TABLE OF TASKS.

Btty.	Time.	Tasks.	Rate of Fire.
A/180	Zero to Zero plus 5.	Barrage Hostile Front Line N.30.c.54.00 - N.36.a.58.70.	4 rounds per per minute.
5 guns	Zero plus 5½.	Lift 50 yards.	
	Zero plus 6½.	Lift 50 yards.	2 rounds per gun per minute.
	Zero plus 7½.	Lift to Hostile Support Line N.30.c.96.00 - N.36.b.10.70.	
	Zero plus 8 to Zero plus 15.	Barrage Hostile Support Line N.30.c.96.00 - N.36.b.10.70.	2 rounds per gun per minute.
	Zero plus 15 to Zero plus 20	-----do-----	(per minute (3 rounds per gun
1 gun Lone gun	Zero to Zero plus 20	Enfilade Hostile Communication Trench from N.36.a.72.55 - N.36.a.92.60.	40 rouds "A"
C/180	Zero to Zero plus 5.	Barrage Hostile Front Line N.36.a.58.70 - N.36.a.60.45	4 rounds per gun per minute
	Zero plus 5½.	Lift 50 yards	
	Zero plus 6½.	Lift 50 yards	
	Zero plus 7½.	Lift to Hostile Support Trench from N.36.b.10.70 - N.36.b.25.40	2 rounds per gun per minute
	Zero plus 8 to Zero plus 15	Barrage Hostile Support Line N.36.b.10.70 - N.36.b.25.40.	2 rounds per gn per minute
	Zero plus 15 to Zero plus 20	-----do-----	3 rounds per gun per minute
B/180			
2 guns	Zero to zero plus 5.	Barrage Hostile Front Line N.36.a.60.45 - N.36.a.80.30.	4 rounds per gun per minute
2 guns	--do--	Barrage Hostile Front Line N.30.c.41.35 - N.30.c.20.54.	
2 guns Det.Sect.	--do--	Enfilade Hostile Front Line from N.30.c.54.00 - N.30.c.25.52.	
	Zero plus 5. to Zero plus 15	As above.	2 rounds per gun per minute.
	Zero plus 15 to Zero plus 20.	As above	3 rounds per gun per minute.

TABLE OF TASKS. (continued)

Bty.	Time.	Tasks.	Rate of Fire.
D/180 2 guns.	Zero to Zero plus 2.	Enfilade NATHAN LANE from N.36.a.57.70 - N.36.b.05.78	3 rounds per gun per minute.
	Zero plus 2 to Zero plus 20.	1 Gun on Trench Junction at N.36.b.05.78. 1 Gun on Trench Junction at N.36.b.18.82.	30 rounds per gun.
4 guns.	Zero to Zero plus 20	Communication Trench from N.36.a.78.32 - N.36.b.49.58.	36 rounds per gun.
D/177. 4 guns	Zero to Zero plus 20.	Communication Trench from N.30.c.54.00 - N.36.a.96.93.	36 rounds per gun.
1 gun	--do--	On SUNKEN ROAD N.30.c.95.08.	36 rounds.
1 gun.	--do--	On Trench Junction at N.36.a.82.40.	36 rounds.

Ammunition 50% "A"   50% "AX" except where otherwise detailed.

-----------------oOo-----------------

M.S. 49

Headquarters
16 D.A.
Headquarters 49th Inf Bde. ✓

Ref. SPANBROEK O.O. No. 12. 1.3.17.

As the LONE GUN A/180 cannot clear the CREST and engage the target allotted, the following target has been substituted.

ENFILADE CUTTING FROM
 N30d 70.60 - N30d 90.87.

Please amend O.O. No. 12 accordingly.

S. Mackay
LT. R.F.A
MARCH 1st 1917   FOR O.C. 180 BDE, R.F.A

Appendix II

SECRET.

Operation Order No. 10.
by
Lieut. Colonel H. G. Gregorie, D.S.O. Commanding,
2nd. Battalion, The Royal Irish Regiment.

Reference Map
WYTSCHAETE & Sheet 28 S.W.

The Field.
1 - 3 - 17.

1. The 47th. Infantry Brigade will relieve the 49th. Infantry Brigade in the SPANBROEK Section tomorrow, the 2nd. March.
   On relief the 49th. Infantry Brigade will move into Divisional Reserve.

2. The Battalion will be relieved in the right sub-section by the 1st. Battalion, The Royal Munster Fusiliers.
   Relief to commence at 5.45 pm.
   On relief the 2nd. Battalion, The Royal Irish Regiment will move to WAKEFIELD and LURGAN Camps.

3. Lewis Guns and teams will be relieved in the morning of the 2nd. March.

4. Movement in daylight east of LOCRE will be by platoons at 300 yards interval.

5. Companies will march by the DAYLIGHT C. DRANOUTRE route.

6. Kits, etc, will be dumped at FORT EDWARD by 5pm.
   O's. C. Coys. will detail 1 man per Coy. to act as guard.

7. French Store lists, signed and countersigned by an Officer, will be rendered to Orderly Room by 9 am. on the 3rd inst.

P. Kehoe,
Lieut. & Adjutant,
2nd. Battalion, The Royal Irish Regiment.

Hour of issue 6.30 pm.

Copy No. 1. War Diary.
2. H.Q., 49th. Inf. Bde.
3. 1/Roy. Munster Fus
4. 7/8th. Roy. Dr. Fus
5. Second-in-Command.
6. O. C. "A" Coy.
7. O. C. "B"
8. O. C. "C"
9. O. C. "D"

Copy No. 10. Bn. Bombing Officer.
11. Lewis Gun Officer.
12. Scout Officer.
13. Signalling Officer.
14. Medical Officer
15. Quartermaster.
16. Transport Officer.
17. Regtl. Sergt. Major.
18. Cook Sergeant.

SECRET.   Operation Order No.11   Copy No. 1
by
Lieut. Colonel F.S. Girgine, D.S.O. Commanding
2nd Battalion, The Royal Irish Regiment.

Reference Maps   The Field.
WYTSCHAETE and sheet 28.S.W.   Appendix III   18-7-17.

1. The 49th Infantry Brigade will relieve the 48th Infantry Brigade in the VIERSTRAAT Section on 19th inst.
   The Battalion will relieve the 9th Battalion, The Royal Dublin Fusiliers in the Right Sub-section.

2. Companies will be disposed as under and will march off at times stated:-
   "D" Coy.   Right Front Line   1 pm.
   "C" "   Left Front Line   1.5 pm.
   "B" "   Right Support   1.10 pm.
   "A" "   Left Support   1.15 pm.

3. Route:- HOSPICE — KEMMEL ROAD.
   "B" and "D" Coys. will relieve via VIA GELLIA.
   "A" and "C" Coys. will relieve via ROSSIGNOL ROAD.

4. 2 platoons of "D" Coy, 2/RI. will relieve 2 platoons of "B" Coy. 9/R.D.F. in the Front Line.
   2 platoons of "D" Coy., 2/RI. will relieve 2 platoons of "B" Coy. 9/R.D.F. in BROADWAY and PARK AVENUE.
   "C" Coy., 2/RI., will have 2 platoons in the Front Line and 2 platoons in PARK AVENUE and will relieve "D" Coy., 9/R.D.F.
   "B" Coy., 2/RI. will relieve 2 platoons of "C" Coy., 9/R.D.F. in ALBERTA DUGOUTS and will have 2 platoons at S.P.11.
   "A" Coy., 2/RI. will relieve "A" Coy. 9/R.D.F. having 2 platoons in BANFF DUGOUTS and 2 platoons in TURNERSTOWN RIGHT.

5. An advance party consisting of No.1's of Lewis Gun Teams, 1 Officer per Coy., 1 N.C.O. per platoon, Coy. Gas N.C.O's., signallers and scouts will be at DOCTOR'S HOUSE at 10 am. where guides will meet them.
   Guides for Coys. will be at DOCTOR'S HOUSE at 2.30 pm.

6. Officers' trench kits, packs, blankets, stores, &c. will be stacked outside the Orderly Room by 12 noon.

7. All troops must be clear of the camp by 1.20 pm.

8. Movement east of a north and south line through LOCRE will be by platoons at 200 yards interval.

9. Trench Store Lists will be rendered to Orderly Room by 9 am. on the 20th. inst.

10. Battalion Headquarters will close in WAKEFIELD HUTS at 1 pm. and will reopen at HARLEY HOUSE at the same hour.

J. Rahilly
Lieut. & Adjutant,
2nd. Battalion, The Royal Irish Regt.

Hour of issue 9 pm.

Copy No.1. War Diary.   10. Lewis Gun Officer.
       2. 49th. Inf. Bde.   11. Bn. Bombing Officer.
       3. 7/8th. R.I. Fus.   12. Signalling Officer.
       4. 9th. R.D. Fus.   13. Scout Officer.
       5. Second-in-Command.   14. Medical Officer.
       6. O.C. "A" Coy.   15. Transport Officer.
       7. O.C. "B" "   16. Quartermaster.
       8. O.C. "C" "   17. Regtl. Sergt. Major.
       9. O.C. "D" "   18. Cook Sergt.

Appendix IV C D
A B

SECRET.   Copy No........

49th. Infantry Brigade Order No. 103 - 16/3/17.

1.   The 49th. Inf. Bde. will relieve the 48th. Inf. Bde. in the VIERSTRAAT SECTION on the 18th. and 19th. March, in accordance with the attached relief table.

2.   Advanced parties of front line battalions, consisting of No.1's of Lewis Gun Teams, 1 officer per company, 1 N.C.O. per platoon, Sergt-Major, Gas N.C.O's, signallers and snipers, will report at Battn. H.Q. of units they are relieving, where necessary guides will be provided 4 hours in advance of the main relief.
        Advance parties of 7/8th. R. Irish Fus. consisting of No. 1's of Lewis Guns, 1 officer per coy., 1 N.C.O. per platoon and signallers, will move up 4 hours in advance of main relief.
        The 7th. R. Innis. Fus. will send an advance party to take over billets at BUTTERFLY FARM at 9.30 a.m. on 19th. inst.

3.   49th. M.G.Hdqtrs. will move to PIONEER FARM on the 18th. inst. and will take over billets there from the 48th. Inf. Bde. Pioneer Coy.

4.   The H.Q. of 49th. T.M.Batty. will move on 18th. inst. to SIEGE FARM and will take over billets occupied by 48th. T.M.Btty.

5.   Details of reliefs to be arranged between commanding officers concerned.

6.   Movement East of a North and South line through LOCRE will be by platoons at 200 yards interval.

7.   All maps, trench stores, defence schemes, etc. will be taken over. Lists of trench stores to be sent to Brigade H.Q. by 6 p.m. 20th. Inst.

8.   Brigade H.Q. will close at LOCRE at 7 p.m. on 19th. and will open at FAIRY HOUSE, BRULOOZE, at the same hour.

9.   The Brigade School will move to FAIRY HOUSE on the afternoon of the 19th. Inst.

10.   Completion of all reliefs to be reported to Bde. H.Q.

11.   ACKNOWLEDGE.

                                                    Captain.
                                        Brigade Major. 49th. Inf. Bde.

Issued through Signals.

Copy No. 1. to 2nd. R. Irish Regt.
" 2. 7th. R. Innis. Fus.
" 3. 8th. R. Innis. Fus.
" 4. 7/8th. R. Irish Fus.
" 5. 49th. M.G. Company.
" 6. 49th. T.M. Battery.
" 7. Z/16. T.M. Battery.
" 8. X/16. T.M. Battery.
" 9. 48th. Inf. Bde.
" 10. 107th. Inf. Bde.
" 11. O.C. VIERSTRAAT GROUP.
" 12. 16th. Division. (G)
" 13. 16th. Division. (Q)
" 14. 16th. Divnl. Arty.
" 15. A.D.M.S. 16th. Div.
" 16. Staff Captain.
" 17. Bde. Signal Officer.
" 18. Bde. Transport Officer.
" 19. 144th. Coy. A.S.C.
" 20. 155th. Fd. Coy. R.E.
" 21. 157th. Fd. Coy. R.E.
" 22. 250th. Tun. Coy. R.E.
" 23. 11th. Hants. (P)
" 24. 49th. Bde. School.
" 25-26. War Diary.
" 27. File.

RELIEF TABLE TO ACCOMPANY 49th INF. BRIGADE ORDER NO. 103.

Date.	Relieving Unit.	Unit to be Relieved.	Guides.	Route.	Remarks.
19th	Right Sub-Section. 2/R. Irish Regt.	9th Dublin Fus.	Doctor's House 2.30 p.m.		1 Guide per platoon under an Officer.
19th	Left Sub-Section. 8/R. Innis. Fus.	2/R. Dublin Fus. (less 1 Coy)	Y.M.C.A. Hut LITTLE KEMMEL 5 p.m.	WATTLING St.	1 Guide per platoon under an Officer.
19th	Support Battalion. 7/8th R. Irish Fus. 1 Coy.	1 Coy 2/R.Dublin Fus. SIEGE FARM Garrison of 9/R. Dublin Fus. in Ft. MOUNT ROYAL. 1 Coy. 8/R.Dublin Fus. ROSSIGNOL.			Guides from each unit concerned will be supplied.
	{1 Platoon	Post of 8/R.Dublin Fus.in Ft. SASKATCHEWAN.	Y.M.C.A. Hut		
	1 Coy. {3 Platoons	In LA POLKA Fm.			
	{1 Platoon	1 Post from this Coy relieves post of 2/R.Dub.Fus. in Ft. HALIFAX.	LITTLE KEMMEL 11 a.m.		There are no men of 48th Inf. Bde in LA POLKA Fm.
	1 Coy. {3 Platoons 1 Coy. to SANDBAG VILLA-QUEBEC VILLA & YORK HOUSE.				
19th	Reserve Battalion. 7/R. Innis. Fus.	8/R. Dublin Fus.			
18th	49th M.G.Coy.	As arranged between C.O's concerned.			BUTTERFLY FARM. Relief to be completed by 11.30 a.m. Relief to commence at 2 p.m.
18th	49th T.M. Battery	As arranged between C.O's concerned.			Relief to commence at 2 p.m.

SECRET.   Copy No. ....1....

Appendix V

49th Infantry Brigade Order No.104 dated 21-3-17.
* * * * * * * * * * * *

1. The following reliefs will be carried out on the 23rd March 1917.

2. RIGHT SUBSECTION.

    The 7/8th R. Irish Fus. will relieve the 2nd R. Irish Regt. Relief to commence 2 p.m.
    On relief the 2nd R. Irish Regt. will move into Brigade Support.

3. LEFT SUBSECTION.

    The 7th R. Innis Fus. will relieve the 8th R. Innis Fus. Relief to commence at 6 p.m.
    On relief the 8th R. Innis Fus. will move into Brigade Reserve. (BUTTERFLY FARM).

4. Gas N.C.O's will accompany advance parties to take over all gas arrangements.

5. All trench stores, details of work and working parties will be handed over to incoming units.
    Trench Store Lists to be rendered to Brigade Headquarters by 6 p.m. 23rd instant.

6. Details of reliefs to be arranged between Battalion Commanders concerned.

7. Completion of Reliefs to be reported to Brigade Headquarters.

8. ACKNOWLEDGE.

McWilliam Captain,

Brigade Major, 49th Infantry Brigade.

Issued through Signals.

        Copy No. 1 to 2nd R. Irish Regt.
        ..   2   7th R. Innis Fus.
        ..   3   8th R. Innis Fus.
        ..   4   7/8th R. Irish Fus.
        ..   5   49th M.G. Company.
        ..   6   49th T.M. Battery.
        ..   7   V/16 T.M. Battery.
        ..   8   107th Inf. Bde.
        ..   9   124th Inf. Bde.
        ..   10   O.C. VIERSTRAAT Group.
        ..   11   16th Division (G)
        ..   12   16th Division (Q)
        ..   13   16th Div. Arty.
        ..   14   A.D.M.S. 16th Division.
        ..   15   Staff Captain.
        ..   16   Bde Signal Officer.
        ..   17   Bde Transport Officer.
        ..   18   144th Coy, A.S.C.
        ..   19   155th Field Coy R.E.
        ..   20   157th Field Coy, R.E.
        ..   21   250th Tunnelling Coy, R.E.
        ..   22   11th Hants (P)
        ..   23   49th Bde School.
        ..   24-25   War Diary.
        ..   26   File.

SECRET. Copy No ......1..

49th Infantry Brigade Order No. 105 - 26-3-17.

1. The following reliefs will be carried out on 29th instant.

2. **RIGHT SUBSECTION.**

    The 2nd R. Irish Regt. will relieve the 7/8th R. Irish Fus.
    Relief to commence at 12-30 p.m.
    On relief the 7/8th R. Irish Fus will move into Brigade Reserve at BUTTERFLY FARM.

3. **LEFT SUBSECTION.**

    The 8th R. Innis Fus. will relieve the 7th R. Innis Fus.
    Relief to commence at 7-30 p.m.
    On relief the 7th R. Innis Fus will move into Brigade Support.

4. Details of relief to be arranged between C.O's concerned.

5. Gas N.C.O's will accompany advance parties to take over all gas arrangements.

6. All trench Stores, details of work, etc, will be handed over to incoming units.
    Trench Store Lists will be sent to Brigade Headquarters by 6 p.m. 30th instant.

7. Completion of relief will be reported to Brigade Headquarters.

8. ACKNOWLEDGE.

　　　　　　　　　　　　　　　　　　　　　　Captain,
　　　　　　　　　　　　　Brigade Major, 49th Inf. Brigade.

Issued through Signals.

```
            Copy No. 1 to 2nd R. Irish Regt.
                 ..  2    7th R. Innis Fus.
                 ..  3    8th R. Innis Fus.
                 ..  4    7/8th R. Irish Fus.
                 ..  5    49th M.G. Company.
                 ..  6    49th T.M. Battery.
                 ..  7    Y/16 T.M. Battery.
                 ..  8    57th Inf. Brigade.
                 ..  9    107th Inf. Brigade.
                 .. 10    O.C. VIERSTRAAT Group.
                 .. 11    16th Division (G)
                 .. 12    16th Division (Q)
                 .. 13    16th Div. Arty.
                 .. 14    A.D.M.S. 16th Division.
                 .. 15    Staff Captain.
                 .. 16    Bde Signal Officer.
                 .. 17    Bde Transport Officer.
                 .. 18    144th Coy, A.S.C.
                 .. 19    155th Field Coy, R.E.
                 .. 20    157th Field Coy R.E.
                 .. 21    250th Tunnelling Coy. R.E.
                 .. 22    11th Hants (P)
                 .. 23    49th Bde School.
                 .. 24-25 War Diary.
                 .. 26    File.
```

SECRET.   Operation Order No. 13.   Copy No.

Lieut. Colonel M. G. Gregorie, D.S.O., Commanding
2nd. Battalion, The Royal Irish Regiment.

Reference Map:
Trench Map   Appendix VII   The Field
                                              28-3-19.

1. The Battalion will relieve the 7/8th. Battalion, The Royal Irish Fusiliers in the Right Sub-Section, VIERSTRAAT Section, tomorrow, the 29th. inst.
   Relief to commence at 12.30 p.m.

2. "A" Coy., 2/R.I. will relieve "D" Coy., 7/8th. R.I.F. in the Left Front Line.
   "C" Coy., 2/R.I. will relieve "B" Coy., 7/8th. R.I.F. in Left Support.
   "B" Coy., 2/R.I. will relieve "A" Coy., 7/8th. R.I.F. in the Right Front Line.
   "D" Coy., 2/R.I. will relieve "C" Coy., 7/8th. R.I.F. in Right Support.

3. Guides, 1 per platoon, for Right Coys. will be at BEAVER HAT at 12.30 p.m.
   Guides, same scale, for Left Coys. will be at HARLEY HOUSE at 12.30 p.m.

4. The relief of the Lewis Guns will be complete by 10.30 a.m.
   Guides for Right Coy. Sections will be at BEAVER HAT at 9 a.m.
   Guides for Left Coy. Sections will be at HARLEY HOUSE at 9 a.m.

5. Advance parties from 7th. Battalion, The Royal Inniskilling Fusiliers will be at Headquarters of Coys. at 11 a.m. to take over trench stores, etc.

6. Advance parties consisting of the usual personnel will arrive at Headquarters of Coys. of 7/8th. Battalion, The Royal Irish Fusiliers at 10.30 a.m.

7. All work, intelligence, etc., will be carefully taken over.

8. O's. C. Coys. will make their own arrangements re conveyance of Kits, etc.

9. Trench Store lists will be sent to the Orderly Room by 9 a.m., 30th. inst.

10. Completion of relief will be reported to Battallion Headquarters in "B.A.B." Code.

11. ACKNOWLEDGE.

                              J. Calverley.
                              Lieut. & a/Adjutant
                              2nd. Battalion, The Royal Irish Regt.

Hour of issue 4 p.m.
Copy No. 1. War Diary.   9. Signalling Officer.
         2. H.Q. 49th. Inf. Bde.   10. Scout Officer.
         3. 7/Roy. Innis. Fus.   11. Medical Officer.
         4. 7/8th. R. Irish Fus.   12. Quartermaster.
         5. O.C. "A" Coy.   13. Transport Officer.
         6. O.C. "B" "   14. Regtl. Sergt. Major.
         7. O.C. "C" "   15. Book Sergeant.
         8. O.C. "D" "

9. SUPPLY, Methods in use—

10. AMMUNITION. Method of Supply and Railhead—

11. R.E. STORES. Supply and Location of R.E. Parks—

12. LOCATION OF SIEGE PARK. Wagon Lines—

13. ORDERS IN CASE OF ALARM, OR GAS—

14. METHOD OF SALVAGE—

15. COLLECTION OF STORES IN CASE OF ADVANCE—

16. TELEPHONES. With Whom Connected and Code Calls—

17. O.P's.—

Appendix VII

SECRET.

Operation Order No. 14
by
Lieut. Colonel A. G. Gregorie, D.S.O., Commanding,
2nd. Battalion, The Royal Irish Regiment.

Copy No. 1

The Field
31-3-17.

Reference Map:
Sheet 28 S.W. (Edition 4a)

1. The 47th. Infantry Brigade will relieve the 49th. Infantry Brigade in the VIERSTRAAT Section on 1st. April.
    The Battalion will be relieved by the 6th. Battalion, The Royal Irish Regiment in the Right Sub-section.
    On relief the Battalion, less "D" Coy. will march to KEMMEL SHELTERS.
    "D" Coy. will be accommodated at BIRR BARRACKS.

2. "A" Coy., 6/R.I. will relieve "B" Coy. 2/R.I. in Right Front Line.
   "C" Coy., 6/R.I. will relieve "D" Coy. 2/R.I. in Right Support.
   "B" Coy., 6/R.I. will relieve "A" Coy. 2/R.I. in Left Front Line.
   "D" Coy., 6/R.I. will relieve "C" Coy. 2/R.I. in Left Support.

3. Guides, 1 per platoon, will be at DOCTOR'S HOUSE at 2.30 pm. Lieut. Pim will be in charge of this party and will be responsible that incoming units get the right guides.

4. Advance Parties and Lewis Gun Sections. Guides, 1 per company and per Lewis Gun Section, will be at DOCTOR'S HOUSE at 10 am.

5. Officers' trench kits, stores, etc., will be dumped at BANDSTAND, KEMMEL, by 1 pm.

6. Movement east of a North and South line through LOCRE will be by platoons at 200 yards interval.

7. All work, intelligence, etc., will be carefully handed over to incoming unit.

8. All maps, trench stores, etc., will be handed over and lists sent to Orderly Room by 9 am on 2nd. April.

9. Completion of relief will be reported to Battalion Headquarters in "B.A.B." Code.

10. ACKNOWLEDGE.

Pulverby Lieut. & Adjutant,
2nd. Battalion, The Royal Irish Regiment.

Hour of issue, 9 pm.

Copy No. 1. War Diary.
2. H.Q. 49th. Inf. Bde.
3. 6th. Bn. The R.I. Regt.
4. Second-in-Command.
5. O.C. "A" Coy.
6. O.C. "B" "
7. O.C. "C" "
8. O.C. "D" Coy.
9. Signalling Officer.
10. Scout Officer.
11. Medical Officer.
12. Quartermaster.
13. Transport Officer.
14. Regtl. Sergt. Major.
15. Cook Sergeant.

S E C R E T.

Appendix VIII

Copy No ...1...

49th Infantry Brigade Order No. 103 - 27-3-17.

Ref. Map 28.S.W.Edn. 4a.
Scale 1/20,000.

1. The 47th Infantry Brigade will relieve the 49th Infantry Brigade in the VIERSTRAAT Section on 1st April, 1917, in accordance with the attached Relief Table.

2. Reconnoitring parties of the front and support Battalions of the 47th Infantry Brigade will report at 49th Infantry Brigade Headquarters, FAIRY HOUSE at 11.30 a.m. on the 31st March. Battalions concerned will send one guide to be at Brigade H.Q. at that hour to conduct parties to their respective Battalion H.Q.

3. Advance parties of front line Battalions consisting of No. 1's of Lewis Gun Teams, one officer per Company, 1 N.C.O per platoon, Gas N.C.O's, Signallers and Snipers will report at Battalion H.Q. of units they are relieving 4 hours in advance of the main Relief on 1st April.
   Advance parties of Support Battalion will report at ROSSIGNOL ESTAMINET 1 hour in advance of the main Relief.

4. All details of Reliefs to be arranged between C.O's concerned.

5. Movement East of a North and South Line through LOCRE will be by platoons at 200 yards interval.

6. All maps, trench stores, etc, will be handed over and lists sent to Brigade Headquarters by 6 p.m. 2nd April.

7. The Brigade School will be discontinued on 1st April. All the Staff and students will return to their units on that date.

8. Brigade Headquarters will close at FAIRY HOUSE at 10 p.m. and will open at M.21.b.5.0. 500 yards West of M in MONT ROUGE at the same hour, on 1st April

9. Completion of all Reliefs to be reported to Brigade H.Q.

10. ACKNOWLEDGE.

Captain,

Brigade Major, 49th Infantry Brigade.

Issued through Signals.

Copy No.				
1	2nd R. Irish Regt.	16	to	Staff Captain.
2	7th R. Innis Fus.	18		Bde Signal Officer.
3	8th R. Innis Fus.	19		Bde Transport Officer
4	7/8th R. Irish Fus.	20		144th Coy, A.S.C.
5	49th M.G.Company.	21		155th Field Coy, R.E.
6	49th T.M.Battery.	22		157th Field Coy, R.E.
7	Y/16 T.M.Battery.	23		250th Tunnelling CoyRE.
8	47th Inf. Bde.	24		11th Hants (P)
9	48th Inf. Bde.	25		49th Bde School.
10	57th Inf. Bde.	26-27		War Diary.
11	107th Inf. Bde.	28		File.
12	O.C. VIERSTRAAT Group.			
13	16th Division (G)			
14	16th Division (Q)			
15	16th Div. Arty.			
16	A.D.M.S. 16th Division.			

RELIEF TABLE TO ACCOMPANY 49TH INFANTRY BRIGADE ORDER NO. 196.

Date.	Unit to be relieved.	Relieving Unit.	Guides	Route.	Destination after relief.	Remarks.
1st.	Right Subsection. 2nd R. Irish Regt.	6th R. Irish Regt.	DOCTOR'S HOUSE 2.30 p.m.	VIA GELLIA and ROSSIGNOL ROAD.	KEMMEL SHELTERS.	One guide per platoon under an officer.
1st.	Left Subsection. 8th R. Innis Fus.	1st R. Munster Fus.	Dressing Stn KEMMEL 7 p.m.	WATLING STREET	BIRR BARRACKS.	One guide per platoon under an officer.
1st.	Support Battalion. 7th R. Innis Fus.	7th Leinster Regt.	Dressing Stn KEMMEL 11 a.m.		CLARE CAMP M.27.c.3.4	One guide for each Coy and post under an officer.
1st.	Reserve Battalion. 7/8th R. Irish Fus.	6th Connaught Rangers.	BRULOOZE Crossroads. 11.30 a.m.		DONCASTER HUTS.	One guide per Company.
1st.	49th M.G.Company.	47th M.G.Company.	As arranged by C.O's concerned.		KLONDYKE FARM.	Relief to be completed by 12 noon.
1st.	49th T.M.Battery.	47th T.M.Battery.	As arranged by C.O's concerned.		DONCASTER HUTS.	Relief to be completed by 12 noon.

13.C.
(37 sheets)

WAR DIARY FOR MONTH OF APRIL, 1917.

VOLUME:-

UNIT:- 2nd R. Irish Regiment

Vol 25

Army Form C. 2118.

2nd BATTALION
The ROYAL IRISH REGIMENT.

WAR DIARY
or
INTELLIGENCE SUMMARY
(Erase heading not required.)

Instructions regarding War Diaries and Intelligence Summaries are contained in F. S. Regs., Part II. and the Staff Manual respectively. Title pages will be prepared in manuscript.

Hour, Date, Place	Summary of Events and Information	Remarks and references to Appendices
April 1st – 6th	The battalion was in billets at KEMMEL SHELTERS and engaged in providing working parties for the front line – 16 other ranks joined today –	J.A.N.
2nd	2/Lieut J.N. TROUGHTON joined the battalion today –	
4th	Capt. W.L.C. MOORE-BRABAZON resumed command & payment of "A" Coy –	
4th	Took over command & payment of "A" Coy.	
5th	The battalion was relieved in KEMMEL SHELTERS by the 7/8. ROYAL IRISH FUSILIERS & moved to DONCASTER HUTS. No more working parties furnished by the battalion. Platoon training (i.e. by Sections) commenced – 7 other ranks joined today –	Appendices 1 + 2
	The battalion was awarded the sum of 135 francs as prize money given for wiring G.H.Q. 2nd line near MILLEKRUIS –	J.A.N.
9th – 12th	Training programme for the period of the 12th is attached as directed by the Army Commander (2nd Army).	Appendix 3
11th	The battalion was inspected by the Army Commander (2nd Army). The weather was very bad. Snow & hail continually – 40 other ranks joined today –	
	Capt. T.A. LOWE then day proceeded to join the 1/18 The LONDON IRISH as attached in command – 5 other ranks joined the battalion today –	J.A.N.
12th		

WAR DIARY or INTELLIGENCE SUMMARY

Army Form C. 2118.

(Erase heading not required.)

Instructions regarding War Diaries and Intelligence Summaries are contained in F. S. Regs., Part II. and the Staff Manual respectively. Title pages will be prepared in manuscript.

Hour, Date, Place	Summary of Events and Information	Remarks and references to Appendices
13th	The 49th Infantry Brigade proceeded to the RECQUES area today. The battalion billeted in HAZEBROUCK on the night of the 13/14th.	Appendices 4 + 5
14th	The battalion billeted for the night at ST MARTIN-au-LAERT.	Appendix 6.
15th	The battalion arrived at NORDAUSQUES about 3 p.m. and was billeted as per attached.	Appendices 7, 8
16th - 28th	The battalion was engaged in platoon, company, battalion and brigade training as per appendices attached. The weather during this period was on the whole favourable to training on the manoeuvre the mornings were devoted to training on the manoeuvre area (about 3 miles from NORDAUSQUES - was attached) and the afternoons to recreational training. Both tug of war teams trained to enjoy themselves thoroughly & returned much healthier for the change.	Appendices 9 - 10, 11, 12 13, 14
16th	5 other ranks joined the battalion.	Appendix - 15
19th	3 other ranks " " "	
24th	The Brigade had an Assault at Arms Competition - The Battalion won 6 events including Tug of war, (ten Africa teen) cross-country, + Retreat Beating	J.A.N.
26th	The Brigade made a practice assault on the WYTSCHAETE RIDGE. The Army Commander, the Divisional Corps Commander, the Brigade	

Army Form C. 2118.

WAR DIARY
or
INTELLIGENCE SUMMARY
(Erase heading not required.)

Instructions regarding War Diaries and Intelligence Summaries are contained in F. S. Regs., Part II. and the Staff Manual respectively. Title pages will be prepared in manuscript.

Hour, Date, Place	Summary of Events and Information	Remarks and references to Appendices
26th	Were present & expressed themselves as fairly satisfied with the performance.	Appendices 16 + 17
28th	3 other ranks joined the Battalion — The battalion marched to ST MARTIN-au-LAERT en route for the front line —	Appendices 18, 19
29th	The battalion billeted in HAZEBROUCK on the night of the 29/30th —	Appendix 20
30th	The battalion marched to the LOCRE area + was billeted at DE ZON camp — 8 other ranks joined the battalion.	Appendix 21. F.F.N.

M. J. Lyons Lt Col
Cmdg. 2nd Bn. The Tyne [illegible] Regt.

WAR DIARY:
---------oOo---------

VOLUME:-

FOR MONTH OF MAY, 1917.

UNIT:- 2nd Royal Irish Regiment

Army Form C. 2118.

WAR DIARY
or
INTELLIGENCE SUMMARY
(Erase heading not required.)

Instructions regarding War Diaries and Intelligence Summaries are contained in F. S. Regs., Part II. and the Staff Manual respectively. Title pages will be prepared in manuscript.

Hour, Date, Place	Summary of Events and Information	Remarks and references to Appendices
May 1st	The battalion relieved the 1/5th Bn. The LOYAL NORTH LANCASHIRE Regt. in the left sub-section of the DIEPENDAHL SECTOR. Capt. C. TAYLOR proceeded to join the 6th Bn. The Royal Irish Regt.	Appendix 1
4th	1 other rank wounded in action.	
5th	The battalion was relieved by the 7/8th The ROYAL IRISH FUSILIERS and moved into brigade reserve at KOKRUH BIDGEE CAMP.	Appendix 2.
6th	KOKRUH BIDGEE camp was shelled by enemy 5"9 Hows. 10 officers slightly wounded. 2/Lieut. W.G. BAILLIE to N.H. COWPER to hospital.	34.N
	2/Lieut W.C.V. GALWEY appointed adjutant of the battalion with effect from 12-4-1917.	IX Corps A/3540 d. 3.4.17
9th	49th Inf. Bde. relieved by the 36th Inf. Bde. in the DIEPENDAHL sector. The battalion moved to WESTON CAMP.	Appendix 3
10th	The battalion relieved the 6th 6th. The ROYAL IRISH Regt. in the right subsection (VIERSTRAAT SECTOR).	Appendices 4, 5
11th	6 other ranks joined as reinforcement today.	
13th	2/Lt. S.B. GRIFFIN rejoined today.	
14th	The battalion was relieved in the right subsection by the 1st Bn. The ROYAL INNISKILLING FUSILIERS. 25 other ranks joined the battalion.	App. 5, 6, 7. 3p.m.

Army Form C. 2118.

WAR DIARY
or
INTELLIGENCE SUMMARY

(Erase heading not required.)

Instructions regarding War Diaries and Intelligence Summaries are contained in F.S. Regs., Part II. and the Staff Manual respectively. Title pages will be prepared in manuscript.

Hour, Date, Place	Summary of Events and Information	Remarks and references to Appendices
16th	S.G. GRIFFIN wounded in action. 1 other rank wounded 1 other rank killed	JAN
18th	The battalion was relieved in brigade support by the 9th Royal DUBLIN FUSILIERS and moved to CLARE CAMP. 1 officer rank joined as reinforcements.	Appendices 8, 9
18th 30th	The battalion was engaged in providing working parties, loading and unloading ammunition for batteries, trench mortars etc. A stationary line. During the nights of the 21st, 28th & 29th the enemy shelled our trench areas in the vicinity CLARE CAMP with a battery of 5.9 How. This battalion incurred no casualties.	JAN
25th 25th	Lieut A.S. FIRE accidentally wounded while on duty. 3 other ranks joined the battalion.	
30th	The Battalion moved to TRALEE LINES "B" (M 28. G 8.1.) near LOERIE.	Appendix 10
	Attached is a congratulatory letter from Major General W.B. HICKIE. C.B. Comdg the 16th (IRISH) DIVISION congratulating the battalion on the guard provided on the occasion of the C in C's visit to 16th Division Head quarters.	Appendix XI

SECRET.   OPERATION ORDER NO. 24.   Copy No. 1
by
LIEUT. COLONEL H. G. GREGORIE, D. S. O., COMMANDING,
2nd. BATTALION, THE ROYAL IRISH REGIMENT.

Reference Map   The Field.
Sheet 28 S.W.2.   1-5-1917.

1. The 49th. Infantry Brigade will relieve the 56th. Infantry Brigade in the DIKKEBUSCH SECTOR on the 1st. May.
2. The Battalion will relieve the 7th. Battalion, The Loyal North Lancashire Regt. in the left sub-section today, the 1st. May.
3. Companies will be disposed as under and will march off at times stated :-
   "C" Company   Left Front Line   6-15 p.m.
   "D"   ,,   Right Front Line   6-25 p.m.
   "A"   ,,   Strong Points and Forts   6-35 p.m.
   "B"   ,,   SLEEPY HOLLOW   6-45 p.m.
4. Guides, 1 per platoon, will meet incoming platoons at HALLEBAST CORNER, R.E. Dump, N.3.c.0.5. at 7-30 p.m.
5. Advance parties consisting of 1 Officer per Company and 1 N.C.O. per platoon, signallers, Coy. Gas N.C.O's. and Nos. 1 of Lewis Gun Teams will meet guides at HALLEBAST CORNER, R.E. Dump, at 2 p.m. today.
6. All movement east of CANADA CORNER will be by platoons at 200 yards interval. If a hostile aeroplane appears troops will halt on the side of the road until the aeroplane has gone.
7. All trench stores, maps, aeroplane photos and Defence Schemes will be taken over.
   Trench Store Lists will be sent to the Orderly Room by 9 a.m. on the 2nd. inst.
8. Rifle Bombers must take 120 rounds S.A.A. into the trenches.
9. Completion of relief to be wired to Battalion Headquarters in Code.
10. Officers valises, etc., will be dumped by Companies at the Quartermasters Stores by 5 p.m.
11. Battalion Headquarters will close in DE ZON Camp at 6 p.m. and open at the BRASSERIE at the same hour.

                                    Lieut. & A/Adjutant,
                      2nd. Battalion, The Royal Irish Regiment.

Hour of issue 12-45 p.m.

Copy No. 1. War Diary.   No. 9. Signalling Officer.
        2. 49th. Inf. Bde.   10. Scout Officer.
        3. O.C., 7/L.N.L.Regt.   11. Medical Officer.
        4. Second-in-Command.   12. Lewis Gun Officer.
        5. O. C. "A" Coy.   13. Quartermaster.
        6. O. C. "B" ,,   14. Transport Officer.
        7. O. C. "C" ,,   15. Regtl. Sergt. Major.
        8. O. C. "D" ,,   16. Cook Sergeant.

SECRET.   OPERATION ORDER NO. 25.   Copy No.
                                by
          LIEUT.COLONEL H. G. GREGORIE, D.S.O., COMMANDING,
             2nd. BATTALION, THE ROYAL IRISH REGIMENT.
Reference Map   The Field.
Sheet 28 S.W.2.   4-5-1917.

1.   The Battalion will be relieved by the 7/8th. Battalion, The
Royal Irish Fusiliers in the left sub-section tomorrow, the
5th. inst.
       Relief to commence at 8 p.m.
       On relief the Battalion will move into Brigade Reserve
at MURRUMBIDGEE CAMP.

2.   "A" Coy.,2/R.I. will be relieved by "A" Coy., 7/8th. R.I.F.
       "B" Coy.,2/R.I. will be relieved by "D" Coy., 7/8th. R.I.F.
       "C" Coy.,2/R.I. will be relieved by "C" Coy., 7/8th. R.I.F.
       "D" Coy.,2/R.I. will be relieved by "B" Coy., 7/8th. R.I.F.

3.   Guides, 1 per platoon, will be at the BRASSERIE at 8 p.m.

4.   The relief of the Lewis Guns will be carried out in the
afternoon.
       Guides, 1 per team, will be at the BRASSERIE at 5-30 p.m.

5.   Officers' kits will be dumped at SLEEPY HOLLOW by 7-30 p.m.
       Companies will detail 3 men per Coy. as guard over kits.

6.   Trench Store Lists will be sent to the Orderly Room by
9 a.m. on 6th. May.

7.   Completion of relief will be reported to Battalion Headquarters in code.

8.   ACKNOWLEDGE.

                                              Lieut. & L/Adjutant,
                              2nd. Battalion, The Royal Irish Regiment.

Hour of issue 6-30 p.m.

Copy No. 1. War Diary.   No. 9. Signalling Officer.
         2. H.Q., 49th. I. Bde.   10. Scout Officer.
         3. 7/8th. Bn. The R.I.F.   11. Lewis Gun Officer.
         4. Second-in-Command.   12. Medical Officer.
         5. O. C. "A" Coy.   13. Quartermaster.
         6. O. C. "B" ,,   14. Transport Officer.
         7. O. C. "C" ,,   15. Regtl. Sergt. Major.
         8. O. C. "D" ,,   16. Cook Sergeant.

SECRET.

Copy No ...1...

Appendix 3

49th Infantry Brigade Order No. 118 dated 8-5-17.

1. The 49th Infantry Brigade will be relieved by the 56th Infantry Brigade in the DIEPENDAAL SECTION on the 9th May and night of 9th/10th May in accordance with the attached relief table.

2. All work, trench stores, etc, will be handed over. Trench Store Lists to be sent to Brigade H.Q. by 6 p.m. 10th May.

3. Surplus men of the 7/8th R. Irish Fus. at present at MURRUMBIDGEE CAMP will be clear of LA CLYTTE by 9 a.m. tomorrow. They will remain at their Transport Lines during the day, and will rejoin their Battalion at CARNARVON CAMP in the evening.

4. Day working parties will continue tomorrow as usual. No working parties will be found after 6 p.m. 9th May.

5. Further details of reliefs will be arranged between C.O's concerned.

6. The 49th Infantry Brigade will relieve the 47th Infantry Brigade in the VIERSTRAAT SECTION on the 10th and night of the 10th/11th May. Details of this relief will be issued later.

7. Brigade Headquarters will remain at SCHERPENBERG.

8. Completion of Reliefs will be reported in code by wire to Brigade Headquarters.

9. The Brigade School will move to a Camp on MONT ROUGE tomorrow morning, 9th instant.

10. Movement East of CANADA CORNER will be by platoons at 200 yards interval.

11. The 49th Machine Gun Company will be under the orders of the G.O.C. 56th Infantry Brigade until relieved in the DIEPENDAAL SECTION.

12. ACKNOWLEDGE.

W. Willcox Captain,
Brigade Major, 49th Infantry Brigade.

Issued through Signals.

Copy No. 1 to	2nd R. Irish Regt.	Copy No. 13 to	16th Div. (Q)
" 2	7th R. Innis Fus.	" 14	16th Div. Arty.
" 3	8th R. Innis Fus.	" 15	A.D.M.S. 16th Div.
" 4	7/8th R. Irish Fus.	" 16	47th Inf. Bde.
" 5	49th M.G. Company.	" 17	56th Inf. Bde.
" 6	49th T.M. Battery.	" 18	123rd Inf. Bde.
" 7	G.O.C.	" 19	180th Bde. R.F.A.
" 8	Staff Captain.	" 20	144th Coy, A.S.C.
" 9	Bde. Signal Off.	" 21-22	War Diary.
" 10	Bde. Transport Off.	" 23	File.
" 11	Bde. Supply Off.	24	Quartermaster 2nd R. Irish
" 12	16th Div. (G)	25	" 7th Innis Fus
28. 250 Tunnelling Coy.		26	" 8th Innis Fus
29. 155 Coy R.E.		27	" 7/8 R. Irish F.

RELIEF TABLE TO ACCOMPANY BRIGADE ORDER NO. 118.

Date.	Unit to be relieved.	Relieving Unit.	From.	To.	Guides. Time & place.	Remarks.
9th.	2nd R.Irish Regt.	7th North Lancs Regt.	MURRUMBIDGEE	WESTCH CAMP M17.d.5.5.	—	Head of Battalion to pass LA CLYTTE Cross Rds at 9.45 a.m.
9th.	8th R.Innis Fus.	7th The King's Own.	RIDGEWOOD.	CURRAGH CAMP.	—	Head of 7th The King's Own will reach RIDGEWOOD at 8.30 p.m.
9th.	7th R.Innis Fus.	7th E.Lanc. Regt.	Right Subsection.	DE ZON CAMP.	1 per platoon at Bn.H.Q. at 10 pm.	
9th.	7/8th R.Irish Fus.	7th S.Lanc. Regt.	Left Subsection.	CARNARVON CAMP M.10.b. 8.6.	1 per platoon at M.G.A Hut, RIDGEWOOD. 7.30 PM	
9th.	49th T.M.Batty.	56th T.M.Batty.	Line.	CURRAGH CAMP.	As arranged between C.O's concerned.	Relief to be completed by 5.30 p.m.
11th	49th M.G.Coy.	56th M.G.Coy.	Line.	VIERSTRAAT SECTION.	As arranged between C.O's concerned.	Details of the relief of 49th M.G.Company by 49th M.G.Coy. will be issued later.

Appendix 3

S E C R E T.   Copy No ......

49th Infantry Brigade Order No. 117 – 8-5-17.

WARNING ORDER.

1. The 19th Division is to relieve the 16th Division in the DIEPENDAAL SECTION by the 12th instant.

2. On relief by the 56th Infantry Brigade in the DIEPENDAAL SECTION the 49th Infantry Brigade will relieve the 47th Infantry Brigade in the VIERSTRAAT SECTION.
    Both reliefs will be carried out simultaneously.

3. On the 9th May and the night of the 9th/10th May the 2nd R. Irish Regt and the 8th R. Innis Fus. will be relieved in Brigade Reserve and Support by two Battalions of the 56th Infantry Brigade.
    On relief the 2nd R. Irish Regt and the 8th R. Innis Fus. will probably move into Reserve and Support respectively in the VIERSTRAAT SECTION.

4. On the 10th the 2nd R. Irish Regt. and the 8th R. Innis Fus. will probably relieve two Battalions of the 47th Infantry Brigade in the line (VIERSTRAAT SECTION).
    On the same date the remaining two Battalions of the 49th Infantry Brigade, 49th Machine Gun Company and 49th T.M.Battery will probably be relieved in the DIEPENDAAL SECTION by the 56th Infantry Brigade, and will move into Support and Reserve in the VIERSTRAAT SECTION, Machine Gun Coy. and Trench Mortar Battery to the line.

5. Detailed orders re the above reliefs will be issued as soon as possible.

6. Brigade Headquarters will close at SCHERPENBERG at 10 a.m. tomorrow, 9th May and will reopen at LA CLYTTE at the same hour.

7. ACKNOWLEDGE.

                                                          Captain,
                            Brigade Major, 49th Infantry Brigade.

```
        Copy No. 1 to 2nd R. Irish Regt.
            ..     2    7th R. Innis Fus.
            ..     3    8th R. Innis Fus.
            ..     4    7/8th R. Irish Fus.
            ..     5    49th M.G. Company.
            ..     6    49th T.M.Battery.
            ..     7    Bde. Signal Officer.
            ..     8    Staff Captain,
            ..     9    16th Div. (G).
            ..    10    180th Brigade R.F.A.
            ..   11-12  War Dairy.
            ..    13    File.
```

SECRET. Copy No ......

49th Infantry Brigade Order No. 119 - 9-5-17.

Appendix 5

1. The 49th Infantry Brigade, less 49th Machine Gun Company, will relieve the 47th Infantry Brigade, less 47th Machine Gun Company, in the VIERSTRAAT SECTION on the 10th and night of 10th/11th May.

2. The 7/8th R. Irish Fus. will relieve the 6th Connaught Rangers in Brigade Reserve at BUTTERFLY FARM. Relief to commence at 11 a.m.

3. The 7th R. Innis Fus. will relieve the 7th Leinster Regt. in Brigade Support. (Headquarters - ROSSIGNOL ESTAMINET). Relief to commence at 1.30 p.m.

4. The 2nd R. Irish Regt will relieve the 6th R. Irish Regt in the Right Subsection (H.Q. CHINESE WALL). Relief to commence at 4 p.m.

5. The 8th R. Innis Fus will relieve the 1st R. Munster Fus. in the Left Subsection (H.Q. YORK HOUSE). Relief to commence at 9 p.m.

6. 49th Trench Mortar Battery, Brigade Observers and Bde. Bombing Officer will arrange to relieve the corresponding units of the 47th Infantry Brigade by 1 p.m. 10th May.

7. Advance Parties and Nos.1 of Lewis Gun Teams of Battalions going into the line will report at the Battalion H.Q. of the units they are relieving 3 hours before their respective reliefs.
   Advance Parties of the Support Battalion will report at ROSSIGNOL ESTAMINET 2 hours before the relief of their Battalion.

8. The 49th Infantry Brigade will take over C.R.E's working parties at 8.30 p.m. Details of the above parties will be sent to units concerned.

9. Further details of reliefs including guides will be arranged by C.O's concerned.

10. Brigade Headquarters will close at SCHERPENBERG at 7 p.m. 10th May and will open at FAIRY HOUSE at the same hour.

11. All movement East of the Line - LOCRE - CANADA CORNER will be by platoons at 200 yards interval.

12. ACKNOWLEDGE.

[Signature] Captain,
Brigade Major, 49th Infantry Brigade.

Issued through Signals. at 12.30 PM

Copy No.			Copy No.	
1	to 2nd R. Irish Regt.		14 to	16th Div. Arty.
2	7th R. Innis Fus.		15	A.D.M.S. 16th Div.
3	8th R. Innis Fus.		16	47th Inf. Bde.
4	7/8th R. Irish Fus.		17	56th Inf. Bde.
5	49th M.G. Company.		18	180th Bde. R.F.A.
6	49th T.M. Battery.		19	144th Coy, A.S.C.
7	G.O.C.		20	Left Bde, 36th Div.
8	Staff Captain.			
9	Bde. Signal Off.			
10	Bde. Transport Off.		21	156th Field Coy, RE.
11	Bde. Supply Off.		22	250th Tun. Coy, RE.
12	16th Div. (G)		23-24	War Diary.
13	16th Div. (Q)		25	File.

Appendix 4

SECRET.   OPERATION ORDER NO. 26.   Copy No. _____
by
LIEUT. COLONEL H. G. GREGORIE, D.S.O., COMMANDING,
2nd. BATTALION, THE ROYAL IRISH REGIMENT.

Reference Map   The Field.
Sheet 28 S.W. (Edition 5A) 1/20,000.   9-5-1917.

1. The Battalion will relieve the 6th. Battalion, The Royal Irish Regiment in the right sub-section (VIERSTRAAT SECTION) tomorrow, the 10th. inst.
   Relief to commence at 4 p.m.

2. Companies will be disposed as follows and will march off at times stated.
   "A" Company   Left Front Line   2-30 p.m.
   "B"   ,,   Right Front Line   2-45 p.m.
   "C"   ,,   Left Support (S.P.12 & BANFF DUG OUTS)   3 p.m.
   "D"   ,,   Right Support (S.P.11 & ALBERTA DUG OUTS)   3-15 p.m.

3. Route - Cross Roads M.18.c.05.50. - MARJORIE LANE - PITT LANE - KIM ROAD - GLEN CORNER (N.20.b.90.55.) - thence overland skirting KEMMEL VILLAGE, to ROSSIGNOL FARM.

4. Guides, 1 per platoon, will be at GLEN CORNER at 4 p.m.

5. Advance parties, usual strength, and Nos. 1 of Lewis Gun Teams will report at Battalion Headquarters, CHINESE WALL at 1 p.m.

6. All movement will be by platoons at 300 yards interval. In the event of the appearance of hostile aircraft troops will immediately halt and take cover.

7. Officers' kits, valises, blankets, company stores, etc., will be dumped outside the Guard Room by 1 p.m.

8. Trench Store Lists will be rendered to Battalion Headquarters by 9 a.m., 11th. May.

9. Completion of relief will be reported to Battalion Headquarters in "B.A.B." Code.

10. Battalion Headquarters will close in WESTON CAMP at 3 p.m. and reopen at CHINESE WALL at the same hour.

11. ACKNOWLEDGE.

                                        [signed]
                                        Lieut. & Adjutant,
                                        2nd. Battalion, The Royal Irish Regiment.

Hour of issue 6 p.m.

Copy No. 1. War Diary.   No. 9. Signalling Officer.
        2. H.Q., 49th. I. Bde.   10. Scout Officer.
        3. 6th. Bn., The R. I.   11. Lewis Gun Officer.
        4. Second-in-Command.   12. Medical Officer.
        5. O. C. "A" Coy.   13. Quartermaster.
        6. O. C. "B" ,,   14. Transport Officer.
        7. O. C. "C" ,,   15. Regtl. Sergt. Major.
        8. O. C. "D" ,,   16. Cook Sergeant.

Appendix 5

Secret.   Operation Order No. 27 Copy No. 1
by
Lieut Colonel H.G. Gregorie D.S.O., Commanding
2/ The Royal Irish Regt
Reference Map - Sheet 28 S.W. Edn 5A   13●7

1. The Battalion will be relieved in the right sub-section (VIERSTRAAT SECTION) by the 7th. Bn The Royal Inniskilling Fus. tomorrow the 14th. inst.

&. Relief to commence at 3 p.m.

2. On relief, the Battalion will move into Brigade Support, companies having the following dispositions:-

"A" Coy - H.Q. & 4 Platoons - SEIGE FARM

"B" " - HQ - DOCTOR'S HOUSE,
— 4 Platoons - LA POLKA.

"C" " - HQ - DOCTOR'S HOUSE,
1 Platoon - FORT HALIFAX
1 " - FORT MOUNT ROYAL
1 NCO & 6 men - FT. SASKATCHEWAN
Remainder of Coy - LA POLKA

"D" " - H.Q. - ROSSIGNOL FARM
— 2 Platoons - ROSSIGNOL FARM
— 2 " - SANDBAG VILLA.

3. Companies will send advance parties to take over trench stores etc. These parties will arrive at their respective positions by 1 p.m.

4. Officers Commanding Companies will make their own arrangements re

- 2 -

conveyance of kits etc.

5. Trench store lists will be rendered to the Orderly Room by gains on the 15th inst.

6. On completion of relief Battalion HQ. will move to ROSSIGNOL ESTAMINET

7. Completion of relief to be reported to Battalion HQ in the usual manner.

8. ACKNOWLEDGE

Rahvey
Lieut. & Adjutant
2/ The Royal Irish Regt

Issued at 6.45 pm.

Copies to :-

No. 1	War Diary	No. 6. O.C. C Coy
2.	O.C. 7/R. INNIS. FUS	7. " D "
3.	Second in Commd.	8. Q.M.
4.	O.C. A Coy	9. T.O.
5.	O.C. B "	10. HQ. MESS.

S E C R E T.   Appendix 7.   Copy No. 1.

49th Infantry Brigade Order No. 120 - 12-5-17.

1. The following reliefs will be carried out on the 14th May.

2. **RIGHT SUBSECTION.**

    7th R. Innis Fus. will relieve the 2nd R. Irish Regt. Relief to commence at 3 p.m.
    On relief the 2nd R. Irish Regt. will move into Brigade Support.

3. **LEFT SUBSECTION.**

    The 7/8th R. Irish Fus will relieve the 8th R. Innis Fus. Relief to commence at 9 p.m.
    On relief the 8th R. Innis Fus will move into Brigade Reserve (BUTTERFLY FARM).

4. All work, trench stores, etc, will be carefully handed over.
    Trench Store Lists will be sent to Brigade Headquarters by 6 p.m. 15th instant.

5. R.E. working parties on the 14th May will be found as under. Details of working parties have been sent to those concerned.

    Party No. B.4.   1st and 2nd reliefs by 7th R. Innis Fus. and 3rd relief by 2nd R. Irish Regt.

    Party No. B.5.   by 2nd R. Irish Regt.

    Party No. B.6.   by 2nd R. Irish Regt.

    Party No. B.8.   by 2nd R. Irish Regt.

    Party No. B.7.   by 7th R. Innis Fus.

    Party No. B.1.   by 7/8th R. Irish Fus.

    Party No. B.3.   by 8th R. Innis Fus.

6. Completion of reliefs to be reported in code to Brigade Headquarters.

7. ACKNOWLEDGE.

                                            Captain,
                            Brigade Major, 49th Inf. Brigade.

Issued through Signals.

Copy No. 1 to 2nd R. Irish Regt.   14 to 16th Div. Artillery.
    "   2   7th R. Innis Fus.   15   A.D.M.S. 16th Division.
    "   3   8th R. Innis Fus.   16   56th Inf. Bde.
    "   4   7/8th R. Irish Fus.   17   109th Inf. Bde.
    "   5   49th M.G. Company.   18   VIERSTRAAT GROUP.
    "   6   49th T.M. Battery.   19   144th Coy, A.S.C.
    "   7   G.O.C.   20   250th Tun. Coy, R.E.
    "   8   Staff Captain.   21   155th Field Coy, R.E.
    "   9   Bde Signal Officer.   22   157th Field Coy, R.E.
    "   10   Bde Transport Officer. 23-24 War Diary.
    "   11   Bde Supply Officer.   25   File.
    "   12   16th Div. (G)
    "   13   16th Div. (Q)

Appendix 8

SECRET.   OPERATION ORDER NO. 28   Copy No.
                                    by
        LIEUT. COLONEL H. F. GREGORIE, D. S. O., COMMANDING,
            2nd. BATTALION, THE ROYAL IRISH REGIMENT.

Reference Map   In the Field
Sheet 28 S.W. 1/20,000.   17-5-18.

1.   The Battalion will be relieved in Brigade Support by the
9th. Battalion, The Royal Dublin Fusiliers tomorrow, the 18th.
inst.
        Relief to commence at 4-30 p.m.

2.   On relief the Battalion will be accomodated in CLARE CAMP.

3.   Route.   Road Junction N.21.d.85.95. - skirt Kemmel Chateau
Cemetery and join KIM ROAD about N.21.a.80.30. - NUT ROAD -
M.24.d.25.95. - BRULOOZE - LOCRE - M.34.c.15.

4.   An interval of 200 yards will be maintained between platoons.

5.   Trench store lists will be sent to the Orderly Room by 9 a.m.
19th. inst.

6.   Completion of relief to be reported by wire in code to
Battalion Headquarters.

7.   ACKNOWLEDGE.

                                                    Lieut. & Adjutant,

                                    2nd. Battalion, The Royal Irish Regiment.

Hour of issue 3 p.m.

Copy No. 1. War Diary.   No. 9. Signalling Officer.
        2. H.Q., 49th. I.Bde.   10. Scout Officer.
        3. 9/R.Dublin Fus.   11. Medical Officer.
        4. Second-in-Command.   12. Quartermaster.
        5. O. C. "A" Company.   13. Transport Officer.
        6. O. C. "B"   ,,   14. Regtl. Sergt. Major.
        7. O. C. "C"   ,,   15. Cook Sergeant.
        8. O. C. "D"   ,,

SECRET.   Appendix 9   Copy No 1

49th Infantry Brigade Order No. 121 - 14-5-17.

1. The 49th Infantry Brigade will be relieved by the 48th Infantry Brigade in the VIERSTRAAT SECTION on the 18th May in accordance with the attached Relief Table.

2. On completion of relief the 49th Infantry Brigade will become Brigade in Divisional Reserve.

3. All work on hand, Trench Stores, etc, must be carefully handed over. Trench Store Lists will be sent to Brigade H.Q. by 6 p.m. 19th instant.

4. Working parties on the 18th May will be found as follows:-

    B.1 by the 8th R. Innis. Fus.
    B.3 by 48th Infantry Brigade.
    B.4 by 2nd R. Irish Regt. (all reliefs).
    B.5 by 48th Infantry Brigade.
    B.6 by 48th Infantry Brigade.
    B.7 by 2nd R. Irish Regt.
    B.8 by 48th Infantry Brigade.

5. The 100 Other Ranks of the 7/8th R. Irish Fus., attached to the 250th Tunnelling Coy. will be relieved by a similar party of 48th Infantry Brigade at 2 p.m. on 18th May. The 40 Other Ranks of the 2nd R. Irish Regt. and the 30 Other Ranks of the 8th R. Innis Fus. attached to the 175th Tunnelling Coy. will be relieved by a similar party of the 48th Infantry Brigade on 18th May.

6. Working parties for the first half of the period in Divisional Reserve will be provided by the 8th R. Innis Fus. and 7/8th R. Irish Fus. The 2nd R. Irish Regt. and 7th R. Innis Fus. will provide the working parties for the 2nd half period.

7. All movement East of a N. and S. line through LOCRE will be by platoons at 200 yards interval.

8. Further details of relief will be arranged between Commanding Officers concerned.

9. Completion of relief will be reported by wire in code to Brigade Headquarters.

10. Brigade Headquarters will close at FAIRY HOUSE on completion of relief and will move to MONT ROUGE, N.21.b.5.0.

11. ACKNOWLEDGE.

                                                    J W W Willan   Captain,
                                            Brigade Major, 49th Infantry Brigade.

Issued through Signals. at 8.50 PM
Copy No.				
1	2nd R. Irish Regt.	14	16th Div. (Q).
2	7th R. Innis Fus.	15	16th Div. Arty.
3	8th R. Innis Fus.	16	A.D.M.S. 16th Div.
4	7/8th R. Irish Fus.	17	48th Inf. Bde.
5	49th M.G. Company.	18	56th Inf. Bde.
6	49th T.M. Battery.	19	177th Bde., R.F.A.
7	G.O.C.	20	144th Coy, A.S.C.
8	Staff Captain.	21	Left Bde. 56th Div.
9	Bde Signal Officer.	22	155th Field Coy, R.E.
10	Bde Transport Off.	23	157th Field Coy, R.E.
11	Bde Supply Officer.	24	250th Tunnelling Coy, R.E.
12	Bde Bombing Officer.	25	175th Tunnelling Coy, R.E.
13	16th Div. (G)	26-27	War Diary.
		28	File.

SECRET.

RELIEF TABLE TO ACCOMPANY 49TH INFANTRY BRIGADE ORDER NO. 121.

Date.	Unit to be relieved.	From	To.	Unit relieving.	Guides and Route.	Remarks.
	RIGHT SUBSECTION					
18th May.	7th R.Innis Fus. Line.	BIRR BARRACKS.	8th R. Dublin Fus.	As arranged between C.O's concerned.	Relief to commence at 3 pm. KEMMEL VILLAGE to be avoided on march back.
	LEFT SUBSECTION					
18th May.	7/8th R.Irish Fus Line.	DONCASTER HUTS	7th R. Irish Rifles	do.	Relief to commence at 8.45 p.m.
18th May.	2nd R.Irish Regt. Bde. Support.	CLARE CAMP.	2nd R.Dublin Fus.	do.	Relief to commence at 4.30 p.m. KEMMEL VILLAGE to be avoided if possible.
18th May	8th R.Innis Fus. Line.	BUTTERFLY FARM	KEMMEL SHELTERS.	9th R.Dublin Fus.	do.	Relief to commence at 4.30 p.m.
18th May	49th M.G. Company. Line.	KILNDYKE FARM	48th M.G.Company.	do.	Relief to be completed by 12 noon.
18th May	49th T.M.Battery. Line.	DONCASTER HUTS	48th T.M.Battery.	do.	Relief to be completed by 12 noon.

Appendix 10

SECRET.   OPERATION ORDER NO. 29   Copy No. 1
by
LIEUT. COLONEL H. G. GREGORIE, D.S.O., COMMANDING,
2nd. BATTALION, THE ROYAL IRISH REGIMENT.

Reference Map   The Field.
Sheet 28 S.W. 1/20,000.   29-5-1917.

1. The Battalion will move to TRAJEE LINES "A" (M.23.b.3.1.) tomorrow, the 30th. inst.

2. Companies will march at 200 yards interval, in the following order, marching off at the times stated :-
   "A" Company   2 p.m.
   "B"   ,,   2-5 p.m.
   "C"   ,,   2-10 p.m.
   "D"   ,,   2-15 p.m.
   Headquarters   2-20 p.m.

3. ROUTE - "A" Route as far as M.22.d.90.45., thence via LOCRE - BRULOOZE Road.

4. Kits, blankets, etc., will be dumped opposite the Guard Tent by 12 noon.

5. ACKNOWLEDGE.

Lieut. & Adjutant,
2nd. Battalion, The Royal Irish Regiment.

Hour of issue 6-30 p.m.

Copy No. 1. War Diary.   No. 8. Signalling Officer.
        2. H.Q., 49th. I.Bde.   9. Scout Officer.
        3. Second-in-Command.   10. Medical Officer.
        4. O.C. "A" Company.   11. Quartermaster.
        5. O.C. "B"   ,,   12. Transport Officer.
        6. O.C. "C"   ,,   13. Regtl. Sergt. Major.
        7. O.C. "D"   ,,   14. Cook Sergeant.

49/16

WAR DIARY.

FOR MONTH OF JUNE, 1917.

VOLUME:-

UNIT:- 2nd Battn Royal Irish Regiment

Army Form C. 2118.

WAR DIARY or INTELLIGENCE SUMMARY

2nd Battalion The ROYAL IRISH REGT.

(Erase heading not required.)

Hour, Date, Place	Summary of Events and Information	Remarks and references to Appendices
June 1st	The battalion was in billets at LOCRE, preparatory to going into the line	Appendices 1, 2
2nd 2-5.6.	The battalion relieved the 9th Royal Dublin Fus: in the trenches — Preparations for the offensive on the 7th were being carried out as per attached programme. On the 3rd the artillery carried out their attack programme from 3 p.m. to 11 p.m. There was an OIL DRUM bombardment on WYTSCHAETE WOOD, UNNAMED WOOD, + GRAND BOIS. A prisoner of the 104th Regt stated that the Germans were expected to attack on the 3rd.	Appendices 3, 4
5.6.	On the 4th in the evening there was a bombardment with flame projectors, designed to set fire to the PETIT BOIS + WYTSCHAETE WOOD. We held a series of outpost posts to prevent the enemy from finding out that our troops were assembled for attack, and to keep his patrols far from our trenches. Our artillery again active from 3 p.m. to 11 p.m. The battalion was relieved at night during a gas shell bombardment by the enemy and moved into support to companies gone to BUTTERFLY FARM.	Appendix 5. Appendix 6. Appendix 7.
	Our casualties during the tour were 2/Lieut W.C.D. GIFFIN wounded in action 1 other rank killed in action 9 other ranks wounded	7.4.1.
6.6.	During the whole day we visited, bombarded the enemy trenches while we retaliated slight with some(?) battery well(?) in bombardment of back areas. At night the battalion moved up to its Assembly position (ci CHINESE WALL) at 2.40 p.m. This was Y/Z night (the night before the attack) —	Appendices 8, 9.

WAR DIARY
or
INTELLIGENCE SUMMARY

(Erase heading not required.)

Army Form C. 2118.

Hour, Date, Place	Summary of Events and Information	Remarks and references to Appendices
y.R.	On the morning of the 1st. at 3.10 a.m. an attack was launched against the WYTSCHAETE RIDGE. To this battalion was allotted the task of capturing the BLACK LINE the second objective to the first day attack. "D" Coys provided the first attacking waves "B" Coy was in support while "A" Coy provided the MOPPERS UP. The battalion left its assembly position along the CHINESE WALL at 5.40 a.m. and captured the BLACK LINE at 4.40 pm on the same day. There was no hitch and all objectives were taken in the time laid down — the men during the day was 'village' but luckily going to shower in the night before there was no dust. It is estimated that the battalion alone captured over 300 prisoners while its casualties were:— Capt. R.A. BELEMORE died of wounds. " J.L. COTTER wounded in action 2/Lieut D.J. KELLEHER " " 17 other ranks killed 130 " " wounded 2 " " missing 3 " " gassed 4 " " shell shock making a total of 3 Officers and 156 other ranks. One of the most pagaining things of the day was the explosion of our land mines, and which went up on our front. It is said by prisoners to have wiped out a whole regiment of Germans —	

WAR DIARY
or
INTELLIGENCE SUMMARY
(Erase heading not required.)

Army Form C. 2118.

Hour, Date, Place	Summary of Events and Information	Remarks and references to Appendices
7th Cont'd	for arrangements for the attack, and operation orders viz 9 other ranks joined the battalion.	Appendices 10, 11
8th	The battalion was relieved and moved into support along YORK ROAD.	
9th	The battalion moved to BIRR BARRACKS. Attached is a Special ORDER of the day issued by Maj Gen W.B. HICKIE CB etc (Commdg 16th (IRISH) DIVISION congratulating the men of the division on their heavy casualties.	Appendix 12.
13th	The 49th Inf. Bde. marches to the MERRIS area and then battalion was billeted just outside METEREN, a village in which they had been stationed in 1914.	Appendix 13, 14
13th - 22nd	The battalion began retraining for the next offensive.	
14th	The battalion marched to CLARE CAMP. It was intended after that the 16th Division should return to trench warfare and hold the line South of YPRES. Afterwards the authorities decided that we should be taken out of the line and reserved for the next offensive. 5 other ranks joined the battalion.	Appendix 15
20th	The 16th Division left the IXth Corps area and proceeded to join the Fifth Army in TILQUES South training area. The battalion was billeted at ST SYLVESTRE CAPPEL (near EECKE).	Appendix 16

Army Form C. 2118.

WAR DIARY
or
INTELLIGENCE SUMMARY
(Erase heading not required.)

Instructions regarding War Diaries and Intelligence Summaries are contained in F.S. Regs., Part II. and the Staff Manual respectively. Title pages will be prepared in manuscript.

Hour, Date, Place	Summary of Events and Information	Remarks and references to Appendices
22nd	The battalion marched to BROXEELE and was billeted there. The following officers joined the battalion. 2/Lieut W.N. Abbott 2/Lieut W. HALL " R.J. O'RIORDON Lieut A.S. PIKE " A.G. O'BRIEN	Appendices 17, 18
23rd - 30th	Battalion in training. Programme of work attached.	App.N. Appendix 19
24th 29th	6 others joined the battalion 5 " " "	App.N.
	The u/m were awarded Parchment Certificates by the Divisional Commander. Capt. The Rev. W.R. FITZMAURICE M.C. Lieut G.H PALKER 2/Lieut J.H.W. TROUGHTON " J.H.L. WATSON " C. HUGHES 25 other ranks	App.N.
30th	The 49th Inf. Bde marched to the TATINGHEM area - The battalion was billeted at TATINGHEM.	Appendices 20, 21

2/7/17

Hude Major
Commanding 2/7th Royal Irish

Appendix XI

G.O.C. 49th Infy Bde.

Please convey to the Officer Cmdg. 2: Royal Irish Regt. my appreciation at the turn out and soldierly appearance of the Guard furnished by his Battalion on the occasion of the C. in C's visit to my Head quarters.

I was exceedingly proud of it -

and I would like my
thanks conveyed to the
N.C.O's and men of the
Guard.

W.B. Hickie; Maj. Gen.
Cmdg. 16° Division.

May 26ᵗʰ 1917

SECRET.

OPERATION ORDER NO. 3

by
CAPTAIN J. D. SCOTT, COMMANDING,
"A" BATTALION, THE ROYAL IRISH REGIMENT.

Copy No. _____

Reference Map
Sheets 27 & 28, 1/40,000.   Appendix 15   The Field.
                                                         16-6-1917.

1. The 49th. Infantry Brigade will march to CLARE CAMP on the 17th. June.
2. Dress - Marching Order. Steel Helmets will be worn.
3. Starting Point - Cross Roads A.15.d.6.8.
4. Route - SCHAEXKEN - CROIX DE POPERINGHE.
5. Order of march - "C", "D", Tums, H.Q., "A", "B".
6. "C" Coy. will pass the Starting Point at 7-8 a.m.
   A billeting party consisting of the 4 Coy. Q. M. Sergts. and Cr. Sgt. Harrison, with bicycle, will report to 2/Lieut. Newsam at "B" Coy's. H.Q. at 6-20 a.m. This party will report to the Staff Captain on CLARE ROAD at M.33.d.65.95. at 7-30 a.m.
7. Intervals of 500 yards will be left between Battalions and 50 yards between Companies.
8. Officers' kits, etc., will be dumped outside the Guard Room by 6 a.m.
9. All transport will be formed up, ready to move off, on the road outside "B" Coy's. H.Q. at 6-45 a.m.
10. Nobody may ride on the lorry except those authorised by the Medical Officer and one man detailed by the Quartermaster.
    1 Lewis Gun limber will load at "D" and "A" Companys' H.Q., commencing at "D" Coy's. H.Q. at 5-45 a.m.
    1 Lewis Gun limber will load at "C" and "B" Companys' H.Q., commencing at "C" Coy's. H.Q. at 5-45 a.m.
11. Great care must be taken to leave billets and their surroundings as clean as possible.
12. Baggage wagons will accompany units.
13. ACKNOWLEDGE.

Lieut. & Adjutant,
"A" Battalion, The Royal Irish Regiment.

Hour of issue 8-30 a.m.

Copy No. 1. War Diary.   No. 7. Signalling Officer.
        2. H.Q., 49th. I. Bde.   8. Intelligence Officer.
        3. O. C. "A" Coy.   9. Medical Officer.
        4. O. C. "B" "   10. Quartermaster.
        5. O. C. "C" "   11. Transport Officer.
        6. O. C. "D" "   12. Regtl. Sergt. Major.
                        No. 13. Cook Sergeant.

SECRET
OPERATION ORDER NO. 3
by
CAPTAIN J. D. SCOTT, COMMANDING,
2nd. BATTALION, THE ROYAL IRISH REGIMENT.

Copy No.

Reference Map.
Sheet 27, 1/40,000.   Appendix 16   The Field.

1. The 16th. Division is to leave the IXth. Corps Area to join the Fifth Army in TILQUES SOUTH Training Area.
2. The above move will be carried out in three stages as follows:-
   20th. June to ECCKE Area.
   21st. June to RENESCURE Area.
   22nd. June to TILQUES SOUTH Training Area.
3. Starting Point - Cross Roads, X.13.b.6.1.
4. Route - COURTE CROIX - ROUGE CROIX - CAESTRE.
5. Order of March - H.Q., Drums, "A", "B", "C", "D".
6. Headquarters will pass the Starting Point at 7-5 a.m.
7. Transport will be formed up on road with head outside Battalion Headquarters at 6-50 a.m.
   Company Cook Carts will rejoin Transport Lines at 6-15 a.m.
8. A billeting party, with bicycles, consisting of the 4 Coy. Q. M. Sergts. and Cr. Sgt. Harrison, will report to 2/Lieut. Newsam at Battalion Headquarters at 5-15 a.m.
   This party will report to the Staff Captain at the Church, EECKE, at 6-15 a.m.
9. Officers' valises, etc., will be dumped at the Quartermaster's Stores at 5-45 a.m.
10. The Brigade will march with intervals of 500 yards between Battalions and 50 yards between Companies.
11. Supply Railhead for 20th. June - , BAILLEUL.
    Supply Railhead for 21st. June - EBBLINGHEM.
.   ACKNOWLEDGE.

                                        Lieut. & Adjutant,
                                2nd. Battalion, The Royal Irish Regiment.

Hour of issue 9 p.m.

Copy No. 1. War Diary.   No. 6. O. C. "C" Coy.
     2. H.Q., 49th. I. Bde.   7. O. C. "D" ,,
     3. Headquarters.   8. Quartermaster.
     4. O. C. "A" Coy.   9. Transport Officer.
     5. O. C. "B" ,,   10. Regtl. Sergt. Major.
            No. 11. Cook Sergeant.

SECRET.   OPERATION ORDER NO. 36   Copy No.
                              by
                 CAPTAIN J. D. SCOTT, COMMANDING,
                 2nd. BATTALION, THE ROYAL IRISH REGIMENT.

Reference Map   Appendix 17   The Field
Sheet 27, 1/40,000.   21- -1917.

1. The 49th. Infantry Brigade will march to the BROXEELE Area on 22nd. June.
2. Intervals of 10 yards will be maintained between Companies.
3. Starting Point - Cross Roads P.30.a.1.4.
4. Order of March - Drums, "A", "B", "C", "D", H.Q.
5. The head of the Drums will pass the Starting Point at 5 a.m.
6. Route.- ST. SYLVESTRE-CAPPEL - Road Junction P.14.a.5.5. - Road Junction P.13.b.5.0. - Cross Roads P.12.d.4.9. - OXELAERE - BAVINCHOVE - ZUYTPEENE.
7. A Billeting Party, with bicycles, consisting of the 4 Coy. Q.M. Sergts. and Cr. Sgt. Harrison, will report to 2/Lieut. Newsam at the Starting Point at 4-30 a.m.
   This party will meet the Staff Captain at NOORDPEENE Church at 6 a.m.
8. The Army Commander will inspect the Brigade as it marches through ZUYTPEENE.
9. Officers' valises of H.Q., "B" and "D" Companies will be dumped at the Transport Lines at 4 a.m.
   The Quartermaster will send a G.S.Wagon to collect Officers' valises of "A" and "C" Companies at 4 a.m. at the respective Coy. H.Qrs.
   Men's packs will be dumped at Coy. H.Qrs. by 5 a.m.
   Dress for March - Fighting Order.
10. Transport. The Transport will be formed up in the Transport Field by 4-45 a.m.
    Company Cookers will report at the Transport Lines at 4-30 a.m.
11. All covers on vehicles must be neatly tied down.
12. Baggage wagons will accompany units.
13. Supply Railhead from 22nd. June inclusive will be ARNEKE.
14. ACKNOWLEDGE.

                                          Lieut. & Adjutant,
                              2nd. Battalion, The Royal Irish Regiment.

Hour of issue 4-30 p.m.

Copy No. 1. War Diary.   No. 6. O. C. "C" Coy.
         2. H.Q., 49th. I. Bde.   7. O. C. "D" ,,
         3. Headquarters.   8. Quartermaster.
         4. O. C. "A" Coy.   9. Transport Officer.
         5. O. C. "B" ,,   10. Regtl. Sergt. Major.
                    No. 11. Cook Sergeant.

16 E.
(Extracts)

WAR DIARY.

FOR MONTH OF JULY, 1917.

VOLUME :-

UNIT :- 2nd Btn Royal Irish Regt.

Army Form C. 2118.

WAR DIARY
or
INTELLIGENCE SUMMARY

2nd Batt. The Royal Irish Reg.

(Erase heading not required.)

Instructions regarding War Diaries and Intelligence Summaries are contained in F. S. Regs., Part II. and the Staff Manual respectively. Title pages will be prepared in manuscript.

Hour, Date, Place	Summary of Events and Information	Remarks and references to Appendices
TATINGHEM Area. (1st July — 7th July 1917)	Battalion & Brigade Training for future operations. Lieut-General H.E. WATTS, C.B., C.M.G., Commander XIX Corps was present at the Brigade Training on the 7th July 1917 and addressed concluding remarks to the troops	See Appendices I — V
ROUBROUCK Area. 8th July 1917	March to ROUBROUCK Area	See Appendix VI
WINNIZEELE Area. 9th July 1917	March to WINNIZEELE Area	See Appendix VII
WINNIZEELE Area. 11th July 1917	Battalion & Brigade training for future operations.	See Appendices VIII & IX
19th July 1917.	Brigade Sports	See Appendices X, XI & XII
20th July 1917	Brigade Inspection by Major-General W.B. HICKIE and distribution of Honours & Awards to recipients mentioned	

Army Form C. 2118.

WAR DIARY
or
INTELLIGENCE SUMMARY

(Erase heading not required.)

2nd Batt The Royal Irish Regt.

Hour, Date, Place	Summary of Events and Information	Remarks and references to Appendices
WINNIZEELE Area. 20th July 1917.	Decorations awarded for Operations of 7th June 1917. Lieut Colonel H.G. GREGORIE. D.S.O. — Legion d'Honneur (Officier) CAPT. J.L. COTTER CAPT. R.R.G. McGRATH — Military Cross CAPT W.B. LOVELESS. R.A.M.C. att 2nd The Royal Irish No. 6112 C.S.M. HAYES P. — D.C.M. No. 10866 Sergt NOTHER, W. " 9545 " HANRAHAM, M. " 8303 " BERGIN, J. " 16101 L/Cpl THOMASON, P. " 2566 " BANKS, F. " 9729 Pte CONWAY, J. " 1559 CM WYATT, W. R.A.M.C. — Military Medal No. 9283 Cpl O'BRIEN, J. — Medaille Militaire.	See Appendix IX XIII
WATOU Area No 2. 26th July 1917.	March to WATOU Area No 2.	9
27th July 1917.	Waking parties totalling 13 Officers & 300 O.R. proceeded to work in YPRES forward Area.	9

Army Form C. 2118.

WAR DIARY
or
INTELLIGENCE SUMMARY

2nd Battn. The Royal Irish Regt

(Erase heading not required.)

Hour, Date, Place	Summary of Events and Information	Remarks and references to Appendices
BRANDHOEK Area. Night 30/31st July 1917.	March to BRANDHOEK Area. Return of Working Parties. Casualties and Re-inforcements to the month, as detailed in	See Appendix XIV. Appendix XV.

M. J. Ryan
Lieut – Colonel
Commanding 2nd Battn. The Royal Irish Regt

SECRET. OPERATION ORDER NO. 41, Copy No. _____
by
LIEUT.COLONEL H. G. GREGORIE, D.S.O., COMMANDING,
2nd. BATTALION, THE ROYAL IRISH REGIMENT.

Reference Maps   The Field.
Sheet 27, 1/40,000.   30-7-1917.
Sheet 28 N.W., 1/20,000.

1. The 49th. Infantry Brigade *(Group)* will move to the BRANDHOEK
   No. 1 Area tonight, the 30th. July.
   The Battalion will move to DERBY CAMP (H.1.a.8.0.)
   Dress - Marching Order.

2. Battalion Starting Point - L.8.d.8.8.
   Brigade Starting Point   - L.9.c.1.0.

3. Order of March - "B", "D", H.Q.
   "B" Company will be at the Battalion Starting Point at 10-30 p.m.

4. East of L.6.c.5.0. a distance of 200 yards will be maintained
   between Companies.

5. Route - L.11.b.8.8. - L.6.c.9.4. - GRAND PLACE, POPERINGHE -
   Main YPRES ROAD.

6. The Transport Lines are at G.4.c.1.8.

7. Lieut. Tod will precede the Battalion, mounted, to warn the
   traffic control.

8. The head and tail of the Battalion will be marked by a lamp.
   One lamp will be issued to O. C. "B" Company and one to the
   Transport Officer.

9. Officers' kits will be dumped at the Quartermaster's Stores by
   8 p.m. tonight.

10. Battalion Headquarters will close at L.7.d.7.5. at 10 p.m. and
    will open at DERBY CAMP on arrival.

11. "A" and "C" Companies will move to the new camp under orders
    already issued to O. C. Detachment.

                                        Lieut. & Adjutant,
                                   2nd. Battalion, The Royal Irish Regiment.

Hour of issue 6 p.m.

Copy No. 1. War Diary.   No. 7. Intelligence Officer.
        2. H.Q., 49th. I.Bde.   8. Lieut. Tod.
        3. Senior Major.   9. Quartermaster.
        4. O.C.Detachment,   10. Transport.
           ("A" and "C" Companies.)   11. Regtl. Sergt. Major.
        5. O. C. "B" Company.
        6. O. C. "D"   ,,

Army Form B. 2069.
(In pads of 50).

Offence Report *(Field Service only)*.

Corps_____

Squadron, Troop, Batty. or Company	Regt. No.	Rank	Name	Place and Date of offence	Offence	By whom reported and Names of Witnesses	Initials of Officer Comdg. Company, &c.	Punishment awarded	Signature of Officer by whom ordered and date of award	Date of entry in Conduct Sheet	Remarks

—A horizontal line should be drawn the whole length of the Return after each day's offences are entered.

49/16

War Diary
of
2nd R. Irish Regt.
for
August 1917

17.C.
(111 sheets)

WAR DIARY.

FOR MONTH OF AUGUST, 1917.

VOLUME.........

UNIT 2nd Royal Irish Regiment

Army Form C. 2118.

WAR DIARY
or
INTELLIGENCE SUMMARY

(Erase heading not required.)

2nd. R. Irish Regt.

Hour, Date, Place	Summary of Events and Information	Remarks and references to Appendices
1st DERBY CAMP (near VLAMERTINGHE)	Battalion in tents at DERBY CAMP. Pouring with rain. Received an order at 3pm to move up to a field in the vicinity of H.16.a.5.5. Battn place of 4.8.2.Bn. who had moved up to Buffert 1st Bn. moved at 10pm. head. Remainder	Appendix 1
2nd H.6.a.5.5.	Returned to DERBY CAMP at 2 noon '16' Echelon moved to T'Hart-Lines.	19
3rd CAMBRIDGE R?	From 16th Bn. relieved 16.15th Div. in the right sector of XIX Corps front. Bn. moved to CAMBRIDGE ROAD (at Pinted Dufford line). Torrential rain. Casualties going up. '13' Echelon moved to BRANDHOEK	Appendices 2, 3, 4, 5
4th "	Torrential rain continued. About 20 Casualties. Many cases of trench feet	19
5th "		19
6th PLUG LINE	Heavy enemy shelling - brightest day 12 O.R. wounded in action. Relieved R. 6" CONNAUGHT RANGERS in support. A Coys. in BLUG LINE. H.Q. in 2/6 German Supports. Capt GORDON RALPH assumed from Leave. Had to advance through a heavy barrage. Enemy barrage mostly on POTIJZE ROAD. Casualties mostly on way up. Heavy enemy shelling - own 16, 5", 4, 4.5. How. (Capt GORDON-RALPH KILLED 2/Lt T.W. MARK WOUNDED 2/Lt C. HUGHES	Appendix 6
7th BLUE LINE	Intense enemy shelling. C.S.M. Power was wounded on July 4/16. Enemy aeroplane & artillery very active. Running aerial attacks to c c (Bay like) 1/4 Battn casualties (3 killed). Retime enemy gas shell bombarded Bn. Battn position began at 10pm. used gases like about 3am.	19
8th BLUE LINE & RAMPARTS	Relieved at 4am by 7/8 ROYAL IRISH FUSILIERS moved to Bivouacs in VLAMERTINGHE (H.K.a.5.5). 70 Battle casualties from 3-7 and about 50 sick (with trench feet).	Appendices 7, 8
9th H.6.5.5.	Inspection for slight wounds of the day. Capt. LORD O. A. V. BERUCLERK and 2/Lt T. L. PILKINGTON joined Battn.	19
10th "	Poured with rain. Relieved Lieut. Colon. d 7/8 R.I.G. in CAMBRIDGE ROAD. Lieut. Colonel G. G. O. RIS went away invalided to England and Major J. D. SCOTT assumed command of the Battalion.	Appendix 9

WAR DIARY
or
INTELLIGENCE SUMMARY

(Erase heading not required.)

Army Form C. 2118.

Instructions regarding War Diaries and Intelligence Summaries are contained in F. S. Regs., Part II. and the Staff Manual respectively. Title pages will be prepared in manuscript.

Hour, Date, Place	Summary of Events and Information	Remarks and references to Appendices
11th H.16, a.5.5.	Battalion relieved 7th ROYAL INNISKILLING FUSILIERS in Support line (BLUE). 11 other ranks wounded in action. Tour quiet going in.	M9
12th BLUE LINE	Enemy aircraft very active over our lines. To-day and for the 3 subsequent days it was a common sight to see our Battalion of 20-25 German aeroplanes flying over our lines and, in many cases, firing M.G. into our trenches. 20 other ranks wounded in action.	M9
13th "	Enemy shelling very severe 2/Lt M.J. HIGGINS wounded. Have getting a very bad time.	M9
14th "	X day. Relieved at night by the 9th and 8th ROYAL INNISKILLING FUSILIERS. - 7th relieves 2 left coys, 8th the two right companies (2+D) in relief turnes to old German and British front lines. A, B (to German), B+D in the British.	Appendix 10
15th German and British F.L.	Y day. 2/Lt BRADY (now S.) and SHIELS (Cook Rank) killed. Full arrangements for attack complete. Battalion moved to assembly positions in Assembly line about commenced at midnight	Appendix 11
16th BLUE LINE	Z day. The attack on the DOTTED RED LINE was made by 16.15-16 Division in conjunction with Brigades on either flank. Zero hour was 4.45am. The Brigade attacked on a 1000 yds frontage with two assaulting Battalions being the 7th INNISKILLING FUSILIERS on the right & the 8th R/Innis Fus on the left. The 1/8 R.I.F was in support, to 2/R.I.F. were in Bde Reserve. At zero hour, three Coys (A,C,D) moved into the front line vacated by the assaulting Battalion. B Coy remained in support in BLUE LINE. The right of Battalion was held by B Coy FDN1+B opposite BLACK House. The left centrally Battalion got in touch forward to BELVA FARM & about gave the German counterattacks The division on our left (The 36th Leat. Bn.) who had lost about so far as GALLIPOLI. The Right Bn of Bde to left (36th Bn) were seen to retire in disorder. This retirement and the fact that knight Battalion were held up at BORRY FARM, caused the Right flank & Brigade to be at this [...]	

WAR DIARY or INTELLIGENCE SUMMARY

Army Form C. 2118.

(Erase heading not required.)

Hour, Date, Place	Summary of Events and Information	Remarks and references to Appendices
16" BLACK LINE	Situation. 'B' Coy were ordered up to the BLACK LINE. The BLACK Line was now held by the 2 R.I. with several parties of 7th Munsters and 7/c R.I.F. 'B' Coy were on the night infiltrating LOW FARM + FROST HO'S in contact and 'A' on the left. 'C' Coy sent a pat of 2 platoons to BEEK HOUSE at 2am about 1am. The greater part of their 2 platoon were either killed or wounded, the remainder owing to the obscurity of the situation and having lost an offr, & were a Captain of the IRISH FUSILIERS, relates to BLACK LINE and attached themselves to 'B' Coy on the right. The shell fire throughout the day was terrific. The 2nd R. Ir. Rgt. held on to the BLACK LINE in front of B...[illegible]...in spite of terrific shell, rifle and M.G. fire at / from the huts & Commander ordered a counter attack to be made in order to help the DUBLINS whose left flank was in the air.— The Germans were holding BREMEN REDOUBT and the Left flank of the DUBLINS were about S26.a.5.7 — just WEST of BREMEN REDOUBT. This order was cancelled at about 3hrs. 11ght. The observer, independent of such sources 9.15 midnight the whole of the Brigade front was taken over by K'6" CONNAUGHT RANGERS and the Bn were back to the old Bn HQrs German front line to known up to the Main "glorious failure" may be attributed mainly to the following causes.—
(1) [illegible]... strong posts [illegible] palisade
(2) want of [illegible] fire all night
the fate for the 2am start
(3) Lack of sufficient [illegible]
Lack of all communications, runners & pigeons	

Army Form C. 2118.

WAR DIARY or INTELLIGENCE SUMMARY

(Erase heading not required.)

Instructions regarding War Diaries and Intelligence Summaries are contained in F.S. Regs., Part II. and the Staff Manual respectively. Title pages will be prepared in manuscript.

Hour, Date, Place	Summary of Events and Information	Remarks and references to Appendices
16 BLACK LINE	A more detailed account of operations on 16th will be allotted and called Appendix 20. The following o/rs in Casualties were sustained on 16th. CAPTAIN. W.B. LOVELESS R.A.M.C att L/LIEUT. P.L. BLAKE L/LIEUT. J.H.W. TROUGHTON " T.L. PILKINGTON. " A.G. O'BRIEN. " A.M.R. HOBBS 110 O.R. Casualties.	Appendices 12,13,14, 15,16,17, 18, 19, 20.
17th GOLDFISH CHAT.	Marched to camp in the vicinity of GOLDFISH CHA.	Appendix 21
18th "	Entrained at VLAMERTINGHE and proceeded in buses via POPERINGHE and ABEELE to WATOU & Area. Coy H.Qrs at MAJOR L.L. FARMER reported from XIX Corps R/joined Camp 2(b) A.B. ELLIOTT (CR) reinforcement. 9.9.17.	
19th WATOU.		Appendix
20th —	Marched to 22 CKE area. 104 O.R. reinforcement.	
21st CCKE.	Marched to BAVINCHOVE and entrained there at 12 midnight noon. Went via HAZEBROUCK, ST POL and ARRAS, detrained at MIRAUMONT and marched to HENMON CAMP, just beside ACHIET-LE-PETIT.	App. 22, 23
22nd - ACHIET-LE-PETIT	Reorganisation. Major F.C. BOWEN D.S.O. joined B.N. 23.9.17. Lt. W.J. ROCHE " " " 24.9.17/any.n.r.	
28 - 31 HAMELINCOURT	Reorganising Battalion and preparing for trench warfare near	

Forms/C. 2118/11.

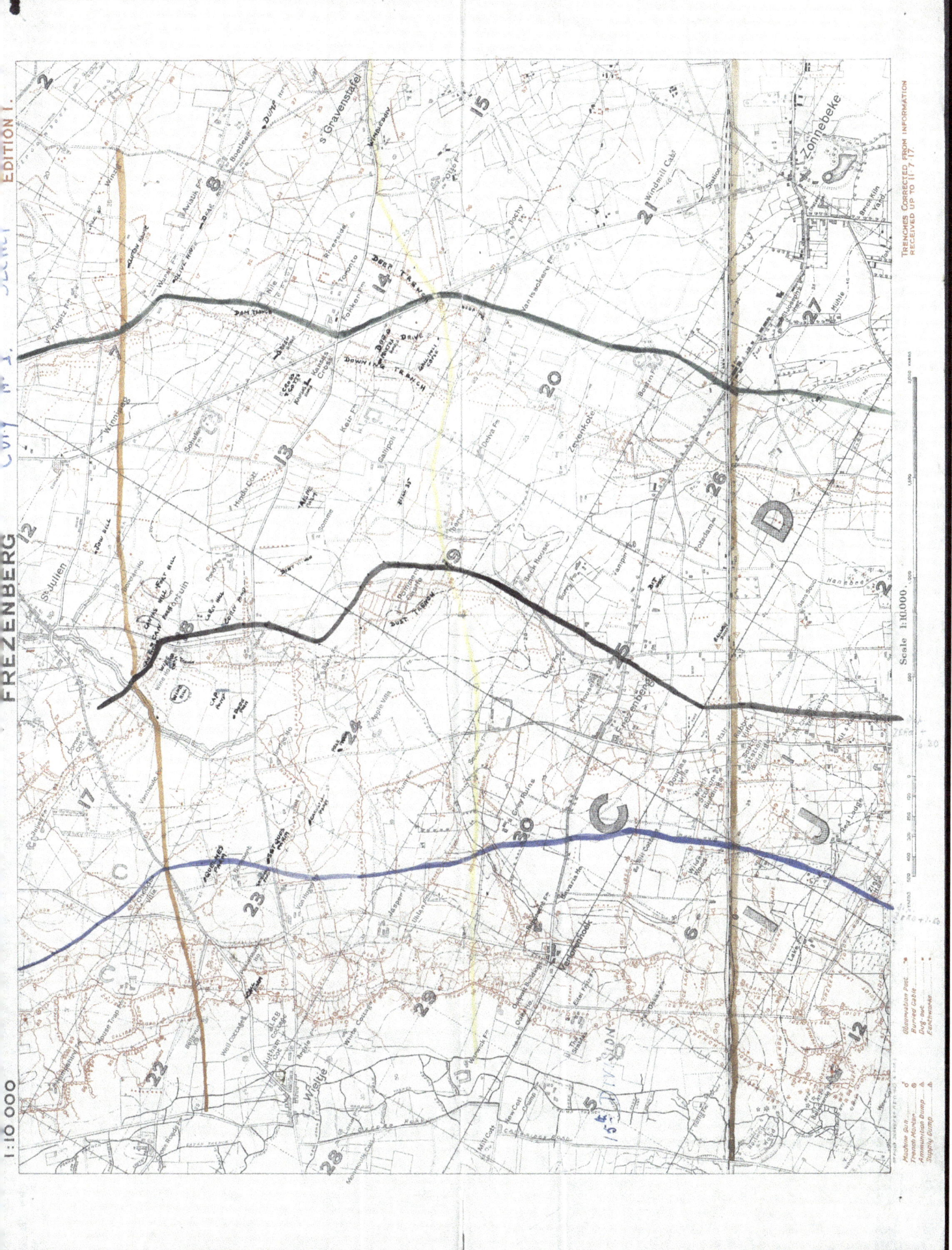

SECRET.   OPERATION ORDER NO. 42   Copy No. 1
                              by
              MAJOR J. D. SCOTT, COMMANDING,
           2nd. BATTALION, THE ROYAL IRISH REGIMENT.
The Field.   15-8-1917.

1. **GENERAL PLAN.**   The 16th. DIVISION, in conjunction with Divisions on either flank, will attack the enemy's positions on 16th. August, 1917.
   The attack will be made in two bounds, each bound is shewn by Coloured Lines on map A.
   First bound   GREEN LINE.
   Second bound   DOTTED RED LINE.

2. **OBJECTIVES OF BRIGADES.**   The 48th. Inf. Bde. (plus 1 Battn.) on the Right, and the 49th. Inf. Bde. (plus 1 Battn.) on the Left will attack up to and including the RED DOTTED LINE. The 47th. Inf. Bde., less 3 Battns. and Machine Gun Company, will be in Divisional Reserve. The Left Battn. of the 48th. Inf. Bde. will be 9th. R. Dublin Fus. The Right Battn. of the 108th. Inf. Bde. will be the 9th. R. Irish Fus.

3. **BOUNDARIES.**   The Boundaries between the 49th. Inf. Bde. and the Brigade on either flank are as follows
   Boundary with 48th. Inf. Bde.
   D.25.a.75.05. - where DOTTED RED LINE crosses the ZONNEBEKE STREAM.
   Boundary with 108th. Inf. Bde.
   D.19.c.7.8. - D.19.b.70.50. - D.14.d.20.40.
   These Boundaries are shewn in BLUE on map A.

4. **TASKS OF BATTALIONS.**   The attack on the GREEN and DOTTED RED LINE will be made by the 7th. R. Innis Fus. on the Left and the 8th. R. Innis. Fus. on the Right. The dividing line between these two Battalions will be -
   D.25.a.80.90. - D.20.b.80.99.
   This boundary is shewn in BLACK on map A.
   There will be a pause of 20 minutes on the GREEN LINE.
   As soon as the RED DOTTED LINE has been captured a line of posts will be pushed out as far as the barrage permits.
   The 7/8th. R. Irish Fus. will support the attack and will find Moppers-Up and Carrying Parties as detailed below.
   (a) One Platoon to Mop-Up BORRY FARM and hold it as a supporting point.
   Two Platoons to Mop-Up ZEVENCOTE and hold it as a supporting point.
   One Platoon to Mop-Up COFFEY FARM, D.20.c.15.15. and then to join the two platoons at ZEVENCOTE.
   The above four Platoons will advance in rear of the first wave of the 8th. R. Innis. Fus.

O.O. No. 42, page 2, after line 13 insert :-

"(d) One Coy. will capture BECK HOUSE and the ground as far East as the Stream, reform and move to IBERIAN in support."

2.

(b) One Platoon to Mop-Up DELVA FARM, and will join the Platoon at IBERIAN when the Hqrs. 7th. R. Innis. Fus. moves to DELVA FARM.

One Platoon to form a supporting point about D.19.d.80.80.

The above two Platoons will advance in rear of the 1st. wave of 7th. R. Innis. Fus. (Right Half Battn.)

(c) One Platoon to Mop-Up IBERIAN and the dug-outs in the vicinity and form a supporting point there.

One Platoon to Mop-Up and hold as a supporting point the clump of trees at D.19.d.70.35.

The above two Platoons to advance in rear of the 1st. wave of the 7th. R. Innis. Fus. (Left Hlaf Battn.)

(d) One Coy. will provide Carrying Parties.

Two Platoons will carry to the 8th. R. Innis. Fus. at COENT FARM; after completing their task they will join the Coy. at ZEVENCOTE.

Two Platoons will carry to 7th. R. Innis. Fus. at DELVA FARM, and will join the two Coys. at IBERIAN on completion of task.

The Battalion will be in Brigade Reserve. At Zero Hour "A" Company, "C" Company (less two Platoons) and "D" Company will advance from their assembly positions and occupy the trenches vacated by the assaulting Battalions from D.25.a.80.05. to D.19.c.60.70.

"D" Company will be on the right from D.25.a.80.05. to D.25.a.80.80.

"C" Company (less two Platoons) in centre from D.25.a.80.80. to D.19.c.60.10.

"A" Company on left from D.19.c.60.10. to D.19.c.60.70.

O.C. "C" Company will detail two Platoons to form a post at BUCK HOUSE immediately it has been taken.

"B" Company will remain in its assembly position.

Battalion Headquarters will move to SQUARE FARM as soon as Hqrs. 7th. R. Innis. Fus. leaves for DELVA FARM.

The 6th. R. Irish Regt. will be in Brigade Reserve in the VLAMERTINGHE Area, and must be prepared to relieve the Assaulting Battalions on the RED DOTTED LINE if required.

5. MOPPING-UP. The 7th. R. Innis. Fus. and 8th. R. Innis. Fus. are responsible for mopping-up all ground in their areas in front of DELVA FARM and ZEVENCOTE. The 7/8th. R. Irish Fus. are responsible for mopping-up in rear of DELVA FARM and ZEVENCOTE (inclusive).

6. CONSOLIDATION. The RED DOTTED LINE, and all supporting points held by the 7/8th. R. Irish Fus. will be consolidated as rapidly as possible after capture.

The R.E. will work under the direction of C.R.E., 16th. Division and will erect wire on the GHELUVELT - LANGEMARCK LINE when captured. They will also prepare certain positions for defence in vicinity of DELVA FARM and IBERIAN.

7. ACTION OF MACHINE GUNS. The Machine Guns will be under the direction of the Div. Machine Gun Officer.

40 guns will form the Machine Gun barrage. After the capture of the final objective they will arrange an S.O.S. barrage to cover the front.

2 guns will move in rear of the attacking Infantry to a position in vicinity of DELVA FARM and two guns will move to a position near HILL 37 (D.20.a.). In case of necessity Battalion Commanders can divert them to other positions for purposes of defence.

8. ACTION OF STOKES MORTARS. Two Stokes Mortars will be attached to each Assaulting Battalion. They will move in rear of the last wave, and will assist the infantry to overcome opposition as required. The remaining four Mortars will be left at Brigade Headquarters.

9. ACTION OF ARTILLERY. The Divisional Artillery will form a creeping barrage covering the advance of the infantry. At zero hour the barrage will be put down as shown on barrage map: BECK HOUSE will be specially dealt with. The first lift will take place at zero plus 5 minutes and it will then proceed forward at the rate of 100 yards in five minutes.

During the 20 minutes pause on the GREEN LINE a protective barrage will be maintained 200 yards in advance of the infantry.

After the capture of the DOTTED RED LINE a standing barrage will be established 300 yards in advance of it for a period of 1 hour, after which it will cease unless recalled by the S.O.S. signal.

10. ACTION OF TANKS. One section of Tanks from "C" Battalion, TANK CORPS, has been allotted to the 16th. Division. These Tanks will not be available unless the weather conditions improve. In any case they are only likely to arrive behind the Infantry in time to act as "Moppers-Up" in cases where isolated positions continue to hold out.

11. COMMUNICATIONS. Brigade Headquarters will remain at MILL COT.

The Bde. Forward Station will advance behind the last wave of the leading Assaulting Battalions, and will be established in the vicinity of IBERIAN.

Battalion Forward Posts will be established as follows :-
7th. R. Innis Fus.   DELVA FARM.
8th. R. Innis Fus.   COFFEE FARM. (D.20.c.2,2.)
7/8th. R. Irish Fus.   IBERIAN.

Battalion Headquarters will not move forward to these positions until communication has been established with them. The attached chart shows the various means of communication except pigeons and runners. As many pairs of pigeons as available will be issued to Brigade Forward Station and Battalions.

Runner Relay Posts will be established at :-
(a) IBERIAN.
(b) SQUARE FARM.
(c) BAVARIA HOUSE.
(d) Brigade Headquarters.

Runners should not be used unless all other methods of communication fail.

The Brigade Forward Station of 48th. Inf. Bde. will be at VAMPIR.

The Brigade Forward Station of 108th. Inf. Bde. will be at SOMME. (D.13.c.4.4.) and later at GALLIPOLI (D.13.d.4.1.).

The Brigade VISUAL STATION and O.P. will be at C.29.d.8.7.

DOGS. Two Message Dogs have been allotted to the Division. All ranks should be warned that dogs carrying message pouches on their collars are not to be detained except for the purpose of having message read by an officer. Messages sent by this means should be in code.

12. CONTACT AEROPLANES. 1 Contact Aeroplane, marked with a BLACK plaque projecting behind the right lower wing and one protective aeroplane will be in the air over the 16th. and 36th. Division Areas from zero hour onwards. Flares will be lit and Watson fans will be waved by the leading troops -

(a) When called upon to do so by means of the contact aeroplane by means of Klaxton horns and very lights. This call will, if the attack proceeds as arranged, only be made at times when the infantry are believed to have reached the GREEN LINE and the DOTTED RED LINE.

(b) When the infantry consider it advisable, to make known the position of their front line.

Red flares will be used.

Flares should not be lit unless the sounding of the Klaxton horn is accompanied by very lights.

13. SYNCHRONIZATION. The Battalion Signalling Officer will arrange to synchronise with Brigade Headquarters at 6 p.m. Y day. He will then send the correct time to all Companies.

14. S.O.S. SIGNAL. The S.O.S. will be GREEN SIGNAL CARTRIDGES.

15. PRISONERS. All prisoners will be sent to BECK HOUSE where they will be collected under the orders of the Officer Commanding the two Platoons of 'C' Company there. He will send them down to the prisoners cage at Brigade Headquarters in batches of thirty under an N.C.O. and 3 men. The Regimental Provost Sergeant and Regimental Police will move up to BECK HOUSE with the C.O.Post for escort duty.

5.

16. **MEDICAL ARRANGEMENTS.** The Regimental Aid Post will be at
BAVARIA HOUSE until Battalion Headquarters moves forward,
when it will be established at SQUARE FARM.
    All cases will be brought to BAVARIA
HOUSE or SQUARE FARM whence they will be evacuated by R.A.M.C.
stretcher bearers to POTIJZE CHATEAU.

17. **ZERO HOUR.** Zero Hour will be notified later.

18. **ACKNOWLEDGE.**

[signature] Lieut. & Adjutant,

2nd. Battalion, The Royal Irish Regiment.

Hour of issue 3 p.m.

Copies No. 1. War Diary.
2. Senior Major.
3. O. C. "A" Company.
4. O. C. "B" Company.
5. O. C. "C" Company.
6. O. C. "D" Company.
7. Signalling Officer.
8. Intelligence Officer.
9. Medical Officer.
10. Regimental Sergeant Major.
11. H.Q., 49th. Inf. Bde.
12. 7th. R. Innis. Fus.
13. 8th. R. Innis. Fus.
14. 7/8th. R. Irish Fus.
15 and 16. File.

5.

16. **MEDICAL ARRANGEMENTS.** The Regimental Aid Post will be at BAVARIA HOUSE until Battalion Headquarters moves forward, when it will be established at SQUARE FARM.

    All cases will be brought to BAVARIA HOUSE or SQUARE FARM whence they will be evacuated by R.A.M.C. stretcher bearers to POTIJZE CHATEAU.

17. **ZERO HOUR.**   Zero Hour will be notified later.

18. **ACKNOWLEDGE.**

                              Lieut. & Adjutant,

                2nd. Battalion, The Royal Irish Regiment.

Hour of issue 5 p.m.

Copies No. 1. War Diary.
          2. Senior Major.
          3. O. C. "A" Company.
          4. O. C. "B" Company.
          5. O. C. "C" Company.
          6. O. C. "D" Company.
          7. Signalling Officer.
          8. Intelligence Officer.
          9. Medical Officer.
         10. Regimental Sergeant Major.
         11. H.Q., 49th. Inf. Bde.
         12. 7th. R. Innis. Fus.
         13. 8th. R. Innis. Fus.
         14. 7/8th. R. Irish Fus.
         15 and 16. File.

SECRET.   Copy No...?......

PROVISIONAL ORDERS FOR THE ATTACK.
8th. R? INNIS. FUSILIERS.      17-8-17.

1. GENERAL PLAN.
    The 16th. Division, in conjunction with Divisions on either flank, will attack the enemy's positions on a date to be notified later.
    The attack will be made in two bounds, each bound is shown by coloured lines on Map "A".
        First Bound   GREEN LINE
        Second Bound   DOTTED RED LINE.

2. OBJECTIVES OF BRIGADES.
    The 48th. Inf. Bde. (plus one Battn.) on the right and the 49th. Infantry Brigade (plus one Battn.) on the left will attack up to and including the RED DOTTED LINE. The 47th. Inf. Bde. less three Battns. and M.G. Coys, will be in Divnl. Reserve. The Left Battn. of the 48th. Inf. Bde. will be 2nd. R. Dublin Fus. The Right Battn. of the 108th. Inf. Bde. will be 9th. R. Irish Fus..

3. BOUNDARIES.
    The boundaries between the 49th. Inf. Bde., and the Bdes on either flank are as follows :-
    Boundary with 48th. Inf. Bde.
    D.25.a.75.05 - where DOTTED RED LINE crosses the ZONNEBEKE stream.
    Boundary with 108th. Inf. Bde.
    D.19.c.7.8. - D.19.b.70.50. - D.14.d.20.40.
    These boundaries are shewn in BLUE on Map "A"

4. TASKS OF BATTALIONS.
    The attack on the GREEN and DOTTED RED LINES will be made by the 7th. R. Innis. Fus. on the Left and the 8th. R. Innis. Fus. on the Right. The dividing line between these two Battalions will be -
    D.25.a.60.90. - D.20.b.80.99.
    This boundary is shewn in BLACK on Map "A".
    The GREEN LINE is to be captured at Zero ZERO PLUS ....
    There will be a pause of 20 minutes on the GREEN LINE.
    The RED DOTTED LINE is to be captured at ZERO PLUS........
    As soon as the RED DOTTED LINE has been captured a line of posts will be pushed out as far as the Barrage permits.

5. DISPOSITIONS.
    "C" Coy. 7/8th. R. Irish Fus. (to be known for these operations as "E" Coy.) are attached and will assist in ATTACK and mop up, up to, and including ZEVENKOTE.
    "C" Coy. and "A" Coy. will supply leading waves, "C" Coy. on RIGHT, "A" Coy. on the LEFT. "D" Coy. and "B" Coy. will be in rear, "D" Coy. on RIGHT, "B" Coy. on the LEFT. Dividing line between Coys. is shewn on Map "A".
    The Battalion will attack in five waves of two lines each.
    Distance between LINES 20 yards
        "   "   WAVES 100 Yards.
    "E" Coy. will form the second WAVE of the ATTACK and are allotted tasks as follows.
    RIGHT PLATOON   (No. 10 2/Lt. YOUNG) will assist in capture of BORRY FARM
                    Mop up and consolidate that position
    RIGHT CENTRE PLATOON (No. 9 2/Lt. COOMBES) will assist in capture of
                    COFFEE FARM and having mopped up will proceed to
                    ZEVENKOTE.
                    These two platoons will follow first WAVE of "C" Coy.
    Nos. 11 and 12 Platoons (2/Lt. DICKSON) will follow 1st. WAVE of "A" Coy.
                    will proceed direct to ZEVENKOTE.
    The three Platoons of "E" Coy. at ZEVENKOTE having completed mopping up will choose and consolidate a suitable position about 250 yards in rear of GERMAN TRENCHES at ZEVENKOTE.
    One Coy. 7/8th. R. Irish Fus. will provide Carrying parties.
    Two Platoons will carry to 5th. R. Innis. Fus. at COFFEE FARM: after completing their task they will join the Coy. at ZEVENKOTE.

- 2 -

5 (contd.).
2 Platoons will carry to 7th R. Innis. Fus. at DELVA FARM, and will join the 2 Coys. at IBERIAN on completion of task.
The 2nd R. Irish Regt., will be in Brigade Reserve. At ZERO Hour 3 Coys. of the 2nd R. Irish Regt., will advance from their assembly positions and occupy the trenches vacated by the Assaulting Battalions, from D.25.a.80.05 to D.19.c.60.70. with a post at BECK HOUSE. 1 Coy. will remain in the assembly position on BLUE LINE.
The 6th R. Irish Regt., will be in Brigade Reserve in VLAMERTINGHE Area, and must be prepared to relieve the Assaulting Battalions on the RED DOTTED LINE if required.

6. MOPPING UP.
The 7th & 8th R. Innis. Fus. are responsible for Mopping Up all ground in their areas in front of DELVA FARM and ZEVENKOTE. The 7/8th R. Irish Fus., are responsible for Mopping Up in rear of DELVA FARM and ZEVENKOTE (inclusive).

7. CONSOLIDATION.
The RED DOTTED LINE, and all Supporting Points held by the 7/8th R. Irish Fus. will be consolidated as rapidly as possible after capture.
"A" & "C" Coys. will consolidate FRONT LINE, pushing forward POSTS as ordered in para 4.
"B" & "D" Coys., will consolidate position in depth approximately along line of GERMAN TRENCHES at ZEVENKOTE.

8. ACTION OF MACHINE GUNS.
The Machine Guns will be under the direction of Divisional Machine Gun Officer.
12 Guns of the 49th M.G. Coy. will assist in the Machine Gun Barrage which will be 200 yards in advance of Arty. Creeping Barrage and will lift in conformity with that Barrage.
2 Guns will move in rear of the Attacking Infantry to a position in vicinity of DELVA FARM and 2 Guns will move to a position near HILL 37 (D.20.a.).

9. ACTION OF STOKES MORTARS.
Two Stokes Mortars will be attached to each Assaulting Battalion. They will move in rear of the last wave, and will assist the Infantry to overcome opposition as required.

10. ACTION OF ARTILLERY.
The Divisional Artillery will form a Creeping Barrage covering the Advance of the Infantry.
At Zero Hour the Barrage will be put down, 300 yards in advance of our present front line: BECK HOUSE will be specially dealt with. The first lift will take place at Zero plus 5 minutes, and it will then proceed forward at the rate of 100 yards in 5 minutes.
During the 20 minutes pause on the GREEN LINE a protective barrage will be maintained 200 yards in advance of the Infantry.
After the capture of the DOTTED RED LINE a standing barrage will be established 300 yards in advance of it for a period of 1 hour, after which it will cease unless recalled by the "S.O.S." Signal.

11. ACTION OF TANKS.
One Section of Tanks, from "C" Battn., TANK CORPS, has been allotted to the 16th Division. These Tanks will not be available unless the weather conditions improve. In any case they are only likely to arrive behind the Infantry in time to act as "Moppers Up", In cases where isolated positions continue to hold out.

12. COMMUNICATIONS.
Brigade Headquarters, will remain at MILL COT.
The Bde. Forward Station will advance behind the last wave of the leading Assaulting Battalion, and will be established in the vicinity of IBERIAN.
Battn. Forward Posts will be established as follows:-
7th R. Innis. Fus.   DELVA FARM.
8th R. Innis. Fus.   COFFEE FARM. (D.20.c.2.2).
7/8th R. Irish Fus.   IBERIAN.
Battn. H.Qrs. will not move forward to these positions until communication has been established with them.
The attached Chart shows the various means of Communication except pigeons and runners.

- 3 -

12 (Contd.)
As many pairs of pigeons as available will be issued to Bde. Forward Station and Battalions. The latter will send half their issue with Battn. Forward Posts.
Runner Relay Posts will be established at -
    (a) IBERIAN
    (b) SQUARE FARM
    (c) BAVARIA HOUSE
    (d) BRIGADE HQRS.
Runners should not be used unless all other methods of communication fail.
The Bde. Forward Station of 48th. Inf. Bde. will be at VAMPIR
The Bde. Forward Station of 108th. Inf. Bde. will be at........
The Bde. Visual Station and O.P. will be at C.29.d.8.7.

13. CONTACT AEROPLANES.
One Contact Aeroplane (Type......) and one Protective Aeroplane will be in the Air over the 16th. and 36th. Division Areas from Zero Hour onwards. Flares will be lit and WATSON FANS will be shown by the leading troops at the following hours

The leading troops will be prepared to light flares and show Watson Fans at other times if asked for by the aeroplane.

14. SYNCHRONISATION.
All Units will send a watch to Bde. S.O. daily at 6 p.m.

15. S.O.S. SIGNAL.
The S.O.S. will be GREEN SIGNAL Cartridges.

16. PRISONERS.
All prisoners will be sent to BECK HOUSE, where they will be collected by the 2nd. R. Irish Regt., and sent down in batches to Bde. Prisoners' Cage at Brigade Headquarters.

17. MEDICAL ARRANGEMENTS.
Regtl. AID POSTS will be established at LOW FARM

18. ZERO HOUR.
Zero Hour will be notified later.

19. ACKNOWLEDGE.

Issued through Signals at

                                                      2/Lieut.,
                          a/Adjutant, 6th. R. Inniskilling Fusiliers...

Copy No. 1 to O.C. "A" Coy.
"   " 2 " " "B" "
"   " 3 " " "C" "
"   " 4 " " "D" "
"   " 5 "   Signalling Officer.
"   " 6 "   H.Q. 49th. Inf. Bde.
"   " 7 "   O.C. 7/8th. R. Irish Fus.
"   " 8 "   " 7th. R. Innis. Fus.
"   " 9 "   " 2nd. R. Irish Regt.
"   " 10 " Medical Officer.
"   " 11 " Quartermaster and Transport Officer.
"   " 12 " O.C. 49th. T.M.B.
"   " 13 " " 49th. M.G.C.
"   " 14 " " 2nd. R. Dublin Fusrs.
"   " 15/16th Retained.

N O T E.

MAP "A" issued to Coys. only.

Officer Commanding 2nd.R.Irish Regt.

Herewith copy No. 16 of Operation Orders No.1. They are not complete and will probably have to be amended as information is received on several points.

Please acknowledge.

August 14th.1917

Lieut & A/Adjutant.
7/8th(S) Battalion The Royal Irish Fusiliers

S.E.C.R.E.T. AUGUST 14th.1917. COPY NO. 16

OPERATION ORDERS No. 4.
BY.
Lieut.Colonel. X.C.WELDON D.S.O. Comdg Royal Irish Fusiliers

PROVISIONAL ORDERS FOR THE ATTACK.

1. GENERAL PLAN
The 16th.Division, in conjunction with Divisions on either flank, will attack the enemy's positions on a date to be notified later.
The attack will be made in two bounds, each bound is shewn by coloured lines on Map "A"
    First Bound   GREEN LINEM
    Second Bound   DOTTED RED LINE.

2. OBJECTIVES OF BRIGADES
The 16th.Division will attack with:-
48th.Infantry Brigade (plus 1 Battalion) on the Right.
49th.Infantry Brigade (plus 1 Battalion) on the Left.
47th.Infantry Brigade (less 3 Battalions) in reserve.
Left Battalion 48th.Infantry Brigade will be 2nd.R.DUBLIN FUSILIERS.
Right Battalion 108 Infantry Brigade will be 9th.R.IRISH FUSILIERS.

3. BOUNDARIES.
The Boundaries between the 49th.Infantry Brigade and the Bde.on either flank are as follows :-
Boundary with 48th.Infantry Brigade.
D.25.a.75.05. -- where DOTTED RED LINE crosses the ZONNEBEKE STREAM.

Boundary with 108th.Infantry Brigade.
D.19.c.7.8. -- D.19.b.70.50. -- D.14.d.80.40.

These boundaries are shewn in BLUE on Map "A"

4. TASKS OF BATTALIONS.
The attack on the GREEN and DOTTED RED LINES will be made by the 7th. Royal Inniskilling Fusiliers on the Left and the 8th.Royal Inniskilling Fusiliers on the Right.
Boundary between Battalions is shewn in BLACK on Map "A"
The GREEN LINE is to be captured at ZERO PLUS.........
There will be a pause of 20 minutes on the GREEN LINE.
The DOTTED RED LINE is to be captured at ZERO PLUS............
As soon as the DOTTED RED LINE has been captured a line of posts will be pushed out as far as the barrage premits.

The 7/8th.Battalion Royal Irish Fusiliers will support the attack and will find "MOPPERS UP" and Carrying Parties as under.

(a) "C"Company (2/Lieut.C.L.HENRY.)
No..10..Platoon (2/LIEUT.A.C.YOUNG.) to Mop Up BORRY FARM and hold it as a Supporting Point
No..11...Platoon (2/LIEUT. W.A.) These two platoons will Mop Up
No..12...Platoon (DIXON.) ZEVENCOTE and hold it as a Supporting Point.
No..9... Platoon (2/LT.G.COOMBES.) to Mop Up COFFEE FARM,D.20.c.15.15. and then join the two platoons at ZEVENCOTE.
These 4 Platoons will move into position on Y/Z Night and will advance in rear of the last wave of the 8.R.Inniskilling Fusiliers.

Continued on Page 2.

SHEET 2. (Part 4. continued)

(b) "B" Company Captain V.J. LYNCH M.C.
No. 5. Platoon (2/Lt.G.W.PICKETT.) to Mop Up DELVA FARM and will join the Platoon at IBERIAN when the H.Q.7th.R.Innis.Fusrs moves to DELVA FARM.
No. 6. Platoon (2/Lt.DICKSON.) to form a Supporting Point about D.19.d.80.80.
The above two platoons will advance in rear of the first wave of the 7th. Royal Inniskilling Fusiliers (Right Half Battalion)

(8) No. 7. Platoon ( ) to Mop Up IBERIAN and the dugouts in the vicinity and form a Supporting Point there.
No. 5. Platoon( ) One to Mop Up and hold as a Supporting Point the clump of trees at D.19.b.70.35.
The above two Platoons to advance in rear of the 1st wave of the 7th. R Innisn Fusrs. (Left Half Battalion)
"B" Company will move into position on Y/Z Night.

(d) "D" Company (Captain E.E.SARGINT M.C.)
This Company will assemble in the Front Line from D.25.a.80.90 to D.19.c.80.30.
At ZERO hour, this Company will advance and capture BECK HOUSE, and the ground as far East as the Stream, reform and on receipt of orders from Battalion H.Qrs. move to IBERIAN in support.

(e) "A" Company. (Captain E.H.FFORDE)
This Company will provide Carrying Parties as under :-
No. 1. Platoon (2/Lt. POWELL.) and No. 2. Platoon (2/Lt SHEPPARD.) will carry to COFFEE FARM.
No.3. Platoon (2/Lieut. Capt OLIVER) and No 4. Platoon (Sgt TIMMINS) will carry to DELVA FARM.
Nos. 1.& 2. Platoons on completion of their tasks will join the Company at ZEVENCOTE.
Nos. 3.& 4. Platoons on completion of their tasks will join the two Coys at IBERIAN.
"A" Coy. will move into position on Y/Z Night

5. LOADS.

	COMPOSITION OF LOAD.	WHERE PICKED UP.
1st. LOAD		
2nd. LOAD.		
3rd. LOAD.		

The Officer or N.C.O i/c of any carrying party, when he has completed his journey will report the fact at the Battalion H'Qrs. of the Unit for which he is carrying and will on no account leave without obtaining the written authority of the O.C. to do so.
A detail of loads will be issued for the first three journeys, but if necessary more journeys will be made. The first load on YUKON PACKS will be picked up as they march past MILL COT. The number of YUKON PACKS available will be......

6. All Companies will remain under the orders of the O.C.7/8th.R.Irish Fusiliers

SHEET 3.

7. ASSEMBLY POSITIONS.

On Y/Z Night the Battalion moves into Assembly Positions.
The order of march on leaving Camp at H.18.a.4.9. will be

        Battalion H.Qrs.
        "D" Company.
        "A" Company.
        "B" Company.
        "C" Company

"D" Company 7/8th. Royal Irish Fusiliers will relieve "C" Coy. 7th. R. Innis. Fusrs. in the front line from D.35.a.80.60. to D.19.c.80.30. Four guides will be sent to BAVARIA HOUSE.

"A" Coy. 7/8th. R. Irish Fusiliers will move to an assembly position in rear of "D" Coy.
  No. 1 & 2. Platoons on the Right
     3. & 4. Platoons on the Left.
No guides will be sent for this Company.

"B" Company 7/8th. Royal Irish Fusiliers will move to assembly positions.
Nos. 5 & 7 Platoons to form up behind the 1st. wave of the 7. R. Innis. Fusrs. Left Half Battalion.
Nos. 6 & 8 Platoons to form up behind the 1st wave of the 7. R. Innis. Fusrs Right Battalion.
4 Guides will be sent to BAVARIA HOUSE.

"C" Company 7/8th. Royal Irish Fusiliers will form up behind the 1st. wave of the 8th. Royal Inniskilling Fusiliers.
4 Guides will be sent to BAVARIA HOUSE.

8. RATIONS.

Rations for "Z" Day will be issued to each man on the afternoon of "Y" Day and will be carried up on the man.

9. SHOVELS.

On moving into Assembly Positions "B", "C" and "D" Coys' will take shovels from the Transport lines on a scale of one every other man. No picks will be taken.

10. LEWIS GUNS.

The Four Lewis Guns of "A" Coy. will be attached :-
(a) Two to the 7. Royal Inniskilling Fusiliers
(b) Two to the 8th. Royal Inniskilling Fusiliers
Only two men with a bag of spare parts and 5 filled drums will accompany each Gun.
(a) These two guns will proceed to SQUARE FARM with Battalion H.Qrs.
(b) These two Guns will proceed with "D" Coy. O.C. "D" Coy will arrange to hand them over to O.C. 8. R. Innis. Fusrs. at LOW FARM.

11. MOPPING UP.

The 7th and 8th. Royal Inniskilling Fusiliers are responsible for Mopping Up all ground in their areas in front of DELVA FARM and ZEVENCOTE. The 7/8th. Royal Irish Fusiliers are responsible for Mopping Up in rear of DELVA FARM and ZEVENCOTE. (inclusive)

12. CONSOLIDATION.

The RED DOTTED LINE and all Supporting Points held by the 7/8th. Royal Irish Fusiliers will be consolidated as possible after capture.
The R.E. will work under the direction of the C.R.E. 16th. Division, and will erect wire on the GHELUVELT — LANGEMARCK LINE when captured. They will also prepare certain positions for defence in vicinity of DELVA FARM and IBERIAN.

SHEET...4.

13. MACHINE GUNS
The Machine Guns will be under the direction of the Divisional Machine Gun Officer.
16 Guns of the 49th.M.Gun Coy. will assist in the Machine Gun Barrage which will be 300 yards in advance of the Artillery Creeping Barrage and will lift in conformity with that Barrage.
Two Guns will move in rear of the attacking Infantry to a position in vicinity of DELVA FARM and 2 Guns will move to a position near HILL 37. (D.20.a.)

14. ACTION OF STOKES MORTARS.
Two Stokes' Mortars will be attached to each assaulting Battalion. They will move in rear of the last wave, and will assist the Infantry to overcome opposition as required. The remaining 4 Mortars will be left at Brigade Headquarters.

15. ACTION OF ARTILLERY
The Divisional Artillery will form a Creeping Barrage covering the advance of the Infantry. At ZERO HOUR the Barrage will be put down 300 yards in advance of our present front line; BECK HOUSE will be specially dealt with. The first lift will take place at ZERO plus 5. minutes, and it will then proceed forward at the rate of 100 yards in 5 minutes.
During the 20 minutes pause on the GREEN LINE a protective barrage will be maintained 200 yards in advance of the Infantry.
After the capture of the DOTTED RED LINE a standing barrage will be established 300 yards in advance of it for a period of one hour, after which it will cease unless recalled by the "S.O.S." Signal.

16. COMMUNICATIONS.
BRIGADE H.QRS. will remain at MILL COT.
The Bde. Forward Station will advance behind the last wave of the leading Assaulting Battalions, and will be established in the vicinity of IBERIAN.
Battalion Forward Posts will be established as follows:-
7th. Royal Inniskilling Fusiliers   DELVA FARM
8th. Royal Inniskilling Fusiliers   COFFEE FARM (D.28.c.2.2.)
7/8th. Royal Irish Fusiliers   IBERIAN.
Battalion H.Qrs will not move forward to these positions until Communication has been established with them.
As many pairs of pigeons as available will be issued to the Battalion half of these will be sent to the Battalion Forward Post.
Runner Relay Posts will be established at:-
(a) IBERIAN
(b) SQUARE FARM
(c) BAVARIA HOUSE.
(d) BRIGADE H.Qrs.
Runners should not be used unless all other means of Communication fail.
The Brigade Forward Station of the 48th. Infantry Brigade will be at VAMPIR.
The Brigade Forward Station of the 108th. Infantry Brigade will be at ....
The Brigade Visual Station and O.P. will be at C.29.d.8.7.

17. CONTACT AEROPLANES.
One Contact Aeroplane (Type............) and One Protective Aeroplane will be in the air over the 16th. Division and 36th. Division Areas from ZERO HOUR onwards. Flares will be lit and WATSON FANS will be shown by the leading troops at the following hours.

The leading troops will be prepared to light flares and show WATSON Fans at other times if asked for by the aeroplane

SHEET. 6.

NO. 18. S.O.S. SIGNAL.
The "S.O.S" will be GREEN SIGNAL CARTRIDGES.

19. PRISONERS
All prisoners will be sent to BECK HOUSE, where they will be collected by the 2nd. The Royal Irish Regt. and sent down in batches to the Brigade Prisoners Cage at Brigade H.Qrs. Only one man to every ten prisoners will be sent down.

20. ZERO HOUR.
ZERO HOUR will be notified later.

21. TANKS. ACTION OF.
One Section of Tanks, from "G" Battalion, Tank Corps, has been allotted to the 16th. Division. These tanks will not be available unless the weather conditions improve. In any case they are only likely to arrive behind the Infantry in time to act as "Moppers Up." In cases where isolated positions continue to hold out.

22. SYNCHRONIZATION.
The Signal Officer will arrange to send a watch to Bde. H.Qrs. at 6.0.P.M. daily for synchronization and will send same round to all Officers daily.

23. HEADQUARTERS
The disposition of all Headquarters is as shown on attached plan.

24. ACKNOWLEDGE.

August 14th. 1917

Lieutenant & A/Adjutant.
7/8th. (S) Battalion The Royal Irish Fusiliers

ISSUED THROUGH SIGNALS AT 5.30 p.m.

COPY NO. 1. "A" Coy.
2. "B" Coy.
3. "C" Coy.
4. "D" Coy.
5. Lewis Gun Officer
6. Intelligence Officer
7. Signalling Officer.
8. Medical Officer.
9. Quartermaster
Copy No. 20. File.

Copy. No. 10. Transport Officer.
11. War Diary
12. War Diary.
13. 49th. Infantry Brigade.
14. 7. R. Innis. Fusrs
15. 8. R. Innis Fusrs.
16. 2. The R. Irish Regt.
17. Spare.
18. O.C. Echelon "B"

WAR DIARY.

FOR MONTH OF SEPTEMBER, 1917.

VOLUME

UNIT: 2nd Battn Royal Irish Regt.

WAR DIARY
or
INTELLIGENCE SUMMARY

Army Form C. 2118.

Month: September

Place	Date	Hour	Summary of Events and Information	Remarks and references to Appendices
HAMELINCOURT	1-3		Very quiet time mainly spent in improving the camp.	
"	4		Relieves 10th R. Dublin Fusiliers in front line - left la Bergere Right Sudrecourt, the line of the HINDENBURG LINE, in front of the German position have being the support line of the Hindenburg Line. The Battalion has about 1108 yds of front with four companies all in the front line, each company having a platoon in support.	App/p 1 App/p —
HINDENBURG LINE	6		Enemy put one barrage 2000/3000 gas shells into new trgts, 3 o/r Ranks died from gas poisoning and about 15 were Gassed. 2/Lt Hillyard gassed.	App/p 2
"	—10		Relieved by the 9/R. Innis Fusiliers. Moves to support positions in neighbourhood of CROISILLES.	App/p 3
CROISILLES	10-16		In support - nothing to report.	
"	16		Relieved by 10th Royal Dublin Fusiliers - moves back to HAMELINCOURT to command Camp.	
HAMELINCOURT	16-28		In camp. Parades every day from 7-1 pm. Recreation in the afternoon. Beat the 1/R Irish Rifles two at football in the Brigade Comp. Schooling up, improving camp, being completed by 5 pm.	App
"	28		Relieved 10th R.D.F. in Right Sub Section.	App
"	29		In the Line.	
"	30		In the Line. 3 killed by "pineapple". We have 8 NCOs + 3 o/r of the 1/4 attached from for instruction in trench warfare.	

The following officers joined the Bn on dates stated.

Capt H. Harrison from Harpenden 10-9-17
" HW Terry Reinforcements 13-8-17
" F.R. Sinclair " 18-9-17
" F.H. Brindley " "
" O.B. O'Brien " 16-9-17
" AB A. Hillyard " 5-9-17
" CB Solomon " "
2/Lt. Gowdy " 7-9-17
" PA Dundas " "

A5834 Wt. W4973/M687 750,000 8/16—D. D. & L. Ltd. Forms/C.2118/13.

2nd R.Irish Regt.
7/8th R.Innis Fus.
7/8th R.Irish Fus.
49th M.G.Company.
Bde. Signal Section.

49th Inf. Bde. No. B.M.C. XII/10 - 1-19-17.

The following awards have been made in connection with operations at YPRES, 1917.

D.S.O.

Captain V.H. Parr, M.C.	7th R.Innis Fus.

M.C.

Lieut. (T.Capt) F.W. Martin.	8th R.Innis Fus.
2/Lieut. F.D. Morphy.	R.Ir.Regt. attd. 7th R.Innis Fus.
Lieut. V. Joyce,	49th M.G. Company.
Lieut. W. Sparks.	7/8th R.Irish Fus.
2/Lieut. G.J. Forbes	7/8th R.Irish Fus.
2/Lieut. A.M.R. Hobbs.	C.R. attd. 2nd R.Ir.Regt.
Rev. E. Kelly C.F.	attd. 7th R.Innis Fus.

D.C.M.

23618 Cpl F. Smith	7th R.Innis Fus.
20655 Sgt R. Kelly.	8th R.Innis Fus.
8907 C.S.M. A. Griffin.	7/8th R.Irish Fus.
8275 Sgt P. Gibson.	2nd R.Irish Regt.

M.M.

75275 Cpl H. Read R.E.	49th Inf. Bde. Sig. Section.

The Brigadier congratulates all recipients, and desires to convey the congratulations of the Army, Corps and Divisional Commanders to them.

T.C. MacDonald
Captain,
Brigade Major, 49th Infantry Brigade.

App. F.

Operation Order to the copy No 1.
by
Lieut. Colonel J. A. Scott, Commanding
2nd Battn. The Royal Irish Regiment.

Reference Map. 3-9-1917.
FONTAINE, 1/2.

1. The 149th Inf. Bde. (less M.G. Coy) will relieve the 48th Inf. Bde. (less M.G. Coy) in the Left Section on the 4th September. The 2nd R. Irish Regt. will relieve the 10th R.D. Fus. in the Right sub-section.

2. The dividing line between Battalions will be LUMP LANE inclusive to Left Battalion.

3. All trench stores, documents, etc. will be taken over.

4. Lewis Gun Sections, L.G. N.C.O., C.S.Ms. 1 N.C.O. per platoon, Bn. and Coy. gas N.C.Os. and C.Q.M.S. Haines, under 2/Lieut. Freeman and Sgt. Dixon will meet guides at QUARRY (T.18.b.8.5) at 11 a.m., leaving camp in 4 parties, 1st party leaving at 8.30 a.m.

5. Lewis Gun limbers will move with L.G. sections to QUARRY and will wait there to take back L.Gs. of 10th R.D. Fus.

6. Companies will move with five minutes interval between platoons, leading platoon of D Coy. will leave camp at 1.30 p.m.
   Order of march - D. H.Q. B. C. A.

7. D Coy. 2/R.I. Rgt. will relieve D Coy 10/R.D. Fus. on left moving from QUARRY via JANET AVE.
   H.Q. will move via JANET AVE.
   C Coy. 2/R.I. Rgt will relieve C Coy 10/R.D. Fus. moving via NELLY AVE.
   B Coy. 2/R.I. Rgt. and 2 platoons, A Coy 2/R.I. Rgt. will relieve B Coy 10/R.D. Fus. on right moving via FACTORY AVE.
   A Coy. 2/R.I. Rgt (less 2 platoons) will relieve A Coy 2/R.D. Fus., LINCOLN TRENCH, moving via FACTORY AVE.
   Guides will meet companies at entrance to trench, T. 24. b. 2.4., 1st platoon at 4 p.m.

8. A carrying party provided by Drums and 6 men per coy. under C.Q.M.S. Haines will live at QUARRY bringing up rations etc from there. C.Q.M.S. Haines will take over accommodation from 10/R.D. Fus. for this party.

-2-

9. Cooks under Cook Sgt. at QUARRY.

10. Rations and water cart will be brought up arriving QUARRY about 3 p.m. daily.

11. Officers' valises, trench kits, mens' packs, will be dumped by coyl. at Q.M. Stores by 12. noon.

12. No maps, other than the undermentioned will be taken into the trenches:-
    HENDECOURT — Ed. 4 d.
    HENINCOURT — Ed. 3 c.
    FONTAINE — Ed. 2
    CHERISY

13. Relief report to Bn. H.Q. at A.p.o.45.

14. ACKNOWLEDGE.

Issued at
8 p.m.
            Malvley,
                Capt. ? Adjt.
            2/ works at Irish Regt.

Copy No. 1 War Diary.   No. 9. Signalling Offr.
    2. H.Q. 49. Inf. Bde.   10. Q.M.
    3. Senior Major.   11. T.O.
    4. O/C "A" Coy   12. R.S.M.
    5.   " "B" "   13. Cook Sgt.
    6.   " "C" "   14. _____
    7.   " "D" "   15. O/C 2/R.D. Fus.
    8. Intell. Offr.   16. " 10/R.I.

Secret   Operation Order No. 47   Copy No. 1
                by
         Lieut. Colonel J. D. Scott, Commanding,
             2/ The Royal Irish Regiment.

Reference Map.
HENDECOURT, 4d.   The Field, 9.9.1917.

1. The 7/8th R. Innis. Fus. will relieve the 2/Rl. Irish Regt. in the right sub sector on 10th September 1917.

2. Companies will hand over to corresponding companies in the 7/8th R. Innis. Fus.

3. Guides, 1 per platoon and 2 per H.Q. as follows:—
"A" & "B" Coys - 5.30 p.m. - Entrance to NELLY AVE. T.24.a.6.5. under 2/Lt. HILLYARD, relief up FACTORY AVE.
H.Q., "C" & "D" Coys - 6.30 p.m. - QUARRY - under 2/Lt. CLANCY - relief up NELLY and JANET AVES.

   Neither "A" & "B" Coys nor "C" & "D" Coys will leave their trenches until communication trenches are cleared by relieving companies.

4. Lewis Gunners will be relieved independently at 2.30
   Guides 1 per ~~coy~~ at entrance to NELLY AVE. - 1.30 p.m.

5. All work, defence arrangements, trench stores will be carefully handed over. Lists of trench stores to be sent to Bn. HQ. by 9 a.m. 11th inst.

6. All movement, when clear of the communication trenches will be by platoons at 5 minutes interval.

7. Completion of reliefs to be reported to Bn. H.Q. in code.

8. On being relieved, the Battalion will be disposed as follows:—
   Bn. H.Q.   T. 22. d. 8. 9.
   "A" Coy   T. 23. d. 9. 1.
   "B" "   T. 23. c. 8. 9.
   "C" "   T. 28. a. 5. 5.
   "D" "   QUARRY.

   C.S.Ms. & 1 N.C.O. per coy., 1 N.C.O. Bn. H.Q. will take over from 7/8th R. Innis. Fus. at 2 p.m. They will arrange to meet their coys. and guide them from entrance to NELLY AVE.

9. Rations for the 11th will be brought up as follows at 8 p.m. 10th inst.—
   H.Q. "B" & "C" Coy — "B" Coys H.Q.
   "A" Coy   — "A"   "
   "D" "   — QUARRY.

-2-

10. Officers' lunch kits, etc. will be dumped at dinner by 7 pm.

11. ACKNOWLEDGE.

[signature]
Capt. & Adjutant
2nd. Bn. Rl. Irish Regt.

Issued at 8 pm.

Copy No. 1	War Diary	No. 8.	O/c "C" Coy
2.	H.Q. 49th Inf. Bde.	9.	" "D" "
3.	7/8 R. K. Innis. Fus.	10.	M.O
4.	7/8th R. Irish Fus.	11.	S.M.
5.	Sec-in-Command	12.	I.O.
6.	O/c "A" Coy	13.	R.S.M
7.	O/c "B" Coy	14.	Cook Sgt.

Secret.   Operation Order No. 48   Copy No.
by
Lieut. Colonel J.S. Scott, Commanding
2nd. Bn. The Royal Irish Regt.

Reference Map
HENDECOURT, 4d.   The Field, 15-9-17.

1. The 49th. Inf. Bde. (less M.G. Coy.) will relieve the 190th. Inf. Bde. (less M.G. Coy.) in the Left sub. sector on the 16th September 1917.

2. The Battalion will be relieved by the 10th. R. Dub. Fus. Relief to be complete by 3 p.m. On completion of relief the Battalion will move to CLONNEL CAMP, HAMELINCOURT.

3. "B" Coy. 10th. R. Dub. Fus. will relieve "D" Coy, 2nd. The Rl. Irish. Rgt.
   "D" "   "   "   "   "   "   "   "C"   "   "   "   "   "   "
   "A" "   "   "   "   "   "   "   "B"   "   "   "   "   "   "
   "C" "   "   "   "   "   "   "   "A"   "   "   "   "   "   "

4. Guides, 1 per platoon and 1 per H.Q. Coy will rendezvous at X roads, ST. LEGER, at 12 noon. 2/Lt. NEWSAM will be in charge and will be responsible that incoming platoons get their right guides.

5. Advance parties from 10th. R. Dub. Fus will take over stores, etc. by 12 noon.

6. Officers' lunch kits, mess boxes, etc. will be dumped at Coy. H.Q. by 2 p.m. The Transport Officer will arrange for the transport necessary transport.

7. All movement will be by platoons at 5 minutes interval.

8. 2/Lt. Godfrey and the usual billeting party will take over CLONNEL CAMP at 12 noon.

9. Completion of relief will be reported to Bn. H.Q. by wire in code.

10. A C K N O W L E D G E.

                                    Rudwley, Capt. & Adjt.,
                                    2nd. The Rl. Irish Regiment.

Issued at 3 p.m.
Copy No. 1. War Diary   No. 5. O/C "A" Coy.   No. 9. M.O.
      2. 49th. Bde.   6. " "B" "   10. Q.M.
      3. 10/R.D.F.   7. " "C" "   11. T.O.
      4. Section Command.   8. " "D" "   12. R.S.M.

2nd R.Irish Regt.
7/8th R.Innis Fus.
7th R.Irish Rifles.
7/8th R.Irish Fus.
49th M.G.Company.
49th T.M.Battery.
Bde. Signal Section.

49th Inf. Bde. No. B.M.C. XII/8 - 29-9-17.

The following awards for gallantry and devotion to duty in action are forwarded for your information :-

MILITARY MEDAL.

5621	Sgt	Crowe	J.	R. Irish Regt.
8371	Pte (L/c)	Nolan	A.	do
9447	Sgt	Brown	W.	do
8393	Pte	Sealy	F.	do
8243	Pte (L/c)	Golding	E.	do
5336	Pte	O'Brien	E.	do
9444	Sgt	Eagar	E.	do
9057	Pte	Lillis	W.	R. Irish Regt. attd. Inf.Bde.Sig. Sect.
7781	"	Condell	R.	do
8455	"	Sawyer	J.	do.
9614	Sgt	Armstrong	W.	R. Innis Fus.
30120	Pte	Thompson	W.	do
26773	"	Ormsby	D.	do
2754	Sgt	Thompson	R.	do
9818	Pte (L/c)	McCormack	T	do
30152	Pte	Duffel	n.	do
10391	Pte (L/c)	Adams	A	do
30095	Pte	Steadman	T	do attd. T.M.B.
8242	Cpl	Smyth	T.J.	R. Innis Fus.
40299	Pte	Cosgrove	W	do
41038	Sgt	Westgate	R.W.	do
43246	Pte	Nash	J.	do
43115	Cpl	Reilly	R.	do
4648	Pte	Doherty	P.	do.
40352	"	Daley	J.	do.
11699	"	Finlay	H.	do
41011	"	Watson	A.	do
24228	"	Lobley	J.	do
5666	Sgt	Young	R.	do
23011	Cpl	Burke	W.	do
28578	Pte	Fenton	J.	do
6574	Sgt	Houston	J.	R.Irish Rifles.
4530	Rfn	MaGuire	H.	do
5070	"	Lloyd	G.H.	do
10659	Sgt	Connolly	H.	do.
6030	Cpl	Thompson	R.A.	do
4133	"	Journeaux	H.F.	do
4152	Pte (L/c)	Luce	J.A.	do
4239	Rfn	Brissett	P.	do
4212	"	Vickers	J.C.	do
41928	"	Truss	T.	do
41772	"	Wilson	T.U.	do
40010	"	House	A.	do
4094	Rfn (L/c)	Drouin	F.T.	do
4236	Rfn (L/c)	Perks	H.	do
4251	Rfn	Giffard	E.	do
41809	"	Boothway	E.A.	do
5606	"	Kelly	D.	do
41894	"	Freeman	H.W.	do
1124	"	Freeney	J.	do

2.

12784 Cpl (L/Sgt)	Daly	M.	R. Irish Fus.
20912 Pte	McKee	P.	do
43119 "	Dalton	E.	do
21495 Pte (L/c)	Laverty	J.	do
16929 Pte	Sweeney	D.	do
24518 "	Loughran	B.	do
18729 "	Grey	F.	do
19091 "	Bishop	R.	do
43117 "	Dobbins	W.	do
24049 "	Robinson	W.	do
20194 "	Finlay	W.	R. Irish Fus attd. L.T.M.Batty.
13366 Sgt	Cragg	G.	M.G.C.
20750 "	Chambers	A.	do
23265 "	Grant	J.	do
31471 Cpl	Blowes	A.	do
6578 Pte	Nickson	A.	do
13355 Pte (L/c)	Snelling	E.D.	do
73147 Pte	Kearny	M.	do
14088 Sgt	Silvester	F.A.	do
14040 "	Baulcombe	C.	do
37215 Pte	Elliot	H.	do

THE BAR TO THE MILITARY MEDAL.

20165 Pte (L/c) McCall W. R.Irish Fus.

Captain,

Brigade Major, 49th Infantry Brigade.

WAR DIARY

FOR MONTH OF OCTOBER, 1917.

UNIT 2nd Btn. R. Irish Regt.

VOLUME NUMBER

Army Form C. 2118.

WAR DIARY
or
INTELLIGENCE SUMMARY.
(Erase heading not required.)

October 1917

Place	Date	Hour	Summary of Events and Information	Remarks and references to Appendices
RIGHT SUB SECTION LEFT SECTION	1		Enemy attack quieter than last time in one other rank killed (A.I. Horse etc.) and 3 O.R. wounded	
"	4		Relieved by 1/8 Royal Dublin Fusiliers. Relief complete by 6 p.m. moved to Support Position in the vicinity of CROISILLES.	App. I
CROISILLES	5		No 3 Special Company R.E. directed Gas and Smoke against enemy trenches opposite the Right Section of Brigade front. Very successful. The enemy sent up a multitude of coloured lights but his retaliation was not heavy.	App. 2
"	10		Relieved in Support Position by the 10th Royal Dublin Fusiliers. Relief complete by 3 p.m. Bn moved back to Clonmel Camp.	App. 3
HAMELINCOURT.			HAMELINCOURT. A strenuous programme of work. Each man in the Battalion had to throw a live bomb during the 12 days in Reserve.	
HAMELINCOURT	18		The good news came that 8614 4/8 Room 'B' Coy had been awarded the V.C. The First V.C. the Regiment has had in the War. Great rejoicings. Beat the R. Irish Fusiliers at Soccer in the CupTie. This is the 2nd time running that we have won the cup.	
"	21		Happy of Weapons. Genrd Hickie thanked Battalion for donation to buy a Redmond memorial. A party of 25 other ranks under 2Lt GODFRAY proceeded by bus to	

WAR DIARY
or
INTELLIGENCE SUMMARY.

Army Form C. 2118.

(Erase heading not required.)

Place	Date	Hour	Summary of Events and Information	Remarks and references to Appendices
HAMEL IN REPORT	21 (Contd)		LOCRE to attend memorial service for Major Redmond 6/R Irish Regt.	
TRENCHES	22		Relieved 10/R Dublin Fusiliers in the Right Sub-Section, left Section.	App 2
"	26		No 3 Special Company R.E. carried out a Gas and Smoke Bombardment of TUNNEL TRENCH with 4" Stokes mortar. Gas cloud drifted well, but the enemy did not show any sign of retaliation – only one red light and a few white Very lights being fired.	Apps 3
"	28		Relieved by 2/6 Royal Inniskilling Fusiliers. An uneventful "tour in" – in Caesar's Nose. W.C.L. SHEE Lieut. reg'ment Battalion	April 6 19
SUPPORT CROISILLES	29		Successful raid carried out by a Company of 1/6 R Munster Fusiliers 3 prisoners taken. Enemy 4 and feeder lines were rushed. Our casualties slight – 8 O.R. wounded + 1 O.R. died of wounds. 21 or so hundreds but at least 24 Germans were killed.	April 7 19
	31		Uneventful.	8

LIEUT. COLONEL,
COMMANDING 2nd Bn. THE ROYAL IRISH REGT.

Army Form C. 2118.

WAR DIARY
or
INTELLIGENCE SUMMARY.
(Erase heading not required.)

Instructions regarding War Diaries and Intelligence Summaries are contained in F. S. Regs., Part II. and the Staff Manual respectively. Title pages will be prepared in manuscript.

Place	Date	Hour	Summary of Events and Information	Remarks and references to Appendices
Line	30		Distribution games by Officers and other ranks for operations at YPRES 1917 are shewn on Appendices 5 & 6	App 5—6

J.P. Scott
Command my 2/4th R Hghrs

Secret   Copy No. 1

Lieut. Colonel F. Alcock Commanding
2nd Bn. The Royal Irish Regiment

Maps: Honnecourt 1:5
Fontaine 1:5   In Field 3.10.17

1. The 7/8 Royal Innis. Fusiliers will relieve the 2nd Royal Irish Regiment in the Right Sub section to-morrow the 4th October. Relief to be complete by 6 p.m.

2. Commencing about 1.30 pm,
   "A" Coy 7/8 R. Innis. Fus. will relieve "A" Coy 2nd R. Irish Regt
   "B"   "   "   "   "   "   "B"   "   "   "
   "C"   "   "   "   "   "   "C"   "   "   "
   "D"   "   "   "   "   "   "D"   "   "   "

   On relief, companies will be distributed as follows:—
   "A" Coy   at   T.23.c.9.9.
   "B" "   "   T.23.d.6.6
   "C" "   "   QUARRY
   "D" "   "   T.23.a.4.2

3. "A" and "D" Coys will not leave Front Line until "A" & "B" Coys of 7/8 R. Innis. Fus. have cleared FACTORY AVENUE.
   "B" and "C" Coys will not leave Front Line until "C" & "D" Coys of 7/8 R. Innis. Fus. have cleared NELL & JANET Lanes.

4. Advance parties of 7/8 R. Innis. Fus, including complete L.G. teams, will take over about 12 noon. On relief, L.G. sections will move back to support positions under arrangements of O.C.'s Coys.

5. No guides will be required.

6. All Trench stores, defence plans, work in progress and counter-attack will be carefully handed over. Trench store lists to be sent to Orderly Room by 9 am, 5 inst. Aeroplane panels will not be handed over.

7. Officers Trench kits/mess boxes will be dumped at QUARRY by 2 pm.

8. Advance parties will be at their respective Support bivouacs by 1 pm.

9. Completion of relief to be reported to Bn. H.Q. in code.

10. All movement will be by platoons at five minutes interval.

11. ACKNOWLEDGE.

                                                        P. Galwey Capt. & Adjutant
                                                        2/The Royal Irish Regiment

Issued at 7 p.m.
         Copy No. 1   to   War Diary
           "   2   "   HQ 49th Infantry Brigade
           "   3   "   7/8 R. Innis. Fus.
           "   4   "   Second in Command
           "   5   "   O.C. "A" Coy
           "   6   "   " "B" "
           "   7   "   " "C" "
           "   8   "   " "D" "
           "   9   "   M.O.
           "   10   "   T.O.
           "   11   "   Adjt.
           "   12   "   Book copy

SECRET.   Copy No .....

49th Inf. Bde. Order No. 168.

4th October 1917.

1. If the weather conditions are favourable a Section of No. 3 Special Coy. R.E. will direct gas and smoke against the following enemy trenches on the night 5th/6th October:-

    (a) Front line from KINGS POINT to junction with OLDENBURG LANE.

    (b) PRINCE TRENCH from KINGS POINT to about U.7.b.80.35.

    (c) New Support line between PRINCE TRENCH and OLDENBURG LANE.

2. The operation will be carried out in two bursts of fire.

    (a) At 7 p.m. on October 5th, when half the available ammunition will be directed against the above targets.

    (b) At 6 a.m. on October 6th, when the programme will be repeated and the remainder of the ammunition expended.

3. The following trenches will be cleared 10 minutes before Zero in each case:-

    (a) LUMP LANE. (Care will be taken to clear LUMP LANE silently and in small parties only).

    (b) Trenches and Saps East of HUMBER SUPPORT.

    Above positions will be reoccupied 5 minutes after the "All Clear" is given by O.C. No. 3 Special Coy, R.E. LUMP LANE will only be reoccupied as far as first sap; a careful reconnaissance will then be made to see if the whole trench is clear of gas; if so, the remaining portion will be again occupied.

4. The Adjutant, Right Battalion, and the O.C. Right Company, Left Battalion will be at the Company H.Q. at junction of LUMP LANE and BURG TRENCH half an hour previous to each shoot, where an officer Special Coy, R.E. will also be sent. The latter officer will report when all is clear. All dugout gas blankets in trenches named in para. 3 will be dropped.

5. Except in case of attack, no firing above the ordinary, that is likely to draw hostile retaliation on the neighbourhood of HUMBER SUPPORT, is to be carried out between the hours of 7 p.m. on October 5th and 10 a.m. on October 6th.
    O.C. Section No. 3 Special Coy. will arrange to withdraw all Mortars, and have any unexpended ammunition properly protected by the latter hour.

6. Should the weather conditions render the shoot impossible, the code word "HERRING" will be sent out before each shoot. The use of this code word before 7 p.m. on October 5th will only refer to first part of programme. The second portion will still take place unless the code word is repeated later.

Should it be necessary to postpone both shoots, the O.C. Right Battalion will arrange to hand over the dugout in BURG TRENCH North of JANET LANE to the O.C. Special Coy. for purposes of storing the unused ammunition. The present occupants of this dugout will be accommodated elsewhere.

7. Extra precautions will be taken to ensure that all ranks carry their Box Respirators in the Alert position ready to put on at once.

8. ACKNOWLEDGE.

T.W. MacDonald. Captain,
Brigade Major, 49th Infantry Brigade.

Issued through Signals.

```
Copy No. 1 to G. O. C.
     ..     2    Staff Captain.
     ..     3    Bde. Intelligence Officer.
     ..     4    Bde. Signal Officer.
     ..     5    2nd R. Irish Regt.
     ..     6    7/8th R. Innis Fus.
     ..     7    7th R. Irish Rifles.
     ..     8    7/8th R. Irish Fus.
     ..     9    49th M.G. Company.
     ..    10    49th T.M. Battery.
     ..    11    16th Div. (G).
     ..    12    47th Inf. Bde.
     ..    13    153rd Inf. Bde.
     ..    14    180th Bde. R.F.A.
     ..    15    No. 3 Special Coy, R.E.
                 (BOISLEAUX-au-MONT).
     ..    16    155th Field Coy, R.E.
     ..    17    157th Field Coy, R.E.
     ..   18-19  War Diary.
     ..    20    File.
```

Secret.   Copy No. 1.

Operation Order No. 51.

by

Lieut. Colonel. J.D. Scott. Commanding.
2nd Bn. THE ROYAL IRISH REGIMENT.

Ref. Map
HANDECOURT. 4. S.   In the field. 9-10-1917.

1. The 48th Inf. Bde. (less M.G. Coy) will relieve the 49th Inf. Bde. (less M.G. Coy) in the left section on 10th October. 1917.

2. This Battalion will be relieved by the 10th Bn. R. DUBLIN FUS. Relief to be complete by 3 p.m. On completion of relief Companies will move to CLONMEL CAMP by platoons at 5 minutes interval.

3. A Coy. 10th R. DUBLIN FUS. will relieve A Coy. 2nd Bn. THE ROYAL IRISH.
   B   "   "   "   "   "   "   "   "   D   "   "   "   "   "
   C   "   "   "   "   "   "   "   "   C   "   "   "   "   "
   D   "   "   "   "   "   "   "   "   B   "   "   "   "   "

4. Officer Commanding D Coy will send 1 guide per platoon under a senior NCO to X Roads ST LEGER 12.30 p.m. to guide B Coy. 10th R.D.F. No other guides are required.

5. Advance parties 10th R.D.F. will take over stores as at the respective Coy. H.Q. 10.30 a.m.

6. All stores, defence schemes, plans of work in progress & proposed, &c. will be handed over and receipts taken. Copies of receipts will be sent to Bn. H.Q. by 12 noon, 11th inst. Aeroplane photographs will not be handed over.

7. Coy. B.M. Sergts. under the Quartermaster will take over CLONMEL CAMP by 12 noon.

8. Officers' trench kits, mess boxes, &c. will be dumped at Coy. H.Q. by 2 p.m. 10th inst. Transport Officer will arrange the necessary transport.

9. Completion of relief will be notified by wire to Bn. H.Q. by code word CLONMEL.

10. ACKNOWLEDGE.

P. Cahndy
Capt. Adjutant.
2nd Bn. THE ROYAL IRISH REGIMENT.

Issued at 3 p.m.

Copy No 1. War Diary.   5. O.C. B Coy.   9. Q.M.
        2. 48th Inf. Bde.   6.   " C   "   10. T.O.
        3. 10th R.D.F.   7.   " D   "   11. Sig. Officer.
        4. O.C. A Coy.   8. M.O.   12. Int. Officer.

SECRET.   Copy No. 1

OPERATION ORDER NO. 52.
by
LIEUT. COLONEL. J. B. SCOTT, COMMANDING,
2nd. Battalion, The Royal Irish Regiment.

Reference Map, HEUDECOURT, 4d.   In the Field, 20-10-1917.

---

1. The 49th. Inf. Bde. (less Machine Gun Company) will relieve the 48th. Inf. Bde. (less Machine Gun Company) in the Left Section on the 22nd. October 1917.

2. The following will be carefully taken over:-
   (a) All trench stores, maps, defence plans.
   (b) All work in progress and proposed.
   A list of all trench stores and ammunition taken over will be forwarded to Battn. H.Q. by 12noon 23rd. October. Aeroplane photographs will not be taken over.

3. 2nd. The Rl. Irish Regt. will relieve 10th. R. Dub. Fus. in right sub-section as follows:-

   "C" Company.   Right.
   "D" Company.   Right Centre.
   "A" Company.   Left Centre.
   "B" Company.   Left.

   marching up in this order by platoons at 500 yards interval, H.Q. last. "A" Company will march off at 12.30 p.m.

4. Advanced parties of Lewis Gun Sections, Scouts, Signallers and one Officer per Coy. and one N.C.O. per platoon, Coy. gas N.C.Os. will take over from 10th. R. Dub. Fus. at 11 a.m. leaving camp in four parties at 500 yards interval, first party at 9-30 a.m.

5. Transport to wait and bring back stores of 10th. R. Dub. Fus.

6. Carrying party,- Drums under Sgt. Drummer to take over from the 10th. R. Dub. Fus. at the QUARRY.

7. Officers valises, etc., to be dumped by 12 noon at the Q.M. Stores.

8. Completion of relief to be sent to Bn. H.Q. by code word THURLES.

9. ACKNOWLEDGE.

                                                Captain & Adjutant,
                                    2nd. Battalion, The Royal Irish Regiment.

Issued at 6 p.m.
Copy No. 1. War Diary.   Copy No. 9. Q.M.
        2. H.Q. 49th. Inf. Bd.   10. T.O.
        3. 10th. R.D.F.   11. Sig. Officer.
        4. O.C. "A" Coy.   12. Int. Officer.
        5. O.C. "B" Coy.   13. R.S.M.
        6. O.C. "C" Coy.   14. Cook Sgt.
        7. O.C. "D" Coy.   15. Sgt. Drummer.
        8. M.O.

SECRET.

Copy No......

49th INFANTRY BRIGADE ORDER No 171.

Ref. map 51.B.S.W.4.
and attached sketch.
                                                            24th October,
                                                            1917

1. On the night 25th/26th October, or on the first suitable night after that date, No. 3 Special Company R.E. will carry out a Gas and Smoke Bombardment with 4" Stokes Mortars of TUNNEL TRENCH from JOVE REBUS (U.20.B.47.70.) to junction with FRINGE TRENCH (U.7.B.45.10.)

2. The front to be dealt with is divided into 4 sectors. A,B,C,D, as shown on the attached map. Ten guns will fire on each sector.

3. The Bombardment will be carried out in 2 shoots as under:-

SHOOT.	TIME.	SECTOR.	MORTARS.	ROUNDS PER GUN.	TOTAL.
(a)	10 p.m. Oct 25th	A.B.C.D.	40.	30.	1200.
(b)	3 a.m. Oct. 26th	A.B.C.D.	40.	30.	1200.

The 30 rounds per gun fired on each occasion will be made up as follows:-

    15 rounds P.S.
    10 rounds C.G.
    5 rounds Smoke.

4. Firing will take place in any wind between W and S.S.W.

5. (a) If weather conditions are clearly unfavourable at 1/30p.m. on October 25th, the code word "CASE" will be sent from Brigade Headquarters to all concerned. This will mean "both bombardments postponed 24 hours".

(b) If the weather conditions appear favourable at 1 p.m. October 25th the code word "JUMP" will be sent out. If subsequently conditions become unfavourable O.C. Special Coy. R.E. will send the code word "RANDOM" from 49th Inf. Bde. H.Q. to Div. H.Q. by whom it will be repeated to all concerned. This will only refer to the first bombardment. The second bombardment will take place unless the word "RANDOM" is repeated a second time.

The final decision will be made by O.C. No.3 Special Coy. in consultation with G.O.C. 49th Inf. Bde. (attention is called to 16th Div. No. A.S. 1091/158 dated 7th Oct. forwarded under 49th Inf Bde. No. S.O. 177)

New code words will be sent out on Oct. 27th and each day following a postponement of both bombardments.

Should it be necessary to postpone one or both shoots, the O.C. Right Sub-Section will arrange to hand over the dug out in BURG TRENCH, N of JANET LANE to the O.C. Special Coy for purposes of storing the unused ammunition.

6. The following trenches will be cleared ten minutes before ZERO in each bombardment.
(a) LUMP LANE (except for sap at U.7.b.10.00.) care will be taken to clear LUMP LANE silently and in small parties only.
(b) Trenches and saps east of HUMBER SUPPORT.
(c) BURG SUPPORT and front line, except for portions shaded in RED on attached map, which will be left garrisoned.

P.T.O.

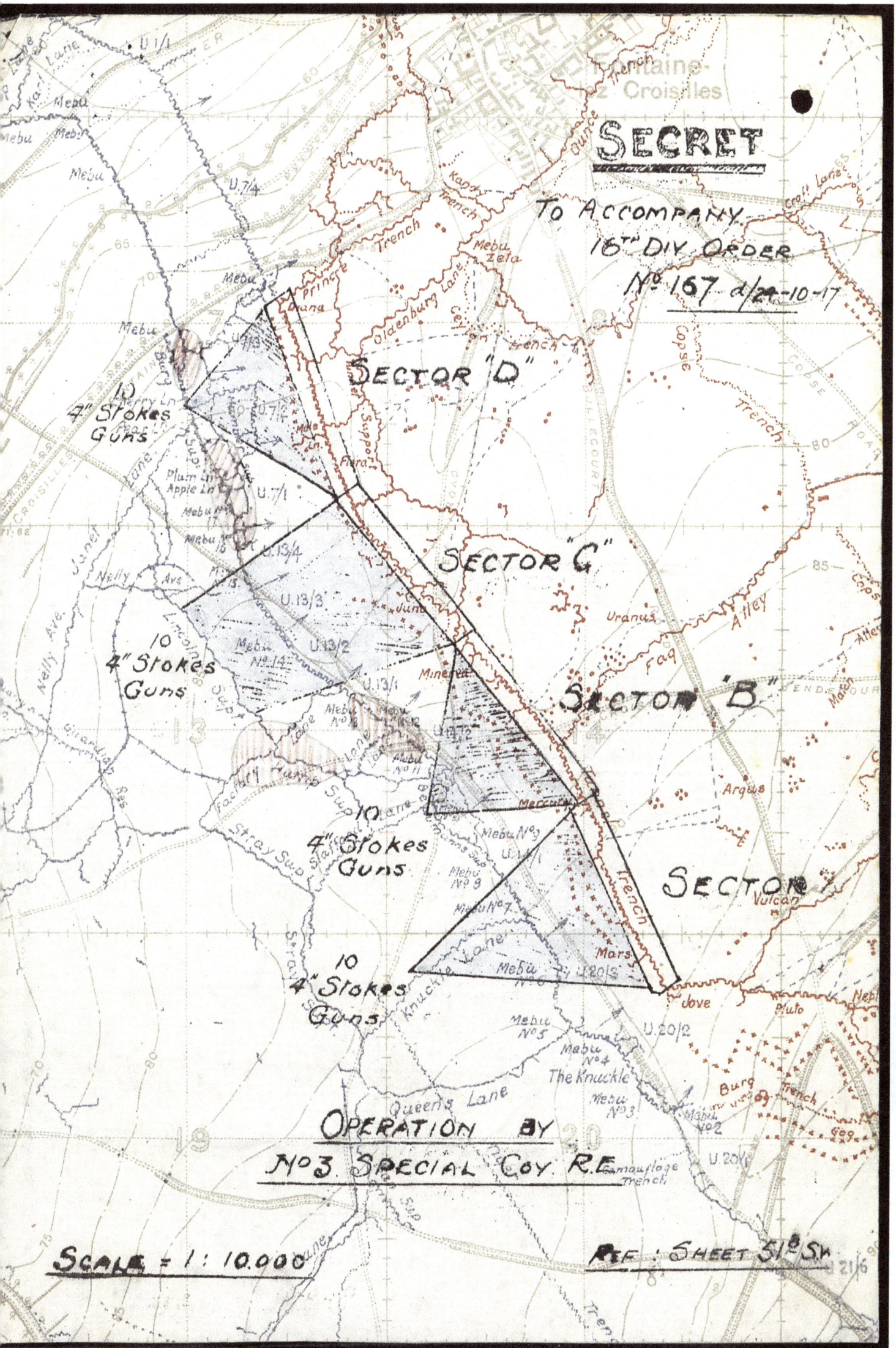

(2)

Troops will as far as possible be accommodated under cover. Above positions will be reoccupied 15 minutes after "all clear" is given by O.C. Special Coy R.E. In all cases a careful reconnaisence will be made of all trenches to see that they are clear of gas.

7. An Officer No. 3 Special Coy R.E. will be sent to Coy H.Q. at junction of LUMP LANE and BURG SUPPORT, and 1 to Coy H.Q. in LINCOLN SUPPORT, where the O.s C left and right Sub-Sections respectively will have a liason Officer, to whom the "all clear" as regards D, and C Sectors will be given. These Officers will report at these places half an hour before ZERO in each bombardment.

8. All dug-out curtains in LINCOLN SUPPORT and N.E. of LINCOLN SUPPORT will be dropped, and extra precautions will be taken to see that all ranks carry their box respirators in the "Alert" position ready to put on at once.

9. The Machine Guns covering the front will enfilade TUNNEL TRENCH, NO MANS LAND and main communication trenches in rear commencing at each ZERO hour under orders to be issued by D.M.G.O.

10. 16th D.A. will arrange for bursts of shrapnel on the main communication trenches and tracks in rear of TUNNEL TRENCH during each discharge from ZERO plus 3 to ZERO plus 15.

11. Signal time will be sent to all concerned at 5 p.m. on the day of bombardment.

12. ACKNOWLEDGE.

signature, Captain.

Brigade Major, 49th Infantry Brigade.

Issued through Signals.

copy No.	1.	to	* G.O.C.
"	2.		Staff Captain.
"	3.		Bde. Intelligence Officer.
"	4.		Bde. Signal Officer.
"	5.		* 2nd R. Irish Regt.
"	6.		* 7th (S.I.H.) R. Irish Regt.
"	7.		* 7/8th R. Innis Fus.
"	8.		* 7/8th R. Irish Fus.
"	9.		* 49th M.G. Company.
"	10.		* 49th T.M. Battery.
"	11.		16th Division. (G)
"	12.		47th Inf. Bde.
"	13.		48th Inf. Bde.
"	14.		152nd Inf. Bde.
"	15.		180th Bde. R.F.A.
"	16.		No. 3 Special Coy. R.E. (BOISLEAUX-AU-MONT)
"	17.		155 Fd.Coy. R.E.
"	18.		157 Fd. Coy. R.E.
"	19-20		War Diary.
"	21.		File.

* Maps to those only.

S563 I. OPERATION ORDER NO. 53.   Copy No. _____
                    by
            LIEUT. COLONEL J.D.SCOTT, COMMANDING,
            2nd. Battalion, The Royal Irish Regiment.
Reference Map. HEUDECOURT, 4d.   In the Field, 27th. October, 1917.
_____

1. The 7/8th. R. Innis Fus. will relieve the 2nd. R. Irish Regt. in
   the Right Sub Section on the 28th. October.
         Relief to be complete by 5 p.m.
2. On relief Companies will be disposed as under:-
         "A" Company,   T.22.b.3.7.
         "B" Company,   QUARRY.
         "C" Company,   T.23.d.8.2.
         "D" Company,   T.23.c.6.8.
3. "A" and "B" Companies will not leave the front line trenches till
   JANET AVENUE is cleared by the R.Innis. Fus. Similarly "D" Company
   till NELLY AVENUE, and "C" Company till FACTORY AVENUE is clear.
   NELLY and JANET AVENUES are placed at the disposal of the left sub-
   section up to 2-30 p.m.
4. Usual advance parties will take over from the 7/8th. R.Innis. Fus.
   at 12 noon.
         Lewis Gunners when relieved will move to new positions under senior
   Lewis Gun N.C.O. of each Company.
5. All trench stores, defence plans, work in progress and contemplated
   will be carefully handed over.
         Lists of trench stores will be sent to Bn. H.Q. by 9 a.m. 28th.
   inst. Aeroplane photographs will not be handed over.
6. All movement will be by platoons at 5 minutes interval.
7. Officers' trench kits etc., will be at QUARRY at 5 p.m.
         Transport Officer will arrange transport.
8. Rations and one blanket per man will be sent up to Coy. H.Q.
   by Quartermaster reaching there by 6-30 p.m.
9. Completion of reliefs, Bn.H.Q. - "KNIFE".
10. ACKNOWLEDGE.

                                        Captain & Adjutant,
                            2nd. Battalion, The Royal Irish Regiment.
Issued at 6 p.m.
         Copy No.1. War Diary.   No.9. Q.M.
              2. H.Q.49th.Inf.Bde.   10. T.O.
              3. 7/8.R.Innis.Fus.   11. Sig. Officer.
              4. O.C."A" Coy.   12. Int. Officer.
              5. O.C."B" Coy.   13. R.S.M.
              6. O.C."C" Coy.   14. Cook Sgt.
              7. O.C."D" Coy.   15. Sgt. Dr.
              8. M.O.

SECRET. App 2 Copy No. 5

49th Infantry Brigade Order No. 173.

Oct. 27th. 1917.

Ref. Map CHERISY
Edn. 3C. 1/10,000.

1.   A raid will be carried out on the 29th October, 1917 by a Company 7/8th R. Innis Fus. (Strength of Raiding Party about 4 Officers and 100 Other Ranks.)
O.C. Raid Captain H.A. GREEN, M.C.

VI Corps Heavy Artillery, 16th Div. Artillery, 49th T.M.Battery, 49th L.G.Company and No. 3 Special Company, R.E. are co-operating.
The 47th Inf. Bde. on the right, and the 153rd Inf. Bde. on the left are making demonstrations.

2.   OBJECT.

To obtain sufficient prisoners for identification purposes and for information, and to inflict damage upon enemy personnel and defences.

3.   RAID AREA.

Trenches to be raided are - Enemy front line and saps from U.7.d.55.85 to U.7.d.70.40 and Support Line about 120 yards in rear of above and two communication trenches connecting front line and support.

4.   ASSEMBLY POSITIONS.

British Front Line from U.7.d.35.75 to U.7.d.35.40.

5.   TASKS.

Raid Company will be devided into 4 parties whose tasks are allotted as follows :-

No. 1.   Deal with OLDENBURG LANE from front line to support, picketing trench junctions at U.7.d.75.85 and U.7.d.85.85 and working South along TUNNEL SUPPORT.

No. 2.   Front line from U.7.d.60.80 to U.7.d.65.65. Special squads to be told off to deal with deep dugouts and prisoners. Tunnel entrances will be dealt with by smoke bombs at alternate entrances, the others being left as "bolt-holes".

No. 3.   Deal with sap and communication trench on South of raid front. Work North along TUNNEL SUPPORT, picketing junction at U.7.d.90.60. One squad of this party will proceed direct to bomb saphead at U.7.d.50.40.

No. 4.   Front line from U.7.d.65.65 to U.7.d.70.40. Special Squads to deal with deep dugouts, (as for No. 2 party) and prisoners.

A covering party of one Lewis Gun and a squad of bombers will protect each flank of the raiding party.

6. ARTILLERY. 18-pdrs.

Zero to Zero plus 2 minutes - Intense barrage on front line from U.7.b.7.3 - U.7.b.4.1. - U.7.d.7.4.

Zero plus 2 minutes - Lift to TUNNEL SUPPORT firing on that trench until Zero plus 5 minutes.

Zero plus 5 minutes and onwards - lift from TUNNEL SUPPORT and form Box Barrage along lines U.7.b.5.0 - U.8.a.1.1 - U.8.c.2.0 - U.7.d.7.3.

Fire will cease at Zero plus 15 minutes, unless artillery are notified to the contrary.

4.5" Howitzers.

Commencing at Zero :-

Two Hows. On trench junctions at U.7.b.7.4, afterwards searching up along trenches running North and North East from this point.
One How. OLDENBURG LANE at U.8.a.2.2.
Two Hows. CEYLON TRENCH U.8.a.4.3 and U.8.a.7.0.
One How. One, U.8.c.4.0.

7. TRENCH MORTARS.

2" Mortars.

Commencing at Zero :-

One Mortar on Sap and MEBU at U.14.a.1.7 (JUNO).
One Mortar on MEBU at U.7.d.7.3. (FLORA).
One Mortar U.13.b.85.90.
One Mortar on MEBU at U.14.a.4.3. (MINERVA).

3" Stokes Guns.

4 guns Zero to Zero plus 1 minute - Intense barrage on front line U.7.b.7.3 - U.7.b.4.1. - U.7.d.7.4.
Zero plus 1 minute to plus 2 minutes guns firing on frontage U.7.b.5.0 - U.7.d.7.4. ~~Cease fire~~ lift on to TUNNEL SUPPORT

2 guns. Traverse enemy front line South of raid front from zero onwards.

4" Stokes Guns.

Will, if wind is favourable, at Zero, form a Smoke Barrage on flanks and support line of raid front.

8. No. 3 SPECIAL COMPANY, R.E.

No. 3 Special Coy, R.E., should the wind be favourable, are co-operating by forming a Smoke Barrage on either flank.

Targets.

1. U.7.b.5.0 to U.7.b.9.1. - 3 guns.
2. U.7.d.7.3 to U.8.c.1.5. - 3 guns.
3. U.8.c.20.50 to U.8.a.1.1. - 4 guns.

9. MACHINE GUNS.

(a) Zero to zero plus 8 minutes - enfilade TUNNEL SUPPORT TRENCH. in U.7.d.
(b) Barrage along general line U.7.b.7.9 - U.8.central.
(c) Sunken Road in U.8.a. and c.
(d) Fire also on U.7.b.4.1, FONTAINE, BUS JUNO and organised shell holes about U.14.a.9.7.
(e) Enfilade FAG ALLEY.
(f) Search SENSEE VALLEY in U.7.b.
(g) Arrange with Division on right to enfilade SUNKEN ROAD in U.14.b and d and TUNNEL TRENCH in U.14.d. and U.20.b.

LEWIS GUNS.

Lewis Guns to fire short bursts at intervals along enemy front line South of Raid Front.

10. WIRE CUTTING.

Artillery and T.M's to cut wire on raid front, and also at other selected places in order to avoid raising suspicion. Gaps to be kept open by Lewis Gun fire at night.

11. DIVISION ON LEFT.

The 51st Division on the left are arranging to put down at Zero a Barrage of H.E. and Smoke on the German front line in U.1.b. which will lift to the enemy support line.

In conjunction with this, the 7th (S.I.H) R. Irish Regt., if wind is favourable, will throw out some "P" Bombs at end of PUG LANE, and open fire with Lewis Guns. in direction of FONTAINE.

47th Inf. Bde. will co-operate by making a feint attack against the right about U.14.d.1.4 to U.20.b.4.7 by putting down a barrage of Stokes Guns and Lewis Guns, and if wind is favourable using smoke and "P" Bombs.

12. RAID HEADQUARTERS.

Headquarters of O.C. Raid will be in deep dugout at U.7.d.15.20. All reports will be sent here and on return raiding party will assemble in this dugout. Prisoners and captured material will be sent to Right Battalion Headquarters.

13. SIGNALS.

The Signalling Officer, 7/8th R. Innis Fus. will arrange for direct communication by telephone and runners between Battalion H.Q. and H.Q. of O.C. Raid. All lines will be left as clear as possible for raid messages.

The Recall signal will be GOLDEN RAIN ROCKETS fired some distance behind our front line.

14. TRAFFIC.

JANET AVENUE, CHERRY, PEAR and PLUMB LANES will be kept clear of all traffic except that which concerns the raid, also BURG SUPPORT between CHERRY and PLUMB LANES.

15. MEDICAL.

The Medical Officer will establish an Adv. Aid Post in deep dugout at U.7.d.15.20 where stretcher cases will be dealt with. Walking wounded will proceed via JANET AVENUE direct to AID POST in QUARRY, first reporting to a N.C.O. who will be posted at junction of JANET AVENUE and BURG SUPPORT.

16. Watches will be synchronized at 12 noon and 2 p.m. at Brigade H.Q. Representatives of following will attend at these times :-

    Divisional Machine Guns.
    7th (S.I.H) R. Irish Regt.
    7/8th R. Innis Fus.
    D.T.M.O.
    49th T.M.Battery.
    16th Div. Artillery.
    No. 3 Special Coy, R.E.
    and SOUTH. I. HORSE.

17. 7/8th R. Innis Fus. will reduce their trench garrison to a minimum. As many men as possible will be accommodated in dugouts.

18. LUMP LANE will be cleared, in small parties and silently, at Zero minus 20, and regarrisoned when the situation quietens down.

19. Zero hour will be notified later.

20. ACKNOWLEDGE.

T. W. MacDonald. Captain,

Brigade Major, 49th Infantry Brigade.

Issued through Signals.

    Copy No. 1 to G. O. C.
    ..   2   Staff Captain.
    ..   3   Bde. Intelligence Officer.
    ..   4   Bde. Signal Officer.
    ..   5   2nd R. Irish Regt.
    ..   6   7th (S.I.H) R. Irish Regt.
    ..   7   7/8th R. Innis Fus.
    ..   8   7/8th R. Innis Fus.
    ..   9   7/8th R. Irish Fus.
    ..   10   49th M.G.Company.
    ..   11   49th T.M.Battery.
    ..   12   No. 3 Special Coy, R.E.
    ..   13   D.T.M.O.
    ..   14   D.M.G.O.
    ..   15   16th Div. Arty.
    ..   16   16th Div. (G).
    ..   17   47th Inf. Bde.
    ..   18   48th Inf. Bde.
    ..   19   153rd Inf. Bde.
    ..   20   180th Bde. R.F.A.
    ..   21   155th Field Coy, R.E.
    ..   22   157th Field Coy, R.E.
    ..   23-24 War Diary.
    ..   25   File.
    ..   26   VIth Corps H.A.

20.B.
(70 sheets)

WAR DIARY

FOR MONTH OF NOVEMBER, 1917.

VOLUME :-

UNIT :- 2nd R. Irish Regiment

Army Form C. 2118.

WAR DIARY
or
INTELLIGENCE SUMMARY.
(Erase heading not required.)

Instructions regarding War Diaries and Intelligence Summaries are contained in F.S. Regs., Part II. and the Staff Manual respectively. Title pages will be prepared in manuscript.

November

Place	Date	Hour	Summary of Events and Information	Remarks and references to Appendices
"	1st-7th	—	Usual routine in Camp. Parades 9-12 afternoon	App I
HAMELINCOURT	7th		Relieved the 8/9th R.D.F. (48th Bde) in left support. Coys in Sunken Roads around CROISILLES — A Coy in SHAFT TR — (Hindenburg line)	App 2
CROISILLES (Left Sector)	8, 9, 10, 11		Rather bad weather. On 10th Nov No 3 Special Company R.E. Carried out a Gas + Smoke Bombardment of TUNNEL TRENCH Very successful. 2 of Enemy came across and gave themselves up as a result.	App 3
"	12		Relieved by the 8/9 Royal Dublin Fusiliers. In relief Bn moved to ENNISKILLEN CAMP, ERVILLERS, a Camp in which we had never been before – much better than CLONMEL CAMP.	App 3 & 4
ERVILLERS	13, 14, 15, 16, 17		Four very pleasant days spent in practising for attack over model trenches on a piece of ground W of ERVILLERS. Had a very successful "dress" Rehearsal on 17th. Conf. own normal Bgde + adj own artillery were present. The afternoons were spent in Coy football and bgt all coys kept fit + well. The men in great fettle.	App 4

WAR DIARY
or
INTELLIGENCE SUMMARY.

(Erase heading not required.)

Army Form C. 2118.

Place	Date	Hour	Summary of Events and Information	Remarks and references to Appendices
ERVILLERS	18	—	Battalion took over a portion of the front and support line from 2/6 R Warks. Killing of Officers and Casualties. 2/Lieut J.A. MANLEY wd and 3 O.R. wd.	App 5
FRONT LINE	19		Day quiet. Hostile artillery slightly active. The casualty last night were caused by pineapples (light T.M - Granatenwerfer) Coys busy in making final preparations. From 6.30 pm until 8 pm gaps were cut in our wire.	
"	20"		At 5.30 a.m. all companies were in their assembly positions. The Battalion attacked with "B" Coy (Capt O'REILLY) on the right, "D" Coy (Capt PIM) on the left, and "A" Coy (2/Lt TERRY) + 2 Platoons from "C" Coy - wiring. Zero hour was 5.30 am TUNNEL TRENCH (subsidiary line) and TUNNEL SUPPORT were captured by 6.30 am. Our casualties were slight. The only offer being hit was 2/Lt M°CLUSKEY "D" Coy. The M.G.R had proven on our left were held up and suffered many casualties the 4th York 2/10 prisoners and killed about 50. Enemy artillery fire was very severe throughout the day - most of it being directed on communication trenches and our original front line. For narrative see App.	App 6
	21		Enemy attempted to counter-attack but his attack double deeper made our artillery W.C. fire shells into suddenly throughout the day	App 7

WAR DIARY
or
INTELLIGENCE SUMMARY.
(Erase heading not required.)

Army Form C. 2118.

Place	Date	Hour	Summary of Events and Information	Remarks and references to Appendices
FRONT LINE	22		At 6 am the S.O.S. was put up but no infantry attack followed. Enemy's artillery very active during night 21/22. Relieved at 7.30 pm by 1/8 R. Innis Fuseliers and marched to CONNEL CAMP. Total casualties for the action of ROEUX HEIGHTS: 3 Officers (2/Lts MAHEY, McCLUSKEY and KELLY) and 80 other ranks.	App 10
HAMELINCOURT	23		Pm Complimented by Major-General HICKIE CB GOC 16 Div for their good work in the last action.	1/2
	24,25,26, 27,28,29		Usual camp routine. Cleaning and remaining up of rifts. 3 hard days in the line.	1/2
	30		Relieved the 8/9 R.D.F. in the right sub-section. No Casualties.	App 8
			For movements of Officers and other ranks reinforcements see App 9 page 1v	App 9

WAR DIARY
or
INTELLIGENCE SUMMARY.
(Erase heading not required.)

Army Form C. 2118.

OFFICERS.
Thereon

Capt H.J.M. O'REILLY M.C.   from Hos. 3.11.17
2/:   C.H. SMITH   "   7.11.17
Major H.G. GREGORIE M.S.O.   Receipt   18.11.17

Officers.

2/: R.A. MANLEY (RMF) W.A-in-Act 19-11-17
2/: B.V. McCLUSKEY (RDF)   "   20.11.17
 "   P. KELLY (C.R.)   "   21.11.17
2/: C.S. SALMON   " to note 25.11.17
2/: O.H. SMITH   to note 1047.17.11.13

All movements attached to the bottom of CROISILLES
HEIGHTS are appended and called appendix 9

SECRET.   Copy No. 19

48th INFANTRY BRIGADE.
OPERATION ORDER No. 170.

8th November, 1917.

1. No. 3 Special Company R.E. will carry out a Gas and Smoke Bombardment at 7 a.m. on 9th November.

2. The front to be dealt with is divided into four sectors A, B, C and D, as shewn on Map "Z" issued with 48th Infantry Brigade Operation Order No. 167 dated 3.11.17.

3. <u>DETAILS OF SHOOT</u> :-

Shoot.	Time.	Sector.	Mortars	Rounds per Gun	Total
No. 3	7 a.m. Nov. 9th 1917.	A, B, C and D.	40	30	1200.

The 30 rounds per gun fired will be made up as follows :-
  15 rounds   P.S.
  10 rounds   C.G.
  5 rounds   Smoke.

4. Firing will take place in any wind between W. and S.S.W.

5. (a) If weather conditions are clearly unfavorable at 5.30 p.m. on November 8th the code word "BRASS" will be sent out to all concerned from Brigade Headquarters. This will mean "Shoot postponed 24 hours."

   (b) If weather conditions are favorable at 6.30 p.m. on November 8th the code word "TIN" will be sent from Brigade Headquarters shortly afterwards.

   (c) If subsequently weather conditions become unfavorable O.C. No. 3 Special Coy. R.E. will send a code word "IRON" from 48th Infantry Brigade Headquarters to Divisional Headquarters, by whom it will be reaported to all concerned.

   (d) O.C. No. 3 Special Coy. R.E. will be at 48th Infantry Brigade Headquarters at 4 a.m. November 9th

6. (a) Officers Commanding 1st R. Dub. Fus. (Right Sub-section) and 8/9th R. Dub. Fus. (Left Sub-section) will arrange to clear the trenches within the area shaded in BLUE on map "Z" published with 48th Infantry Brigade O.O. 167 of 3.11.1917.
   (b) O.C. Special Coy. R.E. will arrange with O's.C. Right and Left Sub-sections to meet them or their representatives at half an hour before Zero at some

SECRET.   COPY NO. _____

OPERATION ORDER NO. 57.

by

LIEUT. COLONEL J. B. SCOTT, COMMANDING,
2nd. Battalion, The Royal Irish Regiment.

In the Field, 11-11-17.
----

1. The Battalion will be relieved by the 8th/9th. R. Dub. Fus. in Left Support, tomorrow, the 12th. inst.
   On relief, the Battalion will move to ENNISKILLEN CAMP, ERVILLERS.
2. Relief will be complete by 5 p.m.
   Advance parties of the 8th/9th. R. Dub. Fus. will take over four hours before the main relief.
3. The usual billeting party under the Quartermaster, will take over the new camp at 11 a.m., on the 12th. inst.
4. All movement will be by platoons at 500 yards interval.
5. All working parties will be cancelled from 8 a.m. on the day of relief to 8 a.m. the following day.
6. Officers' trench kits, mess stores, blankets, etc., will be dumped at ration dumps by 2 p.m. Transport Officer will arrange transport.
7. The following will be handed over to, and receipts obtained from relieving unit:
   (a). Trench maps.
   (b). Defence schemes.
   (c). Trench stores.
   (d). Full statement of work in progress (Company Commanders to note) together with details of any working or carrying parties.
   Receipts and trench stores lists to reach Orderly Room by 9 a.m., the 13th. November.
8. Completion of relief will be wired to Battalion H.Q. using code word, "LENIN".
9. A C K N O W L E D G E.

                                                    F. Gawley.
                                                    Captain,
                                                    Adjutant,
                                          2nd. Battalion, The Royal Irish Regiment.

Issued at. _____

Copy No. 1. War Diary.   No. 9. M.O.
        2. H.Q. 48th. Inf. Bde.   10. Q.M.
        3. H.Q. 49th. Inf. Bde.   11. T.O.
        4. 8/9th. R. Dub. Fus.   12. Signalling Officer
        5. O.C. "A" Coy.   13. Intelligence Officer
        6. O.C. "B" Coy.   14. R.S.M.
        7. O.C. "C" Coy.   15. Cook Sergt.
        8. O.C. "D" Coy.   16. Sergt. Dr.

S E C R E T.

47th Inf. Bde.
48th Inf. Bde.
49th Inf. Bde.

16th Div. Arty.)
Lt. Col. PHIPPS, 39th H.A.G.) for information.
O.C. 4th H.A.G.)

16th Div. No. G.131/17.   14th November 1917.

---

1. The Heavy Artillery hope to start wire cutting opposite the Divisional Front beginning tomorrow 15th instant.

2. This will necessitate frequent clearances of our own trenches opposite the targets on which they are firing. As however firing can only be carried out under favourable weather conditions and time is limited it may be necessary to carry out shoots at short notice whenever a favourable opportunity occurs.

3. To avoid loss of time in arranging clearances the following procedure will be adopted:-

   (a) The Heavy Artillery will inform Infantry Brigadiers direct of any wire cutting that they propose to carry out on their front, giving the target, the clearances that will be necessary and the approximate date and hour. As much warning as possible should be given. Copies of these programmes should be sent to the 16th Division.

   (b) The above information will enable Infantry Brigadiers to make any necessary preparations for clearing their trenches when required to do so.

   (c) As soon after the time fixed as weather conditions are favourable, an officer representing the Heavy Artillery unit which is about to fire will report to the Infantry Officer commanding the portion of the trenches to be cleared and will notify him that the shoot is about to take place. Sufficient warning must be given to enable the clearance to be carried out properly. The Artillery representative will be responsible for ensuring that no firing takes place before the Infantry are ready.

   (d) No clearances will be carried out until the artillery representative informs the infantry commander on the spot that the shoot is going to take place.

4. The Heavy Artillery representative will act as liaison officer with the Infantry Battalion Commander and will inform him or his representative when the shoot is finished and trenches may be reoccupied.

5. ACKNOWLEDGE.

(sd) L.C. JACKSON, Lt. Col.,
General Staff, 16th Division.

2nd R. Irish Regt.
7th (S.I.H) R.I. Regt.
7/8th R. Innis Fus.   1st R. Dublin Fus.
7/8th R. Irish Fus.   8/9th R. Dublin Fus.

49th Inf. Bde. No. S.O. 284 - 15-11-17.

For information.

Captain,
Brigade Major, 49th Infantry Brigade.

SECRET.   COPY NO.

OPERATION ORDERS NO. 58.,
by,
LIEUT. COLONEL, J.D. SCOTT, COMMANDING,
2nd. Battalion The Royal Irish Regiment.
In the Field, 17-11-1917.
----

1. The 2nd. Rl. Irish Regt., will take over a portion of the front line and support from the 7/8th. Rl. Innis. Fus. tomorrow.

2. The Battalion will be disposed as follows:-
   "A" Company plus 2 platoons, 7/8th. Rl. Innis. Fus. - front line and support from junction of NELLY AVENUE and FRONT LINE (inclusive) to U.7.d.30.50. and PEAR LANE - latter exclusive.
   "C" Company - 1 platoon Dug-out, JANET AVENUE, U.7.c.7.2.
                 1 platoon Dug-out, LINCOLN SUPPORT, U.13.a.9.7.
                 1 platoon Dug-out, NELLY SWITCH.
                 1 platoon, Dug-out, BURG SUPPORT.
   "B" Company - SUNKEN ROAD, T.22.a.2.2.
   "D" Company - Support Battalion H.Q., T.22.d.2.9.
   (N.C.Os. and men will only use quarters there provided for them.)

3. Headquarters will be as follows:-
   Bn. H.Q.   - Dug-out, BURG SUPPORT.
   "A" Coy.   - DUG-OUT, BURG SUPPORT.
   "C" Coy.   - Dug-out, JANET AVENUE.

4. Order of march, - "A", H.Q., "C", "B", "D". Leading platoon of "A" Coy. will leave INNISKILLING CAMP at 12 noon and will take over front line by 3-30 p.m.
   The whole relief will be complete at 5 p.m. and will be reported to Battn. H.Q. by code word "DUBLIN". Movement will be by platoons at 500 yards interval. If the weather is clear and enemy's aircraft and Balloons are active use must be made of communication trenches at CROISILLES end.

5. On Y/Z night the Battalion will move into its assembly positions as detailed:-
   "A" Company plus 2 platoons, 7/8th. Rl. Innis. Fus. -
   2 platoons - dug-out, NELLY SWITCH.
   2 platoons - dug-out, BURG SUPPORT.
   "C" Company in BURG SUPPORT. / para 8.
   (This cancels O.O. No. 55/as far as "A" and "C" Coys. are concerned).
   This move is to be complete by 1½ hours before ZERO.
   "C" Coy. on completion of wiring will return to support and be disposed as follows:-
   1 platoon and Coy. H.Q. in dug-out at junction of NELLY AVENUE and LINCOLN SUPPORT.
   2 platoons - NELLY SWITCH.
   1 platoon dug-out, BURG SUPPORT.

6. When companies are in their assembly positions, they will report to Battalion H.Q., using code word, "PAPER".

7. In taking up positions on Y/Z night, great care must be taken that there is no talking, striking of lights or flashing of torches, etc.
   O.C. "A" Coy. will provide two listening posts in the wire to see that patrols of the enemy do not approach our trenches at important places, such as heads of C.Ts. etc. When "A" Coy. is relieved, "B" Coy. will relieve the right listening post, "D" Coy., the left, withdrawing them at ZERO - 15 minutes.

8. ZERO hour and day will be notified later.

-2-

9. All blankets and Officers' valises will be stacked in the space in front of the guard room, by 11 a.m.

10. For the relief of the 18th. inst., the usual advance parties will proceed and take over 4 hours before relief.

11. A C K N O W L E D G E.

                                               Captain,
                                          Adjutant,
2nd. Battalion, The Royal Irish Regiment.

Issued at _____

Copies to:-

	Copy No.1.	War Diary,
	2.	Headquarters, 49th. Infantry Brigade.
	3.	7/8th. Rl. Innis. Fus.
	4.	2/Rl. Dublin Fus.
	5.	Commanding Officer.
	6.	Second in Command.
	7.	Adjutant.
	8.	O.C. "A" Company.
	9.	O.C. "B" Company.
	10.	O.C. "C" Company.
	11.	O.C. "D" Company.
	12.	Intelligence Officer.
	13.	Signalling Officer.
	14.	Medical Officer.
	15.	Lt. McKENNA, 7/8th. Rl. Innis. Fus.
	16.	Quartermaster.
	17.	Transport Officer.
	18.	R.S.M.
	19.	Spare.

SECRET.   COPY NO. _____
                    OPERATION ORDERS,
                              by,
            LIEUT. COLONEL, J. D. SCOTT, COMMANDING,
                2nd. Battalion, The Royal Irish Regiment.
                                                    In the Field,
Reference Map, 1/16,000,   6-11-1917.
Special Sheet, U.1. to C.6.
----

1.   The 16th Division is about to carry out an offensive
      operation with the object of occupying and consolidating the
      TUNNEL TRENCH and TUNNEL SUPPORT from JOVE MEBUS (U.20.b.50.70.)
      to the junction of PRINCE and TUNNEL TRENCHES (U.7.b.45.10.).

2.   OBJECTIVES.
      The final objective is shown in GREEN on attached map.

3.   LINE TO BE CONSOLIDATED.
      The line to be consolidated is that of the final objective.

4.   INFANTRY ATTACK.
      The attack will be carried out by the 47th. Infantry Brigade
      on the right, the 48th. Infantry Brigade in the centre, and
      the 49th. Infantry Brigade on the left.

5.   DISPOSITION OF BRIGADE.
      The 49th. Infantry Brigade will attack with the 2nd. Rl.
      Irish Regt. on the right and the 7th/8th. Rl. Irish Fus. on
      the left.
      The 7th/8th. Rl. Innis. Fus. will be in support.
      The 7th. (S.I.H.) Rl. Irish Regt. will hold the line North
      of the CROISILLES-FONTAINE Road.

6.   BOUNDARIES.
      The boundary between the Battalion and the 2nd. R. Dub. Fus.
      (left Battalion, 48th. Inf. Bde.) will be: communication trench
      from U.8.c.03.18. to U.7.d.83.10. inclusive to the Battalion;
      thence to junction of NELLY AVENUE with front line (inclusive
      to the Battalion), thence in a straight line to U.13.c.60.80.
      The 48th. Inf. Bde. will be allowed to use NELLY AVENUE
      as an OUT trench.
      The boundary between the Battalion and the 7th/8th. Rl.
      Irish Fus. on the left will be U.7.d.86.72. to U.7.d.62.62.
      to PEAR LANE inclusive to the 7th/8th. Rl. Irish Fus.

7.   DISPOSITION OF BATTALION.
      The Battalion will attack with "B" Company on the right,
      "D" Company on the left, and "A" Company in support.
      "B" and "D" Companies will attack in two waves, each
      Company having two platoons in front and two in rear wave.
      The first wave will leave the assembly position at ZERO and
      will take and occupy TUNNEL TRENCH.
      The second wave will pass through them and take and occupy
      TUNNEL SUPPORT, consolidating it as soon as taken.
      The boundary between "B" and "D" Companies will be,
      U.7.d.95.50. to U.7.d.70.38. to U.7.d.20.12.
      O.C."B" Coy. will detail a special party to deal with MEBUS
      "FLORA", U.7.d.70.34.
      O.C. "D" Coy. will detail a special party to deal with
      MOLE LANE.
      "A" Company, (plus Lewis Gunners of "C" Coy.) will remain
      in support in BURG SUPPORT.   O.C. "A" Coy. will detail one
      Lewis Gun Section to move up Sap 1 at ZERO and occupy the
      STRONG POINT which is being formed at the head of the Sap.

-2-

"C" Company (less 4 Lewis Gun Sections) with assistance of R.E. will be held in readiness to wire new front directly it has been occupied.

They will assemble in LINCOLN SUPPORT using deep dug-out at U.13.b.0.6. until ordered to go forward. They will re-assemble here on completion of wiring.

They will follow the second wave of the assault.

R.E. parties will go across with the attack with portable charges to blow in doors or blocks in the shafts.

8. ASSEMBLY POSITIONS.

"A" Coy., BURG TRENCH from U.7.d.22.10. to U.7.d.07.40. using all available MEBUS and space in deep dug-outs.

"B" Coy., front line from top of NELLY AVENUE to U.7.d.29.17.

"D" Coy. from U.7.d.29.17. to U.7.d.15.48.

"C" Coy., LINCOLN SUPPORT from U.13.b.00.53. to NELLY Avenue.

9. HEADQUARTERS.

"A" Coy., deep dug-out, U.7.d.20.15.

"B" Coy., until ZERO. Deep dug-out U.13.b.23.75.
When final objective has been gained, O.C. "B" Coy. will establish his H.Q. in TUNNEL TRENCH about U.7.d.80.20.

"D" Coy., until ZERO, deep dug-out U.7.d.20.15.
When final objective has been gained, O.C. "D" Coy. will establish his H.Q. in TUNNEL TRENCH about U.7.d.66.53.

"C" Coy., deep dug-out, U.13.b.0.6.

Battalion H.Q., deep dug-out, U.7.d.20.15.

7th/8th. Rl. Irish Fus., U.7.d.05.85.

10. The 7th/8th. Rl. Innis. Fus. in support will have two companies in QUARRY, T.18.b.80.35., and two companies in present support positions. One of the companies in QUARRY will find a working party to connect MOLE LANE and Sap 1. When completed, this will form the communication trench for the Battalion.

the 7th.(S.I.H.) Rl. Irish Regt. holding the line will find a working party to connect LUMP LANE with Tunnel Trench.

11. ARTILLERY.

The assault will be made under a creeping barrage of Artillery and under a machine gun barrage. A smoke screen will be produced.

Gas Projectors and drums will be thrown into FONTAINE on the left flank.

12. TRENCH MORTARS.

The 49th. T.M. Btty. will have four Mortars in position to co-operate in attack and will prepare three forward positions from which to help to repel any counter attack that developes.

13. DUMPS.

The following dumps will be available for the use of the Battalion:-

(1) S.A.A. and bombs. South end U.7/2, head of Sap 1 and U.13/4.

(2) Trench Boards. U.7/2.

(3) Wire etc. Junction of JANET AVENUE and LINCOLN SUPPORT. Junction of NELLY AVENUE and LINCOLN SUPPORT.
HUMBER SUPPORT.
U.7/1.
U.7/2.

-3-

(4) Lewis gun drums.
Companies will form dumps of spare Lewis gun drums as follows:-
At junction of front line and Sap 1. (U.7.d.38.42.).
"A" and "D" Coys., 20 drums per section = 160 drums.
At end of sap, post 16. (U.13.b.35.96.).
"B" and "C" Coys., 20 drums per section = 160 drums.

14. COMMUNICATIONS.
All companies up to ZERO, normal. After ZERO, two attacking companies, Fullerphone, Power buzzer and visual (latter will worked by the Bde. Signal Section.).
Report Centre will be in TUNNEL TRENCH about U.7.d.66.53.
The Battalion will be supplied with laddered cable to connect with report centre in TUNNEL TRENCH, and will use fullerphone with earthed circuit.
The Signalling Officer will arrange a visual station about to work back to either of the two 49th.
Inf. Bde. receiving stations which are situated as follows:-
1. CROIS ILLES CHURCH.
2. T.39.b.50.20. (ST. LEGER HILL)
The amplifier of Power Buzzer will be installed in the QUARRY.

15. DRESS.
The following dress will be worn by all ranks during the forthcoming operations:-
Fighting Order.
(a) Clothing, arms and entrenching tool as issued.
(b) Equipment as issued, haversacks will be worn on back and packs will not be carried.
(c) Box Respirators and P.H. Helmets.
(d) Iron rations, unexpended portion of the day's rations, mess tin and cover, Field Dressing.
(e) Waterproof Sheets.
(f) Riflemen, 150 rounds, S.A.A.; 2 Mills Bombs (1 Rifle, 1 Hand).
(g) Lewis Gunners, 50 rounds, S.A.A., 4 Lewis Gun drums.
(h) Bombers, 100 rounds S.A.A., 6 Mills Bombs.
(i) Rifle Bombers, 100 rounds S.A.A., 6 Rifle Grenades.
(j) Signallers, 50 rounds, S.A.A.
(k) The personnel of Company and Platoon H.Q. will carry 50 rounds S.A.A., and 10 "P" Bombs. The "P" Bombs to be distributed as Company Commanders think fit.
(l) Personnel of Battalion and Company H.Q. will carry Very Pistols and ammunition and 6 S.O.S. Rifle Grenades per Headquarters.
(m) Every man will carry 4 sandbags.
(n) Every man will carry a pick or a shovel in proportion 2% picks to 8% shovels.
All Officers will wear men's equipment and will carry M.P. Binoculars, Prismatic Compass and Watch.

16. MEDICAL ARRANGEMENTS.
The Regimental Aid Post will be in the QUARRY, T.18.b.9.4.
Battalion and Company Stretcher Bearers with a certain number of R.A.M.C. bearers will clear to Regtl. Aid Post.
For this purpose 20 extra S.Bs. will be available at QUARRY under orders of the M.O.

17. POSTS.
The Battalion Provost Sergeant will establish a post at MUMPS beside junction of JANET AVENUE, and BRIG SUPPORT, U.7.d.04.50. All prisoners will be sent to him here and he will see that conducting parties at once rejoin their companies.
He will deal with stragglers.
He will send back prisoners under order issued to him.

-4-

18. **RUSES.**
All men should be warned against the probable misuse of white flags and signs of surrender by the enemy. And against the possibility of the enemy using other ruses, such as giving the order "Retire".

19. **BOOBY TRAPS.**
All ranks will be warned of the possibility of booby traps being found in the TUNNEL and steps will be taken to search for these immediately the trench is taken.

20. **GAPS IN WIRE.**
Gaps will be cut in our wire diagonally and will be marked in the trench.

21. **AEROPLANE CONTACT.**
There will always be one contact machine flying on Divisional front.

22. **S.O.S.**
The S.O.S. signal will be as at present.

23. **ZERO.**
Zero hour will be notified later.

24. **SYNCHRONIZATION.**
Watches will be synchronized at Battalion H.Q. at Zero - 3 hours and Zero - 1 hour

25. A C K N O W L E D G E.

Lieut. Colonel,
Commanding 2nd. Battalion, The Royal Irish Regiment.

Issued at _____ p.m.

Copy No. 1. War Diary.
2. H.Q. 49th. Inf. Bde.
3. 7/8 R.I. Regt.
4. 7/8 R. Inn. Fus.
5. 7/8 R. Ir. Fus.
6. 2/R.D.Fus.
7. Commdg. Offr.
8. 2nd.-in-Commd.
9. Adjutant.
10. O.C. "A" Coy.

No. 11. O.C. "B" Coy.
12. O.C. "C" Coy.
13. O.C. "D" Coy.
14. Intell. Offr.
15. Sig. Offr.
16. Med. Offr.
17. Q.M.
18. R.S.M.
19. Spare.

Copy. No 1.

2nd. Battalion, The Royal Irish Regiment.

ADDITIONAL INSTRUCTIONS NO. 1. FOR AN OFFENSIVE ACTION ISSUED IN CONTINUATION OF OPERATION ORDERS NO. 55.

---

1. These instructions are issued to all concerned in addition to and in correction of Operation Orders No. 55.

2. A party of Tunnellers will go over with the attack.
    An Officer of the 174th. Tunnelling Coy. will report to Left Attacking Battalion Headquarters, and will, as soon as the TUNNEL TRENCH has been taken, go forward and make a reconnaissance of the TUNNEL. He will report on completion to Left Battalion Headquarters.
    (a) The Officer in charge of each party of Tunnellers will keep in close touch with the Infantry in whose portion of the TUNNEL TRENCH he is working.
    (b) In clearing the enemy from the TUNNEL as few smoke bombs and 'P' Bombs as possible are to be used on account of the danger to our own men. No 'P' Bombs will be taken forward by the attacking companies, but if required, in case of necessity, a supply will be kept available at Battalion Dump.
    (c) The Infantry Commanders on the spot will inform the Officers in charge of Tunnelling parties when, in their opinion, the TUNNEL has been cleared of the enemy and it is safe for Tunnelling parties to commence their reconnaissance. In the meantime, the latter will search for and destroy any leads which can be connected with the TUNNEL.
    (d) Before the Tunnelling parties enter the TUNNEL, the latter should, as far as possible, be cleared of all Infantry Parties except for those detailed for special duties. Sentries should be posted at each entrance to ensure that no more bombs are thrown down the shafts and that no unauthorised persons enter the tunnel.
    (e) Each party of Tunnellers on entering the TUNNEL will commence on the right of its section and work towards the left.
    (f) The word "SAFE" or "DANGER" will be marked in chalk at the head of each gallery examined.
    (g) On completion of his task, each tunnelling Officer will inform the Infantry of the condition of the Tunnel, and whether it can be occupied by the troops.

3. Communications. Position calls will continue to be used as at present; temporary position calls will be allotted to Companies going over with the attack.
    All messages sent by Power buzzer must be sent either by B.A.B. Code or by Field Cipher.
    As any listening apparatus in use by the enemy is unlikely to be affected or disturbed by the proposed operations, it is most important that every possible precaution should be taken to prevent the Germans from obtaining useful information in this way. This is equally important both <u>before</u> and <u>after</u> the attack.

4. Advanced Headquarters of 157 Field Coy., R.E., will be CROISILLE CAVES, T.24.c.2.8.

5. Add to Operation Orders No. 55, para 15 (b) -
    Every Officer, N.C.O., and man will carry his pack, greatcoat and waterproof sheet into the trenches. Before Zero, packs with greatcoats and waterproof sheets in them will be dumped by platoons in convenient shelters or dug-outs. O.C. Coys. will make arrangements to have them looked after. The remainder of the kit will be placed in sandbags labelled with the number, name and Regt., and left in Q.M. Stores.

6. All Officers will carry the following maps during forth-coming operations :-
    (a) Hectographed sheet issued by Bde. H.Q.
    (b) BULLECOURT Trench Map, 51.B.S.W.4. Edn. 4A.
    (c) CAGNICOURT Trench Map, 51.B.S.E.3. Edn. 3A.

7. "C" Company will be in positions of readiness in BURG SUPPORT at Zero, and will move forward behind the attack to their dumps. They will collect their stores and await orders. They will keep under cover as much as possible. They will await orders from Battalion Headquarters before going forward. On completion of work, "C" Company will return to their Company Headquarters which will be notified later. Officers, N.C.Os. and men of "C" Company will wear a GREEN armlet.
This amendment cancels Operation Orders No. 55 para 7, as far as "C" Company is concerned.

8. Forward dumps of S.A.A., bombs, etc. for the use of the Battalion HAVE BEEN ESTABLISHED AS FOLLOWS:-
    "A" Dump. Trench U 13/4. – U.13.b.27.93.
    "B" Dump. Head of Sap 1. About U.7.d.12.38.
    "C" Dump. South end of trench U 7/2 about U.7.d.33.48.
    These dumps contain Yukon Packs loaded, S.A.A., Mills Hand Grenades, Mills Rifle Grenades, 1" Very Lights and S.O.S. Rifle Grenades.
    O.C. "A" Coy. will detail 1 Officer, 3 N.C.Os. and 24 men to be ready to replenish these dumps when ordered to do so from Advanced Brigade Dump, Junction JANET AVENUE and BURG SUPPORT about U.7.d.0.5.
    Os.C. "B" and "D" Coys. will, as soon as possible, establish dumps in enemy trenches, one dump per company.
    "D" Company, if possible, about junction of MOLE LANE and TUNNEL TRENCH. These dumps to be filled from Battalion dumps, "A", "B" and "C".
    Establishment:-
    S.A.A.,   10 boxes.
    Mills Hand Grenades,   30 "
    Mills Rifle   "   20 "
    1" Very Lights, White.   2 "
    S.O.S. Rifle Grenades   4 " (5 in each box).

9. Water. A reserve of water will be obtainable after Zero hour at Battalion Headquarters.

10. Wounded. It is forbidden for anyone except stretcher bearers to help wounded back to Battalion Aid Post. Walking wounded must make their own way back to dressing station. This order must be thoroughly explained to all ranks, and any infringement of it may involve most serious consequences.

11. Stragglers. Divisional arrangements have been made for straggler posts at T.21.a.4.9. and T.14.b.1.7. Stragglers will not be given orders to rejoin their units. When a sufficient number have been collected they will be marched to Divisional Collecting Station, a special note being made of men without arms. Thence they will be sent under escort to Brigade Headquarters. All ranks must be warned of this order.

12. Prisoners. Officers Commanding "B" and "D" Companies will collect their prisoners and send them back to the Regimental Provost Sergeant who will be in MEBUS about U.7.d.1.4., not as stated in Operation Orders No. 55 para 17. Strength of escort about 15% under N.C.O.
    Tobacco, cigarettes or food are NOT to be given to prisoners. Soldiers are not to take any buttons, caps, or any other articles from prisoners. GERMAN prisoners are not to be allowed to wear any article of ENGLISH uniform.
    Prisoners may keep their personal effects, badges, decorations, etc., unless required by the General Staff. Documents, diaries, etc., are to be handed over to the General Staff without delay.
    Identity discs are not to be taken from them.

13. Burials. The primary duty falls on the Battalion. The usual cemetery will be used.

14. The first line of the attacking Companies will be issued with arm bands. Colour will be notified later.

15. Officers' kits will be cut down to regulation weight before proceeding into the trenches.

All surplus kits and stores will be dumped at Q.M. Stores whence they will, if necessary be removed to CINEMA HALL, ERVILLERS. Every package must be clearly marked and labelled in more than one place with the owners' rank and name, and the unit's title.

Company, etc., blankets will also be dumped at the Q.M. Stores, rolled in bundles by half platoons. Every bundle is to be most clearly marked with the platoon's number, company and unit.

Men's personal effects will be placed in sandbags, each bag to be clearly marked with number, rank, and name of owner. and UNIT

In the event of a hostile withdrawal, every man must carry forward a pick or a shovel.

                         Lieut. Colonel,
       Commanding 2nd. Battalion, The Royal Irish Regiment.

S.A. No.1.
issued to:- Copy No. 1. War Diary.
               2. Commanding Officer.
               3. Second-in-Command.
               4. Adjutant.
               5. O.C. "A" Company.
               6. O.C. "B" ,,
               7. O.C. "C" ,,
               8. O.C. "D" ,,
               9. Intelligence Officer.
             10. Signalling Officer.
             11. Medical Officer.
             12. Quartermaster.
             13. Regtl. Sergt. Major.
             14. Spare.

ADDITIONAL INSTRUCTIONS NO. 2., FOR AN OFFENSIVE ACTION.

16. ACTION OF STOKES MORTARS: The O.C. 49th. T.M. Battery will have 8 Stokes Mortars in position at ZERO hour to open up a rapid barrage on enemy's trenches.
    Zero to Zero plus 2 minutes on TUNNEL TRENCH.
    Zero plus 2 to Zero plus 4 minutes on general line of TUNNEL SUPPORT.
    After the enemy trenches have been captured 4 teams will move forward to more advanced positions for S.O.S. work. Remaining teams will take cover and eventually withdraw to H.Q. of the battery at T.21.b.0.3.

17. O.C. "A" Coy. will be responsible for cutting 16 diagonal gaps in our wire on Y/Z night. These gaps will be marked in our trenches by means of white boards. Steps for exit from trenches will be cut where necessary. These positions of gaps will be shewn to O.C. "A" Coy.

18. No papers or orders likely to give information to the enemy are to be carried by officers or other ranks taking part in the attack.

19. Consolidation of enemy trenches when captured will be carried out as under:-
    1. Form posts along captured trench and make firebays to give good field of fire and to cover all approaches.
    2. Picket entrances to dug-outs until clear and mark them "CLEAR".
    3. Collect S.A.A., bombs, etc., and form dumps at central places.
    4. Every platoon as soon as it has occupied enemy's trench must post sentries and groups to watch for a counter-attack.

20. B.A.B. Code will not be used in front of our present front line. No B.A.B. Code Books are to be taken into action. All such books are to be withdrawn before Zero from Officers taking part in the attack, and sent to Bn. H.Q. by Os.C. Coys. before ZERO.

21. Os.C. "B" and "D" Coys. will provide covering parties to protect the wiring parties.

22. Commencing on Nov. 16th. night firing will be done on a large scale, keeping the wire open and harassing the enemy as much as possible.
    49th. M.G.C. will enfilade the German wire in front of TUNNEL TRENCH in U.7.d., U.13.b., and U.14.a., and also put down a barrage from OLDENBURG LANE at U.8.a.1.1. to SUNKEN ROAD U.8.d.1.4.
    48th. M.G.C. will enfilade OLDENBURG LANE and FAG ALLEY, paying particular attention to the new tracks immediately on the North side of FAG ALLEY, also tracks in U.15.c. and d., and U.14.d.
    8 guns per Coy. will fire intermittently all night.
    From ZERO until ZERO plus 30 minutes all guns allotted for covering and barrage fire will open fire on the barrage lines at the rate of 1 belt per minute. From ZERO plus 30 minutes to ZERO plus 1 hour the rate will be 1 belt per 2 minutes after which 1 belt per 5 minutes will be fired from ZERO plus 1 hour to ZERO plus 1 hour 30 minutes. After ZERO plus 1 hour 30 minutes all barrage guns and teams will be held in readiness to open fire on their barrage lines in case of:-
    (a) The enemy shewing any increased activity with Artillery.
    (b) S.O.S.
    The barrage lines are the final S.O.S. lines on which guns will fire when the objectives have been captured.

23. During the projected operations, the Flares and S.O.S. Signals used will be as under:-
    (a) Infantry will use white flares.
    (b) The S.O.S. Signal for the VI Corps will be a **rifle grenade** bursting into 2 RED and 2 GREEN lights.

24. Tasks of No. 3 Special Coy., R.E., are as follows:-
   1. A very light smoke screen to simulate a lethal shell bombardment will be placed in front of TUNNEL TRENCH from U.20.b.25.60 to U.7.d.30.90. from ZERO to ZERO plus 30 seconds by T.Ms. in Sectors A, B and C. This discharge will take place in any wind.
   2. A similar screen will be placed in the valley N.E. of BULLECOUR by T.Ms. in SECTOR A/1 from ZERO to ZERO plus 1 minute. This discharge will take place in any wind.
   3. A heavy smoke barrage will be placed EAST of TUNNEL TRENCH from ZERO plus 30 seconds to ZERO plus 15 minutes by T.Ms. in SECTORS A, B and C, to cover the objective from the EAST. This discharge will only take place if the wind is between S and E.W. both inclusive.
   4. A heavy smoke screen will be placed in the valley N.E. of BULLECOURT by T.Ms. in SECTOR A/1 from ZERO plus 1 minute to ZERO plus 16 minutes. Wind limits S.S.E. to W. both inclusive.
   5. A smoke screen will be placed about FONTAINE TRENCH in U.1.b. from ZERO to ZERO plus 10 minutes by T.Ms. in SECTOR D. Wind limits S. to N.W. both inclusive

25. PARA 7 OF THESE INSTRUCTIONS IS AMENDED AS FOLLOWS:-
   "C Coy. will leave BURG SUPPORT at ZERO plus 4 minutes for their dumps, pick up their stores and advance to TUNNEL TRENCH and TUNNEL SUPPORT to their tasks and carry out the wiring as fast as possible under the smoke and artillery barrage.

26. The Barrage Map for smoke and M.Guns has been shewn to all concerned and can be seen at Bn. H.Q. if further required.

27. Reference para 14 of these instructions, a white arm band will be worn by first lines of "B" and "D" Coys.

28. The following will be the arrangements for clearing the TUNNEL wh TUNNEL TRENCH is taken. No one will enter the TUNNEL until ZERO plus 8 minutes, but MILLS BOMBS will be thrown down every alternate entrance on company frontages, commencing from Shaft on right of "B" Company.
   At ZERO plus 8 minutes, Capt. HARRISON M.C., with one section of bombers to be detailed by O.C. "B" Coy. will enter the TUNNEL at about U.7.d.70.38. If any enemy are seen or heard in the TUNNEL or any opposition is encountered, Capt. HARRISON, M.C., will at once withdraw his party, inform Company Commanders who will inform Compa Commanders on their flanks, and when the TUNNEL is reported clear of our troops, 'P' bombs will be thrown down alternate entrances as before. The TUNNEL will be afterwards cleared by bags of shavings being lighted inside. These will be available at A, B and C Dumps Coy. H.Q. of "B" and "D" Coys. will carry 18 'P' Bombs which will o be used for this purpose under Capt HARRISONS orders.
   If the TUNNEL is found empty, these 2 sections will move along "B" Coy south till section of 2nd. Rl.Dub. Fus. is met. "D" Coy. North till section of 7/8th. Rl. Irish Fus. is met.
   Each section will carry 4 electric torches. "B" Coy. patrol will be recognised by 2 of these torches having red discs. The sections of the 7/8th. Rl. Irish Fus. and 2nd. Rl. Dub. Fus. will be recognised by similar coloured lights displayed by them.
   These 2 sections will be distinguished by yellow bands instead of white.

Lieut. Colonel,
Issued at _____ Commanding 2nd. Battalion, The Royal Irish Regiment.

Copy No.1.War Diary,   No.7.Commdg.Offr.   13.O.C."D" Coy.   No.19.R.S.M
    2.49.Inf.Bde.   8.Sec-in-Commd.   14.Intell.Offr.   20.Spare
    3. 7/(SIH)R.I.   9.Adjt.   15.Sig. Offr.
    4.7/8 R.Inn.F.   10.O.C."A" Coy.   16.M.O.
    5.7/8 R.Ir.F.   11.O.C."B" Coy.   17.Chapln.
    6.2/R.D.Fus.   12.O.C."C" Coy.   18.C.M.

NOTE. In para 28, line 7 above, after "'B' Coy." add " and 1 section of bombers to be detailed by O.C. 'D' Coy."
   In para 28, line 21 above after "red discs" add "'D' Coy. by 2 of these torches having GREEN discs."

SECRET. OPERATION ORDER No. 8   Copy No. _____
by
LIEUT. COLONEL J. D. SCOTT, COMMANDING,
2nd. Battalion, The Royal Irish Regiment.
Reference: Special Sheet, 1/10.000.   The Field, 29-11-1917.
_____

1. The Battalion will relieve the 8/9th. Bn. The Rl. Dub. Fus. in the right sub-section, of the Left section, tomorrow.
    Right sub-section, U.14.a.7.3. to U.8.c.1.3.
    Battalion H.Q.,   Deep dug-out, U.13.b.9.1.
2. "A" Coy. will relieve "D" Coy., 8/9th. R.D.F. in the front line from U.14.a.7.3. to U.14.a.4.8.
    "B" Coy. will relieve "A" and "B" Coys., 8/9th. R.D.F. in the front line from U.14.a.4.8. to U.8.c.1.3.
    These two coys. will have two platoons each in the front line and two in support.
    "C" Coy. - OLD BRITISH FRONT LINE from U.14.c.2.9. to U.13.b.7.3. and deep dug-out U.13.b.3.1.
    "D" Coy. - OLD BRITISH FRONT LINE from U.14.c.2.9. to NELLY AVENUE exclusive and deep dug-out, U.13.b.6.5.
    Os.C. "C" and "D" Coys. each will detail 1 Officer and 1 Lewis Gun Section to hold MINERVA and JULO MEBUS respectively
    Two platoons (less Lewis Gun Sections) 7/8th Rl. Innis. Fus. (attached - QUARRY. To be utilised as carrying parties rations etc.
    These two Lewis Gun Sections will be attached to "D" Coy.
3. Order of march, - "V.", "B", H.Q., "C", "D", "A" Coy., leaving camp at 2 p.m.
4. (a) All trench stores, plans of defence, No. 9 Periscopes, ammunition, grenades, etc., will be carefully taken over.
   (b) All work in progress and proposed will be carefully taken over in writing to ensure continuity of work.
    Aeroplane photographs will not be taken over.
    A return of the above will be forwarded to Bn. H.Q. by 9 a.m., 1st. December.
5. Advance parties, 1 Officer, 1 N.C.O., and 1 N.C.O. per platoon, from each company will take over at 2 p.m.
    Lewis Gun Sections, scouts, gas N.C.Os., and signallers will take over at the same time.
6. Companies will send to Bn. H.Q. a sketch showing their dispositions to include Headquarters, posts and Lewis Guns as soon as possible after taking over.
7. Relief to be complete by 6 p.m. To be reported to Bn. H.Q. by code word "YORK".
8. Trench kits, blankets, Officers' valises, stores, etc., will be dumped outside Q.Ms. Stores by 12 noon.

                        (sd) V. GALVEY, Captain & Adjutant,
                         2nd. Battalion, The Royal Irish Regiment.

Issued at _____ p.m.
Copy No. 1. War Diary.   10. O.C. "D" Coy.
        2. 7/8th. R. Innis. Fus.   11. Intell. Offr.
        3. 8/9th. R.D.F.   12. Sig. Offr.
        4. Commanding Offr.   13. M.O.
        5. Sec-in-Commd.   14. Chapln.
        6. Adjt.   15. Q.M.
        7. O.C. "A" Coy.   16. T.O.
        8. O.C. "B" Coy.   17. R.S.M.
        9. O.C. "C" Coy.   18. H.Q. 49th. Inf. Bde.

MESSAGE FORM.

No. ....   To ....

1. I am at .... } Note:—Either give Map Reference or mark your position by a 'X' on the Map on back.
2. My Line runs ....
3. My Platoon is at .... Company, and is consolidating.
4. My Platoon is at .... Company, and has consolidated.
5. Am held up by (a) M.G. .... (b) Wire .... ("Place where you are").
6. Enemy holding strong point ....
7. I am in touch with .... on Right at .... on Left at ....
8. I am not in touch with .... on Right, on Left.
9. Am shelled from ....
10. Am in need of :— ....
11. Counter Attack forming at ....
12. Hostile (a) Battery .... active at ....
    (b) Machine Gun
    (c) Trench Mortar
13. Reinforcements wanted at ....
14. I estimate my present strength at .... rifles
15. Have captured ....
16. Prisoners belong to ....
17. Add any other useful information here :—

Time .... m.   Company ....
Date .... 1917.   Battalion ....

(A) Carry no maps or papers which may be of value to the Enemy.
(B) Give no information if captured, except the following, which you are bound to give :—
Name and Rank
(C) Collect all captured maps and papers and send them in at once.

WAR DIARY

FOR MONTH OF DECEMBER, 1917.

VOLUME : -

UNIT :- 2nd. R. Irish Regiment.

Army Form C. 2118.

WAR DIARY
or
INTELLIGENCE SUMMARY.
(Erase heading not required.)

November 1917

Instructions regarding War Diaries and Intelligence Summaries are contained in F. S. Regs., Part II. and the Staff Manual respectively. Title pages will be prepared in manuscript.

Place	Date	Hour	Summary of Events and Information	Remarks and references to Appendices
HINDENBURG LINE – CROISILLES	1		Relieved in the line by the 12th Bn Suffolk Regiment – 40th Division. The Division has been at BOURLON WOOD and was rather tired. Relieved off very quietly – no shelling. On relief we moved back to Clonmel Camp, HAMELINCOURT	App 1, App 2
CLONMEL CAMP HAMELINCOURT	2		In Clonmel Camp. Hear that we are going to BOURLON WOOD – to take an active part in the Battle of Cambrai.	App 3
BARASTRE	3		Battalion marches to BARASTRE area via ERVILLERS – BAPAUME and HAPLINCOURT. Very cold march. Arrives in a camp near BARASTRE about 3.15 pm	App 4
"	4		Packing and unpacking kit. Expected to move to BERTINCOURT, which is just behind HAPLINCOURT WOOD – but this was cancelled	App 4
TINCOURT	5		Marched off at 8.45 am. Route to TINCOURT. Hear that the situation round about MOISLAINS – TEMPLEUX – TINCOURT – GENNELIEVAN VILLERS GUISLAIN is, to say the least, uncertain	
"	6		Embussed at TINCOURT 10.30 am and proceed via HAMEL – MARQUAIX – ROISEL to ST EMILIE where we debussed. Contact up by Company commanders and 1 go off immediately and reconnoitre the new line we are to relieve the 2/5 Lane Fus (55th Bn) at EMPIRE reference (Tenth) Relieve the 2/5 Lane Fus (55th Bn) at EMPIRE. Companies in trenches about 2 foot deep and relieves went nothing of German positions.	App 5
EMPIRE	7		Situation still very obscure. Rumours that the enemy is going to attack in force in this part of the world. Enemy artillery and aircraft very active	
"	8,9,10 & 11		There is still indication that the enemy may attack as lines and new trenches being made every where.	App 6

Army Form C. 2118.

WAR DIARY
or
INTELLIGENCE SUMMARY.

(Erase heading not required.)

Instructions regarding War Diaries and Intelligence Summaries are contained in F.S. Regs., Part II. and the Staff Manual respectively. Title pages will be prepared in manuscript.

Place	Date	Hour	Summary of Events and Information	Remarks and references to Appendices
LEMPIRE	12,13,14,15,16		In support along the EPEHY–LEMPIRE ridge.	App 8
	17		Relieved in support by 10th Royal Irish Fusiliers 48th Brigade. Marches to ST EMILIE where we entrained – Mid. Bn got into open trucks on a small gauge Railway worked by Americans. Detrained at TINCOURT. Good billets.	14
TINCOURT	18, 19, 20, 21, 22		Billets, end. Cleaning up etc.	19
"	23		Left Tincourt by train at about 3 p.m. Relieves 1st 6/Royal Irish Regt in Right Sub-section Right Sector of Peiz Front. 23rd (2nd & 3rd in other units) 49th on our left. 6th Battn very heavy fall, being out for Christmas. Christmas Eve very cold. Heavy snowfall. Enemy artillery activity greatly decreased, although very lively at STAND-TO (6am)	App 9, 19, 14
RONSSOY	24		Enemy again active at STAND-TO. But quiet during the day.	14
	25		Christmas Day. Conditions miserable.	
	26, 27, 28		Same as trench routine. 2 casualties on 26th – other units.	App 10
	29		Relieved by 1/6 R. Innis Fus. Marched to Brigade Reserve in ST EMILIE. Companies in a Railway Cutting near village.	19
	30, 31		Tincourt Rd. A list of decorations awarded to men of the Bn for Operations on 20th Nov. is attached and called App 11. Afternoon splendid.	App 11

During the month CR-R-V-V-V 2/Lt P.T. O'Brien RDF 28-12-17
2/Lt B.A. Routledge Lieut H.B. Patrick R.I. Capt M.E.C. Hannon 31-12-17
Lieut/Capt J.H. Patrick. R.I. 27-12-17

A.S.M.Scott Capt.
Commanding 2/Bn R. Insk. Fus.

SECRET   Operation Orders No. 23   Copy No. —
by
Lieut. Colonel L.D. SCOTT, Commanding
2nd. Bn. The R. Irish. Regt.

Ref: FFEHY. 62.C.N.E.   The Field.
Sh. 2.A. 1:10.000   22.12.1917.

1.   The 49th. Inf. Bde. will relieve the 47th. Inf. Bde. in the right section on 23rd. December, 1917.

2.   The Battalion will relieve the 6th. Bn. The R. Ir. Rgt. in the right sub-section as follows:—
"A" Coy. will relieve "A" Coy. 6th Bn. — Right Front Line.
"B"   "   "   "B"   "   "   — Left   "   "
"D"   "   "   "C"   "   "   — SUPPORT.
"C"   "   "   "D"   "   "   — Reserve by Bn. H.Q.

3.   Advanced parties, constituted as below, will leave TINCOURT, parading at Bn. H.Q. at 9 a.m. and proceeding by march route under the senior officer. Guides, one per coy. and one for Bn. H.Q. will meet these parties at Road Junction - LEMPIRE - RONSSOY, R.15.d.75.75. at 12.30 p.m.
       1 Officer, 1 N.C.O. per platoon, Coy. Gas N.C.O., Nos. 1 and 2 of L.G. Sections, Signallers and 2 runners per coy.
       1 Officer, 1 N.C.O., Bn. Gas N.C.O., Signallers, Scouts and 2 runners for Bn. H.Q.

4.   The Battalion will move by train from TINCOURT Siding at 3 p.m. Bn. H.Q. and Coy's will be ready to entrain by 2.45 p.m.
       From STE. EMILIE, all movement will be by march route by platoons at 5 minutes interval in the order, "A", "B", "D", "C", H.Q.
       No movement E. of STE. EMILIE before dusk.
Guides - Road Junction LEMPIRE - RONSSOY, R.15.d.75.75. - 5.30 p.m. - 4 per coy., 1 for Bn. H.Q.

5.   1 Officer and 1 N.C.O. from each coy and Bn. H.Q. will parade at Bn. H.Q. at 2.15 p.m. under 2/Lt. SANDERSON. This party will report to Staff Captain at entraining point K.13.c.2.2. at 2.30 p.m. Representatives should know the entraining strength of their coy's, etc.

6.   The following will be carefully taken over by relieving units:—
       (a) Trench Stores.
       (b) Ammunition and Grenades.
       (c) Written Defence Scheme.
       (d) Written schemes of work in progress and proposed.
       (e) All maps and other documents connected with the line.
       Copies of (a), (b) and (c) will be forwarded to Bn. H.Q. by 8 a.m. 24th December.

- 2 -

7. Lewis Gun Limbers will leave TINCOURT under the T.O. and will meet the Bn. on arrival at STE. EMILIE at 3.45 p.m. From there they will move with their coys.

 The Maltese Cart and mess cart, cooks cart will move at the same time. T.O. will make all arrangements.

8. One blanket per man will be carried. The remaining blankets in rolls of 10, and packs, will be ready outside their various H.Q's. at 10 a.m. for conveyance to Transport lines. The Q.M. will make arrangements to send up these blankets tomorrow evening to coys. with rations.

9. 15 Petrol Tins per coy. and 15 for Bn. H.Q. will be sent up with rations tomorrow night. Two filled water carts will come up each night with rations.

10. Relief complete will be reported by coys. by following code:-
 "A" Coy : "15."
 "B" " : "21."
 "D" " : "27."

11. A C K N O W L E D G E.

 Roberts
 Captain,
 Adjutant, 2nd. Bn. The Rt. Irish Regt.

Issued at .... p.m.

 Copy No. 1. War Diary
 2. H.Q. 49th Inf. Bde.
 3. 6th R. Irish Regt.
 4. Commanding Officer.
 5. Adjutant.
 6. O.C. "A" Coy.
 7. " "B" "
 8. " "C" "
 9. " "D" "
 10. Medical Officer.
 11. Transport Officer.
 12. Quartermaster.
 13. Sig. Officer.
 14. Intelligence Officer.
 15. R.S.M.
 16. Cook Sergt.
 17. Spare

WAR DIARY,

FOR MONTH OF JANUARY, 1918.

VOLUME :—

UNIT :— 2nd. R. Irish Regiment.

Army Form C. 2118.

WAR DIARY
or
INTELLIGENCE SUMMARY.
(Erase heading not required.)

Place	Date	Hour	Summary of Events and Information	Remarks and references to Appendices
	1918. Jany 1-3		Battalion in Brigade Support at STE EMILIE Railway Cutting. Weather extremely cold. Battalion supplied working parties for work on Support Area Defences.	
	Jany 4-9		49th Infantry Brigade moved out to Brigade Support.	See Appendix No.1.
HAMEL	5.		Christmas Dinner for the men held in the Theatre. The Divisional Commander visited the men while at dinner. The Dinner was a very great success in spite of the difficulties experienced in getting supplies owing to the severity of the weather and transport difficulties. The Divisional Band added considerably to the enjoyment of the entertainment.	
	6.		The Officers held their Christmas Dinner, which was most successful, a most enjoyable evening being spent. The Guests included the Divisional Commander, Brigadier General W.J. DUGAN, D.S.O. C.M.G. 73rd Infantry Brigade and MAJOR MORROW, 6th Batt: R. Irish Regt.	
	7.		The Sergeants held their Christmas Dinner and Concert which also was a very great success.	

WAR DIARY
or
INTELLIGENCE SUMMARY.

(Erase heading not required.)

Army Form C. 2118.

Place	Date	Hour	Summary of Events and Information	Remarks and references to Appendices
HAMEL	1918 Jany. 8.		The 49th Brigade gave a most successful Concert in the Theatre, kindly lent to the purpose by the Division. The Battalion supplied a great deal of the talent and some very good Exhibition Boxing Bouts were given.	
			The work done during this period consisted of Guards, Anti-Aircraft Defences and work on Forward Area Defences.	
	10.		Battalion relieved the 6th Batt. The Royal Irish Regiment in the left Sub. Section moving by train to STE EMILIE thence by march route to the line.	See Appendix No. 2
	10-15		Battalion held the line on the left front, working on Trench repairs, wiring and general improvement to the line. On the whole a quiet time.	
	15.		Battalion was relieved by the 7/8 Royal Irish Fusiliers and moved to left Support with H.Q. at LEMPIRE and Companies in area MALASISSE FARM — LEMPIRE.	See Appendix No 3
LEMPIRE	17-21		Battalion worked on line and Support defences. Activity during this period consisted of Artillery duels.	
	22.		Battalion relieved the 7/8 Royal Irish Fusiliers in the left Sub. Section.	See Appendix No 4
	22-27		Work consisted of Trench repair, wiring and general improvement to the line. Weather greatly improved.	

Army Form C. 2118.

WAR DIARY
or
INTELLIGENCE SUMMARY.
(Erase heading not required.)

Place	Date	Hour	Summary of Events and Information	Remarks and references to Appendices
STE EMILIE.	1918. Jany. 28.		Battalion relieved by 16th/8 Royal Irish Fusiliers and proceeded to Brigade Reserve at Railway Cutting STE EMILIE.	See Appendix No. 5.
	29-31.		Battalion worked on the improvement of the Wilts and supplied parties for work on the EMPIRE defences.	
			The following Honours and Awards were received	
			Lt. Colonel J.D. SCOTT — — — — — — D.S.O.	
			Capt. R.R.C. MacGRATH — — — — — — Bar to M.C.	
			Capt. H. HARRISON — — — — — — Do.	
			Capt. A.S. PIM — — — — — — Do.	
			2/Lt. G. SINCLAIR — — — — — — M.C.	
			Hon. Capt. & Q.M. T. MAHONEY — — — — — — M.C.	
			No. 18004 A/Cpl. WATSON, D. "D. Coy" — — — — — — A.C.M.	
			" 5336 Pte (L/Cpl.) O'BRIEN, E. — — — — — — Bar to M.M.	
			" 9679 Sergt BAILEY, J. "D. Coy" — — — — — — M.M.	
			" 5760 Pte QUINLAN, D. "B" — — — — — — Do.	
			" 1447 " MURPHY, M. "A" — — — — — — Do.	
			" 8585 " JONES, T. "B" — — — — — — Do.	
			" 16671 L/Cpl. MASON, J. "C" — — — — — — Do.	
			" 1115 Sergt BRIEN, M. "D" — — — — — — Do.	
			" 8491 Pte TAAFE, L. "B" — — — — — — Do.	
			" 9712 L/Cpl. FENNEL, T. "C" — — — — — — Do.	

WAR DIARY
or
INTELLIGENCE SUMMARY.
(Erase heading not required.)

Army Form C. 2118.

Place	Date	Hour	Summary of Events and Information	Remarks and references to Appendices
			No. 7803 Cpl. Morris, P. "D" Coy. — — — M.M.	
			" 1718 Pte Hickey, P. "B" — — — Do.	
			" 5962 " O'Brien, J. "A" — — — Do.	
			" 8394 " Seely, J. "A" — — — Do.	
			" 11053 " Ryan, C. "B" — — — Do.	
			" 4944 " Ryan, J. "C" — — — Do.	
			" 8467 Sergt Robinson, J. "B" — — — Do.	
			" 10474 Pte (L/c) Wickham, P. "C" — — — Do.	
			" 9031 Sergt Shanley, W. "D" — — — Do.	
			" 3565 Pte Brennan, J. "A" — — — Do.	
			" 9229 " Russell, T. "D" — — — Do.	
			" 16154 " Box, P. "C" — — — Do.	
			" 8156 Cpl Jones, T. "A" — — — Do.	
			" 11050 Pte English, J. "D" — — — Do.	
			No. 6382 R.S.M. Carew, M.C. — — — G.C.M.	
			" 5984 Pte Weekes, "B" Coy. — — — Do	
			together with twenty six Parchment Certificates.	

Army Form C. 2118.

WAR DIARY
or
INTELLIGENCE SUMMARY.
(Erase heading not required.)

Place	Date	Hour	Summary of Events and Information	Remarks and references to Appendices
	1918 Jany 4.		Greetings to Christmas & New Year Greetings sent to Field-Marshal VISCOUNT FRENCH, G.C.B & Colonel in chief of the Regiment. The following message was received "Field-Marshal VISCOUNT FRENCH begs to thank the Officers Warrant Officers, N.C.Os and men of the 2nd Battalion Thanks of their Regiment for their kind message and wishes for Christmas and the New Year, which he heartily reciprocates."	yes
HAMEL	7.		An most interesting lecture was given by CAPT M.C.C. HARRISON dealing with his capture by the Enemy, his treatment while a Prisoner, his numerous attempts at and eventual successful escape from GERMANY. It was attended by all the Officers N.C.O's of the Brigade.	yes
	10.		A most regrettable feature of the kind was the death of Hon. CAPT and Q.M. T. MAHONEY. Mess the result of an accident. CAPT MAHONEY had been with the Battalion for about three years in FRANCE but it was not due so much to his long association as to his sterling qualities as a Quartermaster in which he excelled, his popularity. He had been with the Regiment to 26 years and its welfare was his first consideration. To his untiring efforts can be ascribed the success and comfort of the Christmas dinners to the men	yes

WAR DIARY
or
INTELLIGENCE SUMMARY.

(Erase heading not required.)

Army Form C. 2118.

Place	Date	Hour	Summary of Events and Information	Remarks and references to Appendices
	1918 Jany 10.		on the 5th January and that the accident should have happened on his return to his billet after an absence of several days at great personal discomfort, and only when he was assured of the success of his attack, makes the incident all the more regrettable.	
			Reinforcements. (Officers)	
	6.		Lt. J.H.W. TROUGHTON. (Transferred to Tank Corps. 17-1-18)	
	17.		CAPT. H. HARRISON. M.C. from Hospital	
	23.		2/Lt. M.J. MULCAHY. from Hospital	
	23.		Lt. F.A. HALL. (ENGLAND (Indian Army))	
			(O.R.)	
	11.		N° 11032. PTE BURKE, J. Wounded in Action	
			" 9057. " LILLIS, W. do	
	12.		" 11655. " BYRNE, J. Killed in Action	
	16.		" 11146. 4/c. O'BRIEN, D. do	
	20.		" 6461 CPL. SAYERS, T. Wounded in Action	
			" 2574 PTE MARSDEN, J. do	
	21.		" 9836 L/c. ANTHONY, T. do	
			" 8582 PTE HILLIER, A. do	

S E C R E T.   OPERATION ORDER No. 65.   Copy No. _____
by
Capt. H. C. C. HARRISON, COMMANDING,
2nd. Battalion, The Royal Irish Regiment.
3rd. January, 1918.
----

1. The 48th. Inf. Bde. (less M.G. Coy.), will relieve the 49th. Inf. Bde. (less M.G. Coy.) in the Right Section on the night 4th/5th. January.

2. The 10th. R. Dub. Fus. will relieve the 2nd. Rl. Irish Regt. in Brigade Reserve. Relief to be complete by 1 p.m. On relief the Battalion will march by companies (order, as relieved by 10th. R. Dub. Fus.) at 200 yards interval, to METZ.

3. Route - VILLERS FAUCON - Rd. Junction N.28.a.9.6. - Road junction N.28.a.9.4. - road junction N.28.a.7.4. - LIEQUAL - Cross road K.13.d.10.25.

4. The usual billeting party under 2/Lieut. STEVENSON will report to Town Major, TINCOURT by 10 a.m., 4th. January. This party will be at Cross roads, K.13.d.10.25. at 2-15 p.m.

5. Officers kits, blankets, etc., will be dumped at Ration Dumps by 10-30 a.m. The Transport Officer will arrange the necessary transport.

7. Relief complete will be wired to Battalion H.Q. using code phrase "Working party cancelled".

8. ACKNOWLEDGE.

Issued at _____ p.m.   Captain & Adjutant,
                    2nd. Battalion, The Royal Irish Regiment..............
Copy No. 1. War Diary.   No. 9. O.C. "D" Coy.
         2. H.Q. 48th. Inf. Bde.   10. Sig. Offr.
         3. 10th. R.D.F.   11. Med. Offr.
         4. Commdg. Offr.   12. Transport Offr.
         5. Sec-in-Commd.   13. Q.M.
         6. O.C. "A" Coy.   14. R.S.M.
         7. O.C. "B" Coy.   15. Cook Sgt.
         8. O.C. "C" Coy.

SECRET.   OPERATION ORDERS NO. 1.   Copy No. _____

by,
Major, W. L. C. MOORE-BRABAZON, COMMANDING,
2nd. Battalion, The Royal Irish Regiment.
The Field, 9-1-1918.

Ref. Map Special Sheet,
LEMPIRE, 1/10,000
---

1. The 49th. Inf. Bde. will relieve the 47th. Inf. Bde. in the left section of the Divisional Front from F.11.a.8.6. to X.26.d.50.45. on the night 10th/11th January.
2. The Battalion will relieve the 6th. Bn. The Rl. Irish Regt. in the left sub-section. Relief to be complete by 8 p.m.
Eight Companies will be disposed as under:-
"A" Coy. - having 2 platoons from F.4.a.6.5. - 13 COPSE, and 1 platoon in No. 12 COPSE. - Coy. H.Q. - F.3.b.5.4.
"B" Coy. on left holding 5 isolated posts in F.3.b. and X.87.c. Coy. H.Q. - X.26.d.4.3.
"C" Coy. in Support - Coy. H.Q. - F.2.b.4.8.
"D" Coy. in reserve - RESERVE RIDGE NORTH, Coy. H.Q. F.2.a.8.5.
Battalion H.Q. F.1.d.7.9.   1 per platoon
Guides for "B", "C", "D", Coys., and H.Q. will be at F.1.c.6.5. at 5-30 p.m. and for "A" Coy. at F.8.a.6.4. at same hour.
3. The usual advance parties will be at Bn. H.Q., 6th.Bn. the Rl. Irish Regt. at 2-30 p.m., leaving TINCOURT at 12 noon.
4. "A" Coy., 2/R.I.Regt. will relieve "C" Coy., 6/R.I.Regt.
    "B"..."A"..................
    "C"..."D"..................
    "D"..."B"..................
Lewis Guns and 24 drums pwr gun will be taken with coys. and not sent up by transport.
5. The Battalion will move by train from TINCOURT SIDING at 3 p.m. Bn. H.Q. and coys. will be ready to entrain by 2-45 p.m.
From STE. EMILIE all movement will be by march route by platoons at 5 minutes interval in the order, "B", "A", "C", "D", H.Q.
No movement E. of STE. EMILIE before dusk.
6. Transport arrangements. Water to "A" Coy. via R. MISSE FM. RD. to F.3.b.2.3.(Transport same route.
Transport for "B", "C", and "D" Coys. to cross rds. F.3.a.7.5. thence by railway cutting to F.5.a.6.8.
Rations etc. for Bn. H.Q. via EPEHI to F.1.d.7.9.
7. The following will be carefully taken over:-
(a) Defence schemes and all documents connected with the line with the exception of aeroplane photographs.
(b) All work in progress and proposed (in writing).
(c) Trench Stores.
(d) Ammunition and Grenades.
Copies of (b) and (c) and a map showing dispositions of coys. after relief will be sent to Bn. H.Q. by 9 a.m. 11th. January.
8. Relief complete will be reported by Coys. using code word "CAMBRAI".
9. ACKNOWLEDGE.

                                                Captain,
Adjutant, 2nd. Battalion, The Royal Irish Regiment.

Copy No. 1. War Diary.
       2. H.Q., 49th. Inf. Bde.
       3. 6/R.I.Regt.
       4. Commdg. Offr.
       5. O.C. "A" Coy.
       6. O.C. "B" Coy.
       7. O.C. "C" Coy.
       8. O.C. "D" Coy.
       9. Signalling Offr.
      10. Medical Offr.
      11. Transport Offr.
      12. Q.M.
      13. R. SER.
      14. Spare.

Army Form W. 3125.

DECLARATION to be made by a soldier of the Regular Forces who is willing to continue to serve until the end of the war under the provisions of section 87, sub-sections (3) and (4) of the Army Act.

I (No.) _____ (Rank) _____

(Name) _____

at present serving in the (Corps) _____

hereby agree to continue as a soldier of the Regular Forces until the end of the war, in the same manner in all respects as if my term of service were still unexpired. Provided that on the termination of the war I shall be discharged with all convenient speed.

_____, Signature of the soldier.

DECLARED before me at _____

on the _____ day of _____ 191___.

_____
Signature of Commanding Officer of the soldier.

SECRET.   OPERATION ORDER NO. 2.   Copy No. ___III___
by
MAJOR J. L. C. MOORE-BRABAZON, COMMANDING,
2nd. Battalion, The Royal Irish Regiment.

Ref. Map, Special Sheet
LEMPIRE, 1/10,000.   The Field, 15-1-1918.
----

1. The Battalion will be relieved in the Left Sub-Section by the 7th/8th. Rl. Irish Fus. tomorrow, the 16th. inst.
2. "A" Coy., 7/8 Rl. Ir. Fus. will relieve "C" Coy., 2/R. I. Regt.
   "B" .... "D" ....
   "D" .... "B" ....
   "C" .... "A" ....
3. On completion of relief the Battalion will move into Brigade Support. Companies will be disposed as under:-
   "A" Coy.   Posts in CATELET VALLEY, F.2.c., Coy. H.Q., cutting in F.2.c.
   "B" Coy.   Cutting in F.2.c.
   "C" Coy.   1 platoon and Coy. H.Q., LEMPIRE, F.15.b.05.25.
              1 platoon, ENFER WOOD, F.9.d.
   "D" Coy.   2 platoons, MALASSISE FARM.
              1 platoon, OLD COPSE, F.9.a.
              1 platoon of "C" Coy. (attached for rations and discipline) - MAY COPSE, F.9.c.
4. Guides.   Guides for "B" Coy., 7th/8th Rl. Irish Fus. will be at MALASISSE FARM at 4-30 p.m.
   Guides for "A", "C" and "D" Coys., 7th/8th Rl. Irish Fus. will be at "C" Coy. H.Q., 7th/8th Rl. Irish Fus., F.2.c.20.40. at 4-30 p.m.
   Guides from 7th/8th Rl. Irish Fus. will be taken from incoming platoons.
5. Advance parties, usual strength, including Nos. 1 of Lewis Guns, will take over new positions in daylight.
6. Transport.   Transport will come via STE. EMILIE - MALASISSE Rd. to F.8.a.60.30. and thence go direct to respective H.Qrs.
7. Water.   Transport Officer will collect all petrol tins and will distribute in equal nos. to Coy. and Bn. H.Qrs. and make arrangements for water cart to fill petrol tins and dixies twice a night.
8. Cooking arrangements.   Cooking is done at each Coy. H.Q., food containers being used for outlying platoons.
9. The following will be carefully handed and taken over:-
   (a) Trench Stores.
   (b) Defence arrangements and all information about the line, except aeroplane photographs.
   (c) Work in progress and work proposed, in writing.
   (d) Working parties.
   (e) Ammunition and Grenades.
   Copies of (a), (c) and (e), to reach this office by 9 a.m., 17th. in
10. Officers' Trench Kits and Mess boxes of "C" Coy. will be dumped at AID POST by 4 p.m. Os. C. "A", "B" and "D" Coys. will arrange to have theirs carried to their new H.Qrs. in CUTTING and MALASISSE FARM.
11. Completion of relief will be notified to Bn. H.Q. using code word, "SOME"
12. A C K N O W L E D G E.

                                                    Captain,
   Issued at ____ p.m.
                    Adjutant, 2nd. Battalion, The Royal Irish Regt..
Copy No.1. H.Q.49.Bde.   6. O. C. "A" Coy. 11. Medical Offr.
        2. War Diary.   7. O. C. "B" Coy. 12. Transport Offr.
        3. 7/8.R.Ir.F.   8. O. C. "C" Coy. 13. Q.M.
        4. Commdg. Offr. 9. O. C. "D" Coy. 14. R. S. M.
        5. Sec-in-Commd. 10. Sig. Offr.   15. Cook Sgt.

OPERATION ORDER N. 5.   Copy No. _____ IV

MAJOR. W. L. C. MOORE-BRABAZON, COMMANDING,
2nd. Battalion, The Royal Irish Regiment.

Ref. Special Sheet,   The Field,
LEMPIRE, 1/10,000   21-1-1918.

----

1. The Battalion will relieve the 7/8th. The Rl. Irish Fus. in the left sub-section tomorrow, the 22nd. inst.
2. "C" Coy., 2/R.I.Regt. will relieve "B" Coy., 7/8th. R.Ir.Fus.-RIGHT.
   "D" .... "A" .... LEFT.
   "A" .... "D" .... SUPT.
   "B" .... "C" .... RES.
3. Guides. Guides, 1 per platoon for "A", "B" and "D" Coys. will be at AID POST in cutting, (F.8.c.1.8.), at 5-30 p.m.
   Guides for "C" Coy. will be at MALASISSE FARM at 5-30 p.m.
4. Usual advance parties, to include Scouts and Nos.1 of Lewis Gun teams, will report at respective Coy. H.Qrs., 7/8th. R. Ir. Fus., at 2 p.m.
5. Mess cart, maltese cart and one limber for Officers' Kits of H.Q., and "C" Coy. will report at Battalion H.Q. at 5 p.m.
6. The following will be carefully handed and taken over:-
   (a)   Trench Stores.
   (b)   Defence arrangements and all information about the line except aeroplane photographs.
   (c)   Work in progress and proposed (in writing).
   (d)   Working parties (according to Bde. List).
   Copies of (a) and (b) to reach xxxxxxxxxxxx Battalion H.Q. by 10 p.m., 22nd. inst. More care is to be taken in the taking over of trench stores, etc. This is to be impressed on the Advance parties detailed in para 4.
7. Working parties will cease at 12 noon on 22nd. January.
8. The 47th. Inf. Bde. is relieving the 48th. Inf. Bde. on the 22nd/23rd. January.
9. Advance parties of the 7/8th. R.Ir. Fus. will report at present Coy. H.Q. at 12 noon on the 22nd. inst.
10. Completion of relief will be reported by wire to Battn H.Q. using code word "No N.C.O. AVAILABLE".
11. A C K N O W L E D G E.

Issued at ___ p.m.   Captain
                Adjutant, 2nd. Battalion, The Royal Irish Regiment.

Copy No.1. War Diary.   No. 9. O.C. "B" Coy.
        2. H.Q. 49th. Inf. Bde.   10. O.C. "C" Coy.
        3. 7/8th. R.Inn.Fus.   11. O.C. "D" Coy.
        4. 7/8th. R. Iri Fus.   12. Sig. Offr.
        5. Commdg. Offr.   13. Med. Offr.
        6. Sec-in-Commd.   14. Transport Offr.
        7. Adjutant.   15. Q.M.
        8. O.C. "A" Coy.   16. R.S.M.
                No. 18. Cook Sgt.

ORDERS No. 4   Copy No. ___

by
LIEUT. COLONEL, J. D. SCOTT, D.S.O., COMMANDING,
2nd. Battalion, The Royal Irish Regiment.

Ref. map Special Sheet,   The Field,
LEMPIRE, 1/10,000.   27-1-1918.
----

1. The Battalion will be relieved in the left sub-section tomorrow night 28th/29th. January by the 7th/8th. The Rl. Irish Fus. On relief the Battalion will move to Brigade Reserve in RAILWAY CUTTING, STE. EMILIE.

2. The 7th/8th. Rl. Irish Fus. will not be East of the LEMPIRE-EPEHY Rd. before 5-30 p.m.

3. "D" Coy. Left front line will be relieved by "C" Coy., 7/8th.R.Ir.F.
   "C" ... Right ... ... "D" ... ...
   "B" ... In reserve ... ... "A" ... ...
   "A" ... In support ... ... "B" ... ...

4. The following will be carefully handed and taken over:-
   (a) Trench Stores.
   (b) Defence arrangements and all information about the line with the exception of aeroplane photographs.
   (c) Work in progress and proposed (in writing).
   (d) Working parties (according to Brigade List).
   Copies of (a) to reach this office by 9 a.m. on the 29th. inst., and copies of (c) by 12 noon, tomorrow the 28th. inst.

5. Taking over party consisting of 2/Lt. CLANCY and the 5 C.Q.M.Sgts. will report at the Reserve Bn. H.Qrs. by 2 p.m. This party will rendezvous at the cross rds. E.24,b,25,95, at 8 p.m. and C.Q.M.Sgts. will guide their respective companies to billets.

6. Completion of relief will be reported to Bn. H.Q. by code message "NOT RECOMMENDED". Companies on arrival in CUTTING will report by runner to Bn. H.Q.

7. Guides 3 per company will meet coys. of 7th/8th. Rl. Irish Fus. as follows:-
   From "C" Coy. MALASISSE FARM. 5-30 p.m.
   From "A", "B" and "D" Coys. on road F.1.c.4.0. at 5-15 p.m.

8. Transport arrangements. Lewis Gun limbers will report to Coy. H.Qrs. at 6 p.m.
   Maltese cart, mess cart and 1 limber at Bn. H.Qrs. at 6 p.m.
   1 limber for cooking utensils, etc., to be at COOKHOUSE in VAUGHAN CUTTING at 6 p.m.

9. Working parties will cease work at 12 noon on 28th. January.

10. A C K N O W L E D G E.

                                                    Captain,
                        Adjutant, 2nd. Battalion, The Royal Irish R.

Issued at ___ p.m.
Copy No. 1. War Diary.   No. 9. O.C. "B" Coy.
       2. H.Q. 49th. Inf. Bde.   10. O.C. "C" Coy.
       3. 7th/8th. R. Ir. F.   11. O.C. "D" Coy.
       4. Commdg. Offr.   12. Sig. Offr.
       5. Sec-in-Commd.   13. Med. Offr.
       6. Adjutant.   14. Transpt. Offr.
       7. O.C. "A" Coy.   15. Q.M.
                                            16. R.S.M.
                17. Cook Sergt.

WAR DIARY.

FOR MONTH OF FEBRUARY, 1918.

VOLUME:-

UNIT:- 2nd Bn. Irish Regiment.

WAR DIARY or INTELLIGENCE SUMMARY

Army Form C. 2118

2nd Bn. Royal Irish Regiment.

Place	Date	Hour	Summary of Events and Information	Remarks and references to Appendices
STE EMILIE	1918. Feby. 1-3.		Battalion in Brigade Reserve in RAILWAY CUTTING at STE EMILIE. The work during this period consisted of work on the Defence Lines and improvement of Billets.	
VILLERS-FAUCON	3-9.		Battalion was relieved by the 2nd Batt. Royal Dublin Fusiliers and moved into Billets at VILLERS-FAUCON the 3rd inst. (Brigade in Support)	Appendix No. 1
	7.		Presentation at Brigade Headquarters by the Army Commander of Medals Ribbons to certain Officers, N.C.Os and men. A Football match between the Battalion and the 6th Connaught Rangers resulted in a loss to the Battalion; Score 2 – Nil. During this period working parties 200 strong were supplied daily working on the Defence Lines wiring at RONSSOY. Anti-Aircraft Lewis Gun Guards were also found at VILLERS-FAUCON and in the neighbourhood.	
HAMEL	9-14		Battalion was relieved by the 7th (S.I.H) The Royal Irish Regiment and moved into Billets at HAMEL on the 9th inst. (Brigade in Reserve)	See Appendix No. 2.

Army Form C. 2118.

WAR DIARY
or
INTELLIGENCE SUMMARY.
(Erase heading not required.)

Instructions regarding War Diaries and Intelligence Summaries are contained in F.S. Regs., Part II. and the Staff Manual respectively. Title pages will be prepared in manuscript.

Place	Date	Hour	Summary of Events and Information	Remarks and references to Appendices
HAMEL	1918 Feby. 10.		The 6th Battalion The Royal Scots Regiment having been broken up about 300 Officers and O.R. were posted to the Battalion and were welcomed by the Commanding Officer. The work during the first week consisted of Battalion Training. Anti-Aircraft Lewis Gun Guards were posted in HAMEL and neighbourhood during this, but great interest was shewn in Inter-Platoon Football Tourney which was held and which resulted in a Win to No. 9 Platoon by 2 goals — 1 in the Finals. Le Temps being No. 9 Platoon -v- No. 2 Platoon.	
	14.		The Battalion relieved the 8th Battalion The K.O.Y.L.I. in the Right Sub. Section of the Left Section Divisional Front, and held the line. Situation quiet though attack anticipated.	See Appendice No. 3
EPEHY 18			The Battalion was relieved by the 7/8th Royal Inniskilling Fusiliers and moved into Brigade Support. Work consisted of work on EPEHY Defences.	See Appendice No. 4

A5834 Wt.W4973/M687 750,000 8/16 D.D. & L. Ltd. Forms/C.2118/13.

Army Form C. 2118.

WAR DIARY
or
INTELLIGENCE SUMMARY.
(Erase heading not required.)

Place	Date	Hour	Summary of Events and Information	Remarks and references to Appendices
	1918. Feby 22.		Battalion relieved Roy^l (S.I.H) Pashyal Irish Regiment in the left Sub-Sector. Situation quiet and normal.	See Appendices No. 5.
	27-28.			
VILLERS-FAUCON.	28.		Battalion moved into Billets at VILLERS-FAUCON as Corps Reserve.	
			DECORATIONS and AWARDS.	
			The following decorations were awarded during the month:-	
			SERG^t (now 2/Lt) A. BURKETT ...... Belgian Croix de Guerre.	
			N° 9886 SERG^t UPSON, A. .... Belgian Croix de Guerre.	
			REINFORCEMENTS. - OFFICERS.	
			LIEUT. T.F. CONNOLLY. Quartermaster.	
			CAPT. A.D. PLACE. On disbandment of 6th Battalion	
			LIEUT. H. JORDAN. "	
			" J.F. O'REILLY. "	
			" S.H. JACKSON. "	
			2/LIEUT. J.A. MOUAT-BIGGS. "	
			" M.J. HUNT. "	
			" J.P. MARREN. "	

Army Form C. 2118.

WAR DIARY
or
INTELLIGENCE SUMMARY.
(Erase heading not required.)

Place	Date	Hour	Summary of Events and Information	Remarks and references to Appendices
	1918. Feby. 10.		REINFORCEMENTS - OFFICERS (cont'd)	
			2/Lieut J.T. FARRELL. On attachment from 6th Battalion.	
			" L. O'KEEFFE. "	
			" R.T. HAMILTON. "	
			REINFORCEMENTS — OTHER RANKS.	
	2.		19.	
	10.		270.	
	17.		3.	
			DECREASE — OFFICERS	
	2.		MAJOR. W.L.C. MOORE - BRABAZON... 6 months tour of duty at home	
	6.		2/Lieut. J.G. MAHAFFY.... Hospital.	
	13.		LIEUT. G.J.H. PALMER..	
	16.		CAPT. R.R.C. MACGRATH, M.C..	
	18.		2/Lieut. R. ADAMSON..	
	24.		CAPT. D. FOULKES..	
	26.		" H. HARRISON, M.C..	
	28.		" A.D. PLACE, M.C.... As Instructor to American Army.	

Army Form C. 2118.

WAR DIARY
or
INTELLIGENCE SUMMARY.
(Erase heading not required.)

Instructions regarding War Diaries and Intelligence Summaries are contained in F.S. Regs., Part II. and the Staff Manual respectively. Title pages will be prepared in manuscript.

Place	Date	Hour	Summary of Events and Information	Remarks and references to Appendices
	1918 Feby 28.		INCREASE — OFFICERS CAPT. R.R.C. MACGRATH, M.C. ... From Hospital LIEUT. G.J.H. PALMER " " " CASUALTIES — OTHER RANKS. 14. 1 O.R. Wounded in Action 16. 2 " " " 21. 2 " " "	

Lieut Colonel
Commanding 3—6—1918

Appendix No. 1

SECRET.   OPERATION ORDER NO. 5.   Copy No. _____
by,
LIEUT. COLONEL, J. D. SCOTT, D.S.O.,
Commanding, 2nd. Battalion, The Royal Irish Regiment.

Reference Map. Sheet,   The Field,
62. C. N.E., 1:20,000.   2-2-1918..

1. The 48th. Inf. Bde. (less M.G. Coy.) will relieve the 49th. Inf. Bde. (less M.G. Coy.) in the left section on the night 3rd./4th. February.

2. The Battalion will be relieved by the 2nd. R. Dub. Fus., relief to be completed by 1 p.m. On relief companies will proceed by march route to billets in VILLERS FAUCON (E.26.b.4.9.).

3. C.Q.M.Sgts. under 2/Lt. SANDERSON will report to Town Major, VILLERS FAUCON, at 10 a.m. on the 3rd. February.

4. Companies will hand over their defence scheme, work in progress and proposed (in writing), trench stores and working party lists.

5. The following anti-aircraft Lewis Guns will be relieved by the Battalion by 12 noon 3rd. February.
E.27.b.8.7. one gun to be relieved by one L.G. Section, "A" Coy.
E.27.d.4.9. (Bde. Transpt. Lines) one gun to be relieved by one L.G. Section, "D" Coy.
An Officer will be sent by companies to take over each position from 2nd. R. Dub. Fus.
Rations will be sent under company arrangements. Complete Coy. H.Q. Lewis Gun Sections will be sent.

6. The Transport Officer will send one L.G. limber to each Coy. H.Q. One limber for cooks, one limber, maltese cart and mess cart, Bn. H.Q., 11 a.m. If fine, this transport will remain on road at LEVEL CROSSING E.28.d.2.1. and will be loaded there.

7. After relief the Battalion will be prepared, in case of emergency, to man the STE. EMILIE DEFENCES as laid down in EMERGENCY DEFENCE SCHEME.

8. Completion of relief will be reported by runner to Bn. H.Q.

9. A C K N O W L E D G E.

                                                Captain,
         A/Adjutant, 2nd. Battalion, The Royal Irish Regiment

Issued at _____

Copy No.		Copy No.	
1.	H.Q. 49 Inf. Bde.	10.	Intell. Officer.
2.	2/R.D.Fus.	11.	Lewis Gun Officer.
3.	Bmbg. Officer.	12.	Quartermaster.
4.	Sec-in-Command.	13.	Transpt. Officer.
5.	O.C. "A" Coy.	14.	R.S.M.
6.	O.C. "B" Coy.	15.	Cook Sergt.
7.	O.C. "C" Coy.	16.	War Diary.
8.	O.C. "D" Coy.	17.	2/Lt. SANDERSON.
9.	Signalling Officer.	18.	File.
		19.	Spare.

Appendix No 2

S E C R E T.   OPERATION ORDER No. 6.   Copy No _____
by
Lieut. Colonel J.D. Scott, D.S.O.
Commanding 2nd Battalion The Royal Irish Regiment
The Field 7-2-18.

---

1. The 7th (S.I.H.) Royal Irish Regiment will relieve the 2nd Bn. The Royal Irish Regiment at VILLERS FAUCON on the 9th February. Relief to be complete by I p.m.

2. On completion of relief the Battalion will proceed to H___ Companies.

3. Advance party consisting of C.Q.M.Sergts under 2/Lt Sanderson will report to the Town Major HAMEL at IO a.m. on the 9th Feb.

4. Lewis Gun Sections on Anti-Aircraft duty will be relieved by the 7th(S.I.H.)Royal Irish Regt. before II a.m. under Bn.L.G.Officer.

5. The Transport Officer will send one L.Gun limber to each Company H.Qrs. One limber for Cooks, one limber, Maltese Cart and Mess Cart to Bn.H.Qrs at II a.m.
Two G.S.Wagons will be available to carry down Blankets.

6. The working party on the 9th will be as usual. A train will be at siding (C.Y.II) VILLERS FAUCON at 4 p.m. to carry this party back.

7. Packs and Blankets will be dumped outside Company H.Qrs by II a.m.

8. Completion of relief will be notified to Bn. H.Qrs.

9. ACKNOWLEDGE.

                         Captain
a/Adjutant 2nd Battalion The Royal Irish Regiment.

Issued at _____

Copy No			
1.	H.Q.49th Inf.Bde.	10.	Intell.Officer.
2.	7th(S.I.H.)R.I.Regt.	11.	Lewis Gun Officer.
3.	Cmndg.Officer.	12.	Quartermaster.
4.	Sec-in-Command	13.	Transport Officer.
5.	O.C. "A" Coy.	14.	R.S.M.
6.	O.C. "B" Coy.	15.	Cook Sergt.
7.	O.C. "C" Coy.	16.	War Diary.
8.	O.C. "D" Coy.	17.	2/Lt.Sanderson.
9.	Signalling Officer.	18.	File.
	19. Spare.		

Appendix No. 3.

S E C R E T. OPERATION ORDER No. 7.   Copy No _____
                        by
            LIEUT.COLONEL J.D.SCOTT,D.S.O.,Commanding
                   2nd Battalion The Royal Irish Regiment.
Ref.Special Sheet   The Field
LEMPIRE 1/10,000   12-2-18.
_____

1. The Battalion will relieve the 9th Battalion The K.O.Y.L.I.in
    the right sub-section of the left section Divisional Front on
    night 14/15th February.
2. Each Company will relieve the corresponding Company of 9th
    K.O.Y.L.I.
3. The following will be carefully taken over:-

        (a) Trench Stores.
        (b) All defence Schemes and documents connected with the
            line
        (c) Aeroplane Photographs.
        (d) Work in progress and proposed (in writing)
        (e) Maps.
        (f) Working Parties.
    Copies of (a) and (d) and a list of (e) and a sketch showing dis-
    positions of Companies will be sent to Bn.H.Q. before 12 noon 15th
    February.
        One Officer per Company, one N.C.O. per Platoon and No's 1 of
    L.G. Teams will proceed to the Line on the night 13/14th February
        The Battalion will arrange to take over all patrols on night of
    relief and will send 50% of the strength of this party out with
    patrols of 9th K.O.Y.L.I. An Officer will accompany each patrol
    which should consist of at least 12 O.Ranks per Company in the Front
    Line. This Party will parade at 3 p.m. on the 13 th inst:
4. All anti-aircraft Lewis Guns will be relieved by 12 noon 14th Inst.
    Should they not be relieved by that hour they will be with-drawn.
5. Battalion Snipers and Observers, one N.C.O. per Company, one N.C.O. for
    Battalion H.Q. and Bn Signallers will leave HMTL under Capt.H.Harrison
    at 10 a.m. 14th inst. and will take over by day-light.
        The Bn.Scouts will furnish the patrol mentioned in para 3 strenght-
    ened by 1 Officer and 2 N.C.O's per Company in Front Line.
6. The Battalion will entrain at HMTL 4-30 p.m. detraining at ST.EMILIE
    EMMY must not be entered before 6 p.m. Movement will be by Platoon
    at 5 minutes intervals.
        Companies to be ready to entrain by 4-20 p.m.
7. The T.O. will have one L.G.Limber at each Company H.Q, one Limber
    and Maltese cart, Mess Cart at Bn.H.Q. at 3 p.m. 14th Inst.
        Officers valises, packs and Blankets will be dumped outside Coy H.
    at 11 a.m. One Blanket per man will be carried
8. Arrangements about rations, water, cooking etc will be notified when
    known.
9. Completion of relief will be wired to Bn.H.Q. by code message
    "Forms not required".
10. Bn.H.Q. Fld.8.8.
11 ACKNOWLEDGE.

                                            E.MacVeeth
Issued at _____   Captain.
            a/Adjutant 2nd Battalion The Royal Irish Regiment.
    Copy No 1. War Diary.   9. O.C. "C" Coy.
            2. H.Q.49th Inf Bde.   10. O.C. "D" Coy.
            3. 9th K.O.Y.L.I.   11. Sig.Officer.
            4. Commdg Officer.   12. Med.Officer.
            5. Sec-in-Command.   13. Transport Officer.
            6. Adjutant.   14. Quartermaster.
            7. O.C. "A" Coy.   15. Int.Officer.
            8. O.C. "B" Coy.   16. R.S.M.
                    17. Cook Sergeant.

Appendix No 4.

S E C R E T   OPERATION ORDER NO.8.   Copy No____
by
LIEUT COLONEL J.D.SCOTT.D.S.O.Commanding.
2nd Battalion The Royal Irish Regiment,..

Special Sheet   The Field.
LEMPIRE 1/10,000   17-2-18.

1. The Battalion will be relieved by the 7/8th Rl.Inniskilling Fus. on the night 18/19th February.
   On relief the Battalion will move into Brigade Support in EETHY.

2. "A" Coy 7/8th Rl.Inniskilling Fus will relieve "C" Coy 2nd R.I.Rgt.
   "C" Coy   "   "   "   "   "   "   "D" Coy 2nd R.I.Rgt.
   "B" Coy   "   "   "   "   "   "   "B" Coy 2nd R.I.Rgt.
   "D" Coy   "   "   "   "   "   "   "A" Coy 2nd R.I.Rgt.

3. Guides 1 per platoon for 7/8th Rl.Innis.Fus will be at level crossing F.1.b.4.3.at 6-30 p.m. on the 18th.

4. Advance parties from 7/8th Rl.Innis,Fus. will report at Bn.H.Q.at 2 p.m.18th inst and will be met by 1 guide per Company.
   Advance parties from 2nd Rl.Irish Regt. to consist of 1 Officer and 1 N.C.O. per Company and 1 N.C.O. per platoon will report at Bn H.Q. at 9-30 a.m. to take over Billets etc. Companies will take over Billets as in para 2.

5. TRANSPORT. Lewis Gun limbers will be at Coy ration dumps at 6-30 p.m Maltese cart, Mess cart and 2 limbers will be at Bn.H.Q. at 6-30 p.m.

6. Patrols will cover the relief. 2 N.C.O's and 8 Other Ranks 7/8th Rl Innis Fus will be attached to "D" Coy night 17/18th for patrol work.

7. All trench stores,work in progress and proposed working parties, information about the line etc will be carefully handed and taken over. Trench Store Lists to reach Bn.H.Q. by 9 a.m. on the 19th.

8. Completion of relief will be notified to Bn.H.Q. using code word "HOME".
   Companies will report arrival in support positions by runner.

9. Rations will arrive at ration dumps in support at 9 p.m.

10. A C K N O W L E D G E.

                                        Captain.
       Adjutant 2nd Battalion The Royal Irish Regiment.

Issued at ____

Copy No 1. War Diary.   9. O.C."C" Coy.
      2. H.Q.49th InfBde.   10. O.C."D" Coy.
      3. 7/8th Rl.Innis.Fus.   11. Sig.Officer.
      4. Commdg Officer   12. Med.Officer.
      5. Sec-in-Command.   13. Int.Officer.
      6. Adjutant.   14. Transport Officer.
      7. O.C."A" Coy.   15. Quartermaster.
      8. O.C."B" Coy.   16. Cook Sergeant.

Appendix No. 5.

OPERATION ORDER NO. 9.   Copy No ____
by
Lieut Colonel J.D.SCOTT, D.S.O., Commanding
2nd Battalion The Royal Irish Regiment.

Map Sheet   The Field
SHEET 1/10,000   21-2-1916.
----

1. The Battalion will relieve the 7th(S.I.H.) Royal Irish Regt. in the left sub-section to-morrow the 22nd instant.

2. "A" Coy 2nd Rl.Ir.Regt will relieve "B" Coy 7th Rl.Ir.Regt. in right Front Line.
   "C" Coy -------------------------------- "B" Coy 7th Rl.Ir.Regt in left Front Line
   "B" Coy 2nd Rl.Ir.Regt will relieve "A" Coy 7th Rl.Ir.Regt in Support.
   "D" Coy -------------------------------- "C" Coy 7th Rl.Ir.Regt in Reserve.

3. Guides one per platoon from S.I.H. will be at cutting X.25.c.4.9. at 6-30 p.m.. Guides for advance parties will be at same place at 1.p.m.

4. Advance parties of S.I.H. will report at Bn.H.Q. REMY at 10 a.m. 22nd instant. O.C A and B Coy will send Platoon guides to be there at that hour - O's. C C and D will send one guide per Company.

5. The following will be carefully handed and taken over:-
   (a) Trench Stores.
   (b) Information about the line except aeroplane photographs.
   (c) Work in hand and proposed (in writing)
   (d) Working Parties.
   Copies of (c) to include work done on working parties will be sent to Orderly Room by 10 a.m. to-morrow. Copies of (d) to reach Bn.H.Q. by 9 a.m.the 23rd inst.

6. Advance parties consisting of snipers, observers, No's I of L.G. Teams, Officer and I N.C.O. per Company, I N.C.O. per platoon, Coy. and Bn. Gas N.C.O's will be met at X.25.c.4.9 at 1 p.m. by guides from S.I.H.

7. TRANSPORT. Mess cart and 2 limbers to be at Bn.H.Q. 6 p.m.
   Lewis Gun Limbers to be at Coy H.Q. at 6 p.m.
   Maltese cart at Aid Post at 6 p.m.

8. Rations will arrive at 9 p.m.

9. The relief will be covered by a patrol which will leave Right of Right Company at 6-30 p.m.

10. The Lewis Guns of A and B Coy's at Brigade Transport Lines will be relieved by the S.I.H. by 12 noon the 22nd inst.

11. Completion of relief to be wired to Bn.H.Q. using code word "BUBBLY"

12. A C K N O W L E D G E

                                                Captain
                Adjutant 2nd Battalion the Royal Irish Regiment.

Issued at
Copy No.1 War Diary.   9.O.C. "C" Coy
       2.H.Q. 49th Inf.Bde.   10.O.C. "D" Coy.
       3.7/8th Rl.Innis.Fus.   11.Sig.Officer.
       4.7th(S.I.H.)Rl.Ir.Regt.   12.Med.Officer.
       5.Commdg Officer   13.Int.Officer.
       6.Sec-in-Command   14.Transport Officer.
       7.O.C. "A" Coy   15.Quartermaster.
       8.O.C. "B" Coy   16.

16th Division.

49th Brigade.

2nd BATTALION

ROYAL IRISH REGIMENT

MARCH 1918

Appendix :-

    Extract from private diary 25.3.18-3.4.18.

WAR DIARY or INTELLIGENCE SUMMARY

Army Form C. 2118.

2 R. Ir. R. 1918

Place	Date	Hour	Summary of Events and Information	Remarks and references to Appendices
	1918. March			
VILLERS- FAUCON	1		Battalion at HQ in GRANGE CAMP	
RONSSOY	4		Battalion relieved R.S.Batt. The Connaught Rangers in LEMPIRE DEFENCES	
			Companies and H.Q. occupying the village of RONSSOY	
	5		Our Artillery commence programme of heavy harassing fire on probable enemy assembly positions, tracks, communications &c.	
	7	8 pm 10 pm	Enemy Artillery carried out concentrated shoot on RONSSOY in retaliation for our harassing fire.	
BASSE-	8		Battalion relieved the 7/8 Royal Inniskilling Fusiliers in the right subsector.	
BOULOGNE			H.Q. at BASSE-BOULOGNE	
	13		Anticipated attack by enemy did not materialise. Heavy harassing bombardments commenced by our Artillery	24 A (11 thirty)
	16	6.30 am	S.O.S. signal put up by troops on our left. The Battalion harassed battle stations but nothing transpired	
			On relief by the 7/8 Batt. (C.I.H.) The Royal Irish Regiment the Battalion moved	

Army Form C. 2118.

WAR DIARY
or
INTELLIGENCE SUMMARY.
(Erase heading not required.)

Instructions regarding War Diaries and Intelligence Summaries are contained in F. S. Regs., Part II. and the Staff Manual respectively. Title pages will be prepared in manuscript.

Place	Date	Hour	Summary of Events and Information	Remarks and references to Appendices
RONSSOY.	1918 Mar 16		to LEMPIRE DEFENCES occupying RONSSOY village	
	18		Harrassing fire by Enemy Artillery caused casualties on tank Area roads	
	20		Battalion relieved R.W.R. Royal Inniskilling Fusiliers in left sub Section. Hostile attack anticipated.	Apps xx x1
	21	4:30 AM	Enemy put down heavy Artillery barrage on LEMPIRE consisting of a large percentage of gas shells. All telephone wires to out almost immediately — communication by visual was impossible owing to the mist.	
		9.30 AM	The Barrage eased, and on emerging from Batt. H.Q. dug out Rifle firing was heard quite close to Batt. H.Q. Col. SCOTT at once ordered all others of Batt. H.Q. to man ROSE TRENCH	
		10 AM	The Germans were rallying at entrance to dug out which Key proceeded to bomb. This party was easily disperced by bombs and rifle fire. Our left flank Serrus Kavanelly Serrus as H.Q. details sent on to 2 Platoons of "D" Coy. (Reserve Coy.) who were in touch with Brigade on my left. The Germans who had broken through on our right took up a position between ROSE TRENCH and LEMPIRE DEFENCES. We were then fired ups	

WAR DIARY
or
INTELLIGENCE SUMMARY.
(Erase heading not required.)

Army Form C. 2118.

Place	Date	Hour	Summary of Events and Information	Remarks and references to Appendices
RONSSOY	1918 Mar. 21	10 AM	on fire both sides of ROSE TRENCH at a range of about 100 yds. but managed to keep the enemy at bay till 1-30 p.m.	
		1:30 PM	At this hour the enemy broke through on our right and also pushed forward in mass on our right. The remnants of ROSE TRENCH in order to avoid getting completely cut off at once withdrew to reform in IRISH TRENCH: those who succeeded in reaching the Trench obtained a fresh supply of ammunition. Here we looked at LIEUT PALMER and 2ND LIEUT SINCLAIR who had been billetted in LEMPIRE on the previous evening. The Trench was deserted when we got there. We remained in the village had been in German hands for some time	
		2:15 PM	The Germans started bombing the Northern End of IRISH TRENCH and used a machine Gun in Southern End. We immediately charged the machine Gun which the garrison left on seeing us take a determined attack.	
		2:30 PM	We started to retire on STE EMILIE. As we emerged from RONSSOY it was observed that the Germans were almost half way between RONSSOY	

Army Form C. 2118.

WAR DIARY
or
INTELLIGENCE SUMMARY.
(Erase heading not required.)

Instructions regarding War Diaries and Intelligence Summaries are contained in F. S. Regs., Part II. and the Staff Manual respectively. Title pages will be prepared in manuscript.

Place	Date	Hour	Summary of Events and Information	Remarks and references to Appendices
	1918.			
RONSSOY	March 21	2.30 P.M.	and ST. EMILIE on our left as we retired. Machine Guns opened fire on us at about 300 yards range. Very few succeeded in reaching ST. EMILIE - Approxte numbers 3 Officers (including LIEUT PALMER wounded) and about 15 O.R.	
VILLERS-FAUCON	22.	3 AM	The 49th Infantry Brigade left VILLERS-FAUCON at 3 A.M. reaching Div. H.Q.	
TINCOURT		5 AM	at TINCOURT at 5 AM	
		10 AM	Took up position in GREEN LINE support to Pioneer Battalion. During afternoon attacked repeatedly by enemy low-flying aircraft: otherwise quiet day.	
		4.30 P.M.	1 Batt: The Black Watch took up a position between GREEN FRONT LINE and GREEN SUPPORT in Brigade Sector	
		10 P.M.	CAMBRIDGESHIRE REGT. SHERWOOD FORRESTERS and RIFLE BRIGADE	
		12 M.N.	took up a position immediately in rear of GREEN SUPPORT in our Sector.	
	23.	6.30 A.M.	Order to retire received. H.Q. Infantry Brigade and Entrenching Battr. retires through other Regiments in same sector at 7.30 A.M	

WAR DIARY
or
INTELLIGENCE SUMMARY.
(Erase heading not required.)

Army Form C. 2118.

Place	Date	Hour	Summary of Events and Information	Remarks and references to Appendices
TINCOURT	1918 Mar.23	10 AM	The HQ of Infantry Brigade took up a position in KARKOS TRENCH about 10 AM to cover retirement of the 117th Infantry Brigade.	
DOIGT		11 AM.	Retired to Trench running through BOIS de FLAQUES.	
		12 Nday	Machine Gun fire was opened on Trench	
		1 P.M.	The 39th Division on Brigade left was forced to retire leaving a large gap on our left. As the Germans were advancing on his flank I considered it necessary to withdraw my left and endeavour to get touch with next unit. I was in the process of carrying out this movement when an order was received to retire if necessary on BIACHES. This order was received at 1-30 p.m. I issued an order to retire at once as both flanks were being turned. It was impossible to follow the direction laid down by Brigade H.Q. — almost Southerly course was taken via PERONNE	
LA CHAPELETTE		3 PM	The River was crossed by bridge at LA CHAPELETTE. An attempt to cross by Railway Bridge near LA CHAPELETTE failed as latter had been blown up. The country between the Bridge and Road Bridge was impassable owing to marsh. Brigade was accordingly obliged to use bridge	

Army Form C. 2118.

WAR DIARY
or
INTELLIGENCE SUMMARY.
(Erase heading not required.)

Place	Date	Hour	Summary of Events and Information	Remarks and references to Appendices
	1918 Mar 23		PERONNE before reaching this Road Bridge. The Bridge was not reached till most of the covering party of the 48th Brigade had already crossed.	
BIACHES			All units of 16th DIVISION assembled on high ground covering BIACHES	
		5.30 P.M.	49th Infantry Brigade reached here at 5.30 p.m. in company with 1st Batt: The Inniskilling Fusiliers.	
			The Division proceeded to take up a defensive position in H.30.a	
			The 49th Infantry Brigade was on the extreme right of this line	
	24	12.20 AM	Orders were received that the 16th DIVISION was to retire	
		6 A.M	They reached their Transport Lines between CAPPY & BRAY about 6 A.M.	
CAPPY-BRAY		6 P.M	49th Infantry Brigade moved off to guard crossings over RIVER SOMME between ETINEHEM & MERICOURT. The 2nd Batt: The Royal Irish Regt. was in reserve to the 7th (S.I.A) The Royal Irish Regt. and 7/8 th Inniskilling Fusiliers	Appdx FRANCE Sheet N° 62 g 3
	25	5. A.M.	The 16 Division is transferred from VIIth to XIXth CORPS	See Appendix N°.2
			Battalion moved via MERICOURT-CHUIGNOLLES to Prisoners of War Cage 3/4 mile South of FROISSY. 1 Coy. 7/8th Inniskilling Fusiliers on Outpost	N° 3

WAR DIARY
OR
INTELLIGENCE SUMMARY.
(Erase heading not required.)

Army Form C. 2118.

Place	Date	Hour	Summary of Events and Information	Remarks and references to Appendices
	1918		Duty guarding crossings over River and Canal	
	Mar 25			
	26.	10 AM	hurried into position by Railway in R.L.C. & with Regt (S.I.H) Dublin Fus Regt on left and 4/8th Infantry Brigade on right. 7/8th Royal Inniskilling Fus were moving into support after the 39th Div had withdrawn. Throughout the afternoon large bodies of the enemy including Cavalry are observed to be moving to Cot on flanks. Mobile guns are brought into action and high ground to hills N.E. of our position.	Appx 5 Aus ORRS 5
		7 PM	withdrew to old French line trench 3000 yards EAST of MERICOURT owing to left flank being partially turned. Dispositions 7/8 Royal Inniskilling Fusiliers on left, Royal Irish on right, S.I.H. in support. During night one company Hull Pioneers reinforced and took up a position between the R. Inniskilling Fus and the Royal Irish.	
	27	10 AM	48th Infantry Brigade prolonged the line on the right. Attacked in morning. Owing to good field of fire on right Enemy failed to get within 1000 yards of our trench but on left flank they managed to	Aus ORRS A 17-23 W3

Army Form C. 2118.

WAR DIARY
or
INTELLIGENCE SUMMARY.
(Erase heading not required.)

Instructions regarding War Diaries and Intelligence Summaries are contained in F.S. Regs., Part II. and the Staff Manual respectively. Title pages will be prepared in manuscript.

Place	Date	Hour	Summary of Events and Information	Remarks and references to Appendices
	1918			
	Mar 27		Got into with trench occupied by 7/8 Royal Inniskilling Fus where they commenced to Trench Mortar	Appendix No 24
		2:10 PM	Orders to withdraw on MORCOURT was received.	
		2:15 PM	Orders were issued to all units in this area to this effect. S.I.H. did not at first act as a previous order stated that they were to be in to prevent hostile attacks onward at MORCOURT, it was found that the enemy were already in possession of CERISY a further retirement became necessary. This was carried out under very heavy machine gun and Artillery fire at short range on LAMOTTE to HAMEL line.	No 25
	28	7:30 PM	Orders were received to proceed to FOUILLOY, hence to billets in AUBIGNY.	No 26
		8:30 AM	49th Infantry Brigade concentrated EAST of HAMEL in support to CAREY'S FORCE. 2nd Royal Irish Regt x 7/8th (S.I.H.) Royal Irish Regt x 7/8 R Inniskillings Fus. were formed into a composite Battn. under Major HARRISON	
		4:50 PM	Owing to heavy bombardment it became necessary to reinforce front line with Inniskilling Coy & Royal Irish Coy. S.I.H. Coy remaining in support.	No 27
	29.		Comparatively quiet day. S.I.H. relieving 7/8 Inniskilling Fus. in evening	No 28

Army Form C. 2118.

WAR DIARY
or
INTELLIGENCE SUMMARY.
(Erase heading not required.)

Place	Date	Hour	Summary of Events and Information	Remarks and references to Appendices
	1918.			
	Mar. 30	1 P.M.	Line very strongly attacked after intense bombardment on front line trench. 7/8 Inniskilling Fus. move from Rein Position in support to use from which a counter attack could be delivered. Attack successfully repulsed. In evening 7/8 R. Inniskilling Fus. relieve 2nd Royal Irish.	
	31.		Comparatively quiet day. In evening moved into position in support NORTH of HAMEL in order to re-organise line to fill a gap in front line between relieved following night when Bay moved to support line.	
	April 1		Quiet day.	
	2		Quiet day.	
	3		Quiet day. Relieved by 14th Div. Relief complete at 10.30 P.M. moved via AUBIGNY en-bussed at BLANGY-TRONVILLE to billets at SALEUX	

Army Form C. 2118.

WAR DIARY
or
INTELLIGENCE SUMMARY.
(Erase heading not required.)

Place	Date	Hour	Summary of Events and Information	Remarks and references to Appendices
	1918. March 21st		CASUALTIES LT. COL. T.D. SCOTT, D.S.O. Killed in Action.	
			LIEUT. G.J.H. PALMER Wounded in Action.	
			2/LT. G. SINCLAIR (Roy. Munster Fus.) Missing.	
			" J.M. TERRY (Do.) Do.	
			" W.N. ABBOTT (Conn. Rangers) Do.	
			" J.H. MAHAFFY (Roy. Dub. Fus.) Do.	
			LIEUT. J.A. MOUATT-BIGGS Do.	
			2/LT. J.T.P. FARRELL Do.	
			" L. O'KEEFFE Do.	
			" D.E. STANFORD Do.	
			LIEUT. J.J. DONOVAN Do.	
			" W.J. ROCHE Do.	
			" H. JORDAN Do.	
			CAPT. A.S. PIM, M.C. Do.	
			LIEUT. V.W.F. HICKS Do.	
			2/LT. A.J. McCANN (Roy. Dub. Fus.) Do.	

WAR DIARY
or
INTELLIGENCE SUMMARY.
(Erase heading not required.)

Army Form C. 2118.

Place	Date	Hour	Summary of Events and Information	Remarks and references to Appendices
	1918			
	March		CASUALTIES (cont'd) CAPT. R.W. FITZ MAURICE M.C. missing	
	9th		1st LIEUT. R.H. JEFFREY (M.O.R.C. U.S. Army) Do.	
	26th		LIEUT. W.C.L. SHEE Wounded & missing	
			2/LIEUT. C.H. SMITH missing	
			CASUALTIES — O.Ranks	
	21		3 O.R. Killed in Action	
			12 " Wounded in Action	
			499 " missing	
			9 " Wounded in Action	
	26			
			REINFORCEMENTS — Officers Nil	
			— O. Ranks	
	21		80 O.R. joined the Battalion	
	22		16 " do.	

M.C.C. Harrison Lt Col.
Cmdg 2nd Royal West Kent Regt

ACCOUNT OF THE ACTION OF
2/Royal Irish Regiment, 49th Brigade, 16th Division,
VII Corps, FIFTH ARMY from 25th March
to 3rd APRIL 1918.

Extracted from Private Diary of Major M.C.C. Harrison.

COPIED FROM PRIVATE DIARY OF

MAJOR M.C.C. HARRISON, D.S.O., M.C. (at that time with

2/R.Irish R. 49th Bde. 16th Div. VII Corps, Fifth Army).

MARCH 1918.

25th. 5 p.m.	16th Division is transferred from VII to XIX Corps. Battn. moved via Mericourt and Chuignolles to Prisoner's of War cage ¾ mile south of Froissy. 1 Coy 7/8th Inniskilling Fus. on outpost duty guarding crossings over river and canal.
26th. 10 a.m.	Moved into position by railway in R.4.c. and 10.a with S.I.H. on left and 48th Bde. on right. 7/8th Inniskilling Fus. moved into support after 39th Division had withdrawn. Throughout the afternoon large bodies of enemy including cavalry are observed to be moving to both our flanks. Hostile guns are brought into action on high ground ½ mile N.E. of our position.
7 p.m.	Withdraw to old French trench 3000 yards East of Mericourt owing to left flank being partially turned. Dispositions: 7/8th Inniskilling Fus. on left, Royal Irish on right, S.I.H. in support. During night one coy. Hants Pioneers reinforced and took up a position between Inniskillings and Royal Irish. 48th Bde. prolonged the line on the right.
27th. 10 a.m.	Attacked in morning. Owing to good field of fire on right enemy failed to get within 1000 yards of our trench, but on left flank they managed to get level with trench xxxx occupied by 7/8th Inniskilling Fus. whom they commenced to trench mortar.
2.10 p.m.	Orders to withdraw on Morcourt was received.
2.15 p.m.	Orders were issued to all units in this area to this effect. S.I.H. did not retire as a previous order stated that they were to hold on to present position at all costs. On arrival at Morcourt it was found that the enemy were already in possession of Cerisy. A further retirement became necessary. This was carried out under very heavy machine-gun and artillery fire at close range, via Lamotte to Hamel line.
7.30 p.m.	Orders were received to proceed to Fouilloy, thence to billets in Aubigny.
28th. 8.30 a.m.	49th Bde. concentrated East of Hamel in support to Carey's Force. 2nd ~~23rd~~ Royal Irish Regt, 7th Royal Irish Regt (S.I.H.) and 7/8th Inniskilling Fus. were formed into a composite battalion under Major Harrison.
4.50 p.m.	Owing to heavy bombardment it became necessary to reinforce front line with Inniskilling Coy and Royal Irish Coy. S.I.H. remaining in support.

March 1918.

29th. — Comparatively quiet day. S.I.H. relieving 7/8th Inniskillings in evening.

30th.
1 p.m. — Line very strongly attacked after intense bombardment on front line trench. 7/8th Inniskillings move from their position in support to one from which a counter-attack could be delivered.
Attack successfully repulsed.
In evening 7/8th Inniskilling Fus. relieve 2nd Royal Irish.

31st. — Comparatively quiet day. In evening moved into position in support north of Hamel in order to reorganize line. 7/8th Inniskilling were obliged to fill a gap in front line but were relieved following night when they moved to support line.

APRIL.

1st. — Quiet day.

2nd. — Quiet day.

3rd. — Quiet day. Relieved by 14th Division. Relief complete at 10.30 p.m. Moved via Aubigny embussed at Blangy Tronville to billets at Saleux.

M.C.C. Harrison,
Major.

49th Brigade.

1. Method of holding the line in depth.

Our method was not satisfactory as our resisting power did not increase as the enemy pushed forward past our advanced posts.

Owing to ~~intense~~ dense fog, and telephone wires being cut, inter-communication became impossible soon after commencement of preliminary bombardment.

It is more than probable that several groups of men were caught while changing from their night dispositions to the "Man Battle Stations".

A more formidable resistance could have been put up had all battalions commanders in the line been able to keep a reserve of two companies in the RED LINE and make a continuous strong line of resistance.

All posts or trenches in front of this 1st main line of resistance I consider are best held in depth.

NOTE BY TYPIST.

The above report was copied from diary but seems to be embodied in the report which follows.

49th BRIGADE.

1. **Method of holding the line in depth.**

   I consider our method was unsatisfactory:

   (a) Our power of resisting did not increase as the enemy advanced. A more formidable resistance could have been put up had all battalion commanders in the line been able to keep 2 companies in reserve to form a strong continuous line of defence along the red line. Any posts or trenches in front of this line I consider are best held in depth.

   Each brigade to have one battalion in the Yellow or Red support line and the third in reserve to be used as opportunity may demand, i.e. either to reinforce red or yellow lines, or for local counter-attack should the opportunity occur.

   (b) It has been proved that it is impracticable to have different day and night dispositions. With the increased amount of artillery now employed it is a very simple matter for the enemy to put an end to all movement at any moment. On 21st March it is more than probable that several groups of men were caught in the act of moving from their night dispositions to their Man Battle Stations.

   All communications being cut off directly the preliminary bombardment started, battalion commanders had no means of finding out whether their advanced posts had been able to effect the change or not.

2. As far as I know our M.G's did not come into action during the preliminary battle. Owing to mist S.O.S. signal was probably not seen. If M.G's were firing on their S.O.S. lines throughout bombardment, it is probable that their fire was not very intense after 3 or 4 hours. I take it the M.G's had no means of finding out when the enemy past (? passed) our front line trench. Consequently the enemy was able to continue his advance more or less unmolested as far as machine-gun fire was concerned.

   Had the bulk of the machine guns been in the red line with a few to strengthen our advanced posts and front line we might have got far more value out of them.

   It is very demoralizing to come under heavy machine-gun fire and the fact of having the M.G's with the infantry gives the men increased confidence.

   During the retirement more motor machine guns or small armoured cars were very badly needed. I must mention here that I consider it almost impossible to have too many of these vehicles, either in a retirement or an advance.

   On one occasion at least the Germans could have broken clean through had they not hesitated in shoving their motor machine guns in amongst the retreating infantry.

3. With the exception of about 15 men, mostly from headquarters, the whole of the Royal Irish Regt. was missing after 21st March.

   Subsequently as drafts arrived and casualties occurred it frequently became necessary to reorganize platoons, sections, and even companies according to the strength of the battalion.

The battalions of the brigade were on two occasions organised as companies.

4. Bombs were used in large quantities by the headquarters party of the Royal Irish Regt. who were defending Rose Trench. The enemy had elected to reassemble at one end of this trench and owing to mist it was impossible to tell who they were within 25 yards of us, when bombs were freely used by us. As the enemy was in mass their casualties were heavy.

The enemy eventually bombed this party out of the trench, but this could not have taken place had not our supply of S.A.A. run out.

Stokes mortars were used against us with some effect.

I saw none of ours in action.

I did not see any Rifle Grenades used. Had the men had more experience in firing these I think they might have been employed with great advantage on one or two occasions.

5. LEWIS GUNS.

75% of the value of a Lewis Gun is wasted by each team not being supplied with at least one good pair of binoculars.

Drums were always hard to obtain - ammunition was generally plentiful.

6. Communication forward of Bde. H.Q. was invariably too slow. Visual was seldom possible - the battalion had no bicycles, and battalion could only communicate with Bde. H.Q. by runner, which is not a satisfactory way of getting an important message back.

I would suggest that motor cycles be allotted to battalions, but as this is probably impossible, if Bde. H.Q. were alloted more than one, they could have one sent forward to an advanced position to collect important messages from battalions in the line.

M.C.C. HARRISON, Major,

Commanding 2nd Royal Irish Regt.

7/4/18.

~~49/18~~
~~188th Inf.Bde.~~
~~63rd Div.~~

Transferred from ~~49th~~
Inf.Bde. ~~16th~~ Div.
23.4.18.

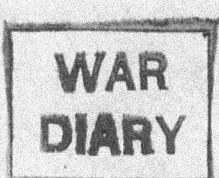

2nd BATTN. THE ROYAL IRISH REGIMENT.

A P R I L

1 9 1 8

WAR DIARY
or
INTELLIGENCE SUMMARY.
(Erase heading not required.)

Army Form C. 2118.

2 R Irish R
96/4/37

Place	Date	Hour	Summary of Events and Information	Remarks and references to Appendices
	1918 April			
SALEUX	4th		Battalion moved to VISMES-AU-VAL detraining at BLANGY and marching from there	
VISMES-AU-VAL	8th		Inspection by the Brigadier General Commanding 49th Infantry Brigade	
	9th		Battalion left VISMES-AU-VAL and marched to BERTHEN-SUR-MER via FEUQUIERES — FRESSENVILLE — WOINCOURT arriving in Billets at 5 P.M.	
		12 M.N.	Party of 150 (practically whole Batt) leave for WOINCOURT to act as Entraining party	
	10th	9 P.M.	Battalion marched to WOINCOURT and entrained at 11 P.M. for WIZERNES.	
WIZERNES	11th	11 A.M.	Battalion detrained and marched to ELNES via HALLINES — SETQUES — LUMBRES	25.0. trabats
ELNES	14th		A Composite Battalion is made up from the Remnants of the 49th Infantry Brigade and leaves to digging work on line	
	18th	9.30 A.M.	Battalion H.Q. move to STEENBECQUE where Composite Battn is at work. Spending the night at AIRE. Route WAVRANS — REMILLY — CREHEM — CIAREQUES — REBECQ	

Army Form C. 2118.

WAR DIARY
or
INTELLIGENCE SUMMARY.
(Erase heading not required.)

Place	Date	Hour	Summary of Events and Information	Remarks and references to Appendices
	1918. April			
AIRE	19th	10 AM	Continued march to STEENBECQUE via BOESEGHEM.	
STEENBECQUE	20th		The Battalion is reformed from Composite Battn. and reinforced by the 7/8 Royal Inniskilling Fusiliers, 7th (S.I.H.) Dublin Fusiliers Regt. and 2nd Royal Dublin Fusiliers.	
	20-23		Reorganisation of Battalion	
	23	9 AM	The Battalion entrains to ARQUEVES via LILLERS — DOULLENS — RAINCHEVAL area. The G.O.C. 16th Division, B.G.C. 49th Infantry Brigade with their Staffs come to the Starting point to wish the Commanding Officer and Battalion "Good Bye and Good Luck" on leaving the 16th Division and join the 63rd (R.N.) Division 188th Infantry Brigade Vth Corps IIIrd Army.	
RAINCHEVAL	23rd	6 PM	Arrive and find Tents.	
	29th		Inspection of Battalion by the Army Commander	

Army Form C. 2118.

WAR DIARY
or
INTELLIGENCE SUMMARY.
(Erase heading not required.)

Instructions regarding War Diaries and Intelligence Summaries are contained in F. S. Regs., Part II. and the Staff Manual respectively. Title pages will be prepared in manuscript.

Place	Date	Hour	Summary of Events and Information	Remarks and references to Appendices
	1918 April			
	18th		REINFORCEMENTS – OFFICERS	
			CAPT J.C. ST J PIKE, M.C.	
	21		E.C. MARSH from 16th DWs	
	22		2/LT W.R. SIMMONDS, M.M. (S.L.H)	
	23		CAPT G.O.F. ALLEY, M.C. (RAMC)	
			2/LT W.H. BROWN (Con Rangers)	
	25		" E.W. HARPER	
			LT L.L. WHITE (RDLI)	
	28		" E.A.W. SMITH (Con Rangers)	
			CAPT REV FR E.T. KANE	
	29		2/LT E.T. McWEENEY (Con Rangers)	
			REINFORCEMENTS – OTHER RANKS	
	8		30 O.R. Joined the Battalion	
	9		3 " do	
	10		3 " do	

Army Form C. 2118.

WAR DIARY
or
INTELLIGENCE SUMMARY.
(Erase heading not required.)

Place	Date	Hour	Summary of Events and Information	Remarks and references to Appendices
	1918 April 25.		REINFORCEMENTS — OTHER RANKS (cont.) 25 O.R. Joined the Battalion	
	22		232 " (R. Inniskilling Fus.) do 132 " (S I H) do 119 " (R. Dublin Fus.) do	

M.C.C. Harrison Lt Col
Comdg 2nd Royal Irish Regt